Corporate Strategy and the Search for Ethics

Corporate Strategy and the Search for Ethics

★ ★ ★ ★ ★ ★ ★ ★ ★ ★ **R. Edward Freeman**

The Colgate Darden Graduate School
of Business Administration
University of Virginia

Daniel R. Gilbert, Jr.

Bucknell University

 Prentice Hall, Englewood Cliffs, New Jersey 07632

Library of Congress Cataloging-in-Publication Data

Freeman, R. Edward.
    Corporate strategy and the search for ethics / R. Edward Freeman
and Daniel R. Gilbert, Jr.

    p.   cm.
    Bibliography: p.
    Includes index.
    ISBN 0-13-175472-6
    1. Corporate planning.   2. Strategic planning.   3. Business
ethics.   4. Industry—Social aspects.   I. Gilbert, Daniel R.
II. Title.
HD30.28.F729   1988
658.4'012—dc 19

Editorial/production supervision
  and interior design: **Cheryl L. Smith**
Cover design: **Ben Santora**
Manufacturing buyer: **Ed O'Dougherty**
Photo credit: **Slide Graphics of New England, Inc.**

Printed in the United States of America

10 9 8 7 6 5 4 3 2 1

ISBN 0-13-175472-6

Prentice-Hall International (UK) Limited, *London*
Prentice-Hall of Australia Pty. Limited, *Sydney*
Prentice-Hall Canada Inc., *Toronto*
Prentice-Hall Hispanoamericana, S.A., *Mexico*
Prentice-Hall of India Private Limited, *New Delhi*
Prentice-Hall of Japan, Inc., *Tokyo*
Prentice-Hall of Southeast Asia Pte. Ltd., *Singapore*
Editora Prentice-Hall do Brasil, Ltda., *Rio de Janeiro*

To our parents
Joan T. Gilbert and Daniel R. Gilbert, Sr.
and in memory of
Wynelle A. Freeman and Frank P. Freeman, Jr.

★ ★ ★ ★ ★ ★ ★ ★ ★ ★ ★ ★ ★ CONTENTS

PART III: THE SEARCH FOR ETHICS

★ ★ ★ ★ ★ ★ ★ ★ ★ ★ ★ ★ ★ PREFACE

This book is the result of a collaboration that began several years ago in a seminar on business ethics. We became convinced that there needed to be a complete revision in our thinking about the concept of corporate strategy. Ethics and strategy go together, and we need to tell a radically different story about organizational life to connect these concepts. We begin telling that story here.

We are grateful to a number of colleagues at a variety of institutions for listening and helping us to clarify and sharpen our ideas. At the top of the list are the members of the original business ethics seminar at the Carlson School of Management, University of Minnesota: Ron Dykstra, Barbara Edwards, Paula King, William Roering, and Shannon Shipp. Others at the Carlson School have been a constant source of conversation. In particular we are grateful to Ian Maitland, Harold Angle, Dawn Elm, Carol Jacobson, Raghu Garud, S. Venkataramen, Doug Polley, Bala Chakravarthy, Paul Johnson, Ken Roering, and a host of undergraduates who took our business ethics courses. Dean Pete Townley has given us financial support as well as the benefit of his experience as a decision maker connecting ethics and strategy.

Our present homes have also been supportive. Bucknell University is a scholar's dream, and special thanks go to Timothy Sweeney, Dean Larry Shinn, John Miller, and Arthur Sterngold.

It seems only fitting to offer a defense of individual rights and self-governing communities, as applied to the corporation, from among the shadows of Mr. Jefferson's University. The Darden School is perhaps the best model for what we call, in Chapter 8, the Personal Projects Enterprise Strategy. Dean John Rosenblum and the sponsors of the Darden School have generously given financial support for the completion of this book. In addition, teaching the ideas in the book to Darden students, along with Rosenblum and Alexander Horniman, has been a rewarding experience. Both have given us the insightful criticism and warm friendship that is necessary for scholarship to thrive. Patricia Bennett, Karen Dickinson, and Henry Tulloch of the Olsson Center for Applied Ethics, as well as numerous other Darden colleagues, have made writing this book a real joy.

A number of other people are partially responsible for the ideas in this book. Executives such as Marvin Standley, Robert Herson, Jim Pottorf, Ron LeMay, David Nicol and countless others have suffered through versions of our argument here. On the academic side are Mark Pastin, Arizona State University; Ed Epstein, University of California, Berkeley; Mike Hoffman, Bentley College; Norman Bowie, University of Delaware; Thomas Donaldson, Loyola University; Jagdish Sheth, University of Southern California; Lee Preston, University of Maryland; Bill Frederick and Donna Wood, University of Pittsburgh; and William Evan, University of Pennsylvania. Without the special effort of Lisa Romanoff and Alison Reeves of Prentice Hall we would not have attempted this book.

A number of other institutions have provided the necessary ambiance for the realization of this project. In Minneapolis, we are grateful to Lotus and The New French Cafe. In Charlottesville, the Charlottesville Book Gallery and the Coffee Connection have been more than tolerant. A good deal of the work on this book was done in Section 132, Row 5, Seats 26 and 27, at the Metrodome, home of the Minnesota Twins. Tom Kelly, Gary Gaetti, and Kirby Puckett have provided us with countless examples of the importance of individual excellence in the context of a community.

A special debt is owed to Tom Peters for starting the revolution in management, making this book possible, and then encouraging us to write it, while making ludicrous predictions about the yearly baseball pennant races.

In addition, we have greatly benefited from a long and fruitful collaboration with Professor Edwin Hartman of Rutgers University. He has forced us to be clearer about a number of points while laboring under the extreme handicap of being a San Francisco Giants fan.

Finally, in writing this book we have had the chance to reflect on our understanding of the concept of the person. By example, Gregory Shea has taught us about authenticity, and Gordon Sollars has taught us about liberty. Maureen Wellen and Benjamin Wellen Freeman have taught us about support and community. Our debt to these people simply cannot be repaid.

Our parents began the process of teaching us about ethics, and are responsible for all of the errors of character shown in this book. It is only fitting that we dedicate it to them.

Charlottesville, Va. and Lewisburg, Pa. 1987

★ ★ ★ ★ ★ ★ ★ ★ ★ INTRODUCTION

This book is about a revolution that is going on in management. Spurred by the publication of *In Search of Excellence*, managers and theorists alike are beginning to focus on values as one of the most important concepts in understanding today's business world. As a consequence of scandal, bad press, and the filing of criminal charges against a host of executives, business ethics has also become a frequently debated subject. Our point of view is quite simple: the search for excellence and the search for ethics amount to the same thing, and both have to be connected to our concept of corporate strategy. We must learn to build corporate strategy on a foundation of ethical reasoning, rather than pretending that strategy and ethics are separate.

In this book we shall demonstrate that questions and issues of corporate strategy are fundamentally ethical issues. We shall argue, too, that we must get much better and more sophisticated in our understanding of ethics. Finally, we shall try to articulate and defend one view of the connection between strategy and ethics, based on the notions of individual rights. Our argument is divided into three parts.

Part I: Ethics and Strategy: The Real Revolution

In Part I, we shall introduce some fundamental ideas to enrich our understanding of corporate strategy. The four chapters in this part explain why ethics and strategy are connected and give some ways to improve the way that we reason about ethics in business. Part I addresses the need to use the language of ethics in understanding corporate strategy. In Chapter 1 we give a number of examples of how ethics and strategy are connected, and we say why the search for ethics is a task of the highest importance. We develop several principles, including the Values Principle and the Interdependence Principle, to explain why our concept of corporate strategy needs to be revised.

In Chapter 2 we address the commonly held belief that ethics is subjective and that no progress can be made. We show how this view, known as "relativism," is mistaken, and how the kernel of truth in relativism—that morality is personal, serious, and complex—implies that we must reason about moral and ethical issues.

In Chapter 3 we explain the fundamentals of ethical reasoning. Using a simple framework of harms and benefits, values, rights, rules, and principles, we give examples of how to use the language of ethics to tackle business problems.

In Chapter 4 we explore seven different ways to systematically connect ethics and strategy, using the concept of "enterprise strategy." Enterprise strategy allows us to combine the principles of values and interdependence in several unique ways.

Part II: How Not to Connect Ethics and Strategy

The chapters in Part II address the current literature on corporate strategy and show how attempts to deal with ethics are implicit in various models of strategy, and are inadequate.

In Chapter 5 we analyze one recent attempt to link strategy and ethics, the so-called corporate social responsiveness approach. Using some simple game theory, we look at the Procter and Gamble Rely tampon case to show the shortcomings of the corporate social responsiveness model.

In Chapter 6 we analyze the economic view of strategy. We begin by deducing the ten commandments of capitalism. We show how corporate strategy conceived as a solution to market failure is suspect. We examine portfolio approaches such as the Boston Consulting Group matrix, and the recent work of Michael Porter on competitive analysis. We find that there are implicit ethical assumptions in all of these theories, and that these assumptions cannot be defended.

In Chapter 7 we turn our attention to the planning process, and offer a sweeping critique of "process theories" of strategy. We find them inadequate in terms of their attention to individual persons.

Part III: The Search for Ethics

In Part III we defend one view of ethics and strategy. We argue in Chapter 8 that the best view of the connection of ethics and strategy is in terms of individual rights. We articulate a concept of the person in terms of beings who commit themselves to the achievement of projects, in cooperation with others. Therefore we must think about the corporation as a set of voluntary agreements among human persons each of whom is seeking to accomplish certain projects of importance to him or her. We explain this view in terms of several moral principles which we hope will continue to be debated for years to come. None of these principles is new, yet their application to corporate strategy is in its infancy.

A Word of Caution about Our Methods

A brief word of caution is in order. In the chapters of this book, we shall present arguments; that is, connected series of statements in which conclusions seem to follow from premisses. Above all, we shall strive for clarity and simplicity in our exposition. So, of practitioners, we ask that you be patient and follow all of the logic, not just the punch lines. There are some useful ideas, but they are useful precisely because they are the valid conclusions from premisses that we believe are true. Of academics, we ask that you follow the endnotes. We have eschewed the method of appeal to authority that is implicit in multiple citations and have adopted instead a more discursive style in rather lengthy endnotes. Again, the important part is the logic of the argument. We believe that the key to sound management practices begins with sound principles. The absence of the latter in corporate strategy, and the real message of those principles that *can* be found, compel our efforts in this book.

Corporate Strategy and the Search for Ethics

★ ★ ★ ★ ★ ★ ★ ★ ★ CHAPTER **1**

The Revolution
in Management

ETHICS AND STRATEGY

Business ethics is hot. There are daily stories in *The Wall Street Journal* and the popular press.[1] Television news carries the latest scandal, and eagerly depicts the current "robberbarons." Consider some of the recent events:

1. Dennis Levine and a host of others are accused and later convicted of insider trading. Speculation centers on the motivations of well-to-do Wall Streeters engaging in criminal activity.[2]

2. Ivan Boesky pleads guilty to trading stocks on insider information, in part on tips from convicted inside-trader Levine. Boesky goes on to cooperate with the SEC and allegedly tapes conversations with other business associates.[3]

3. T. Boone Pickens, Irwin "The Liquidator" Jacobs, Carl Icahn, and their fellow mavericks launch numerous takeover bids for firms they believe are mismanaged and undervalued. The results are a wave of corporate restructurings. The language of mergers and acquisitions becomes "white knights," "greenmail," "shark repellent," and "poison pills."[4]

4. General Motors, IBM, Honeywell, Exxon, and other major firms decide to divest their operations in South Africa. After a decade-long attempt to abide by the Sullivan principles, executives admit that doing business in South Africa no longer makes sense. Meanwhile, a senior executive from Mobil Corporation resigns from the board of the Duke University business school because of Duke's decision to divest stock of companies such as Mobil that still operate in South Africa.[5]

5. Johns Manville files for bankruptcy in an attempt to avoid liabilities stemming from the asbestos controversy. Executives claim that court protection is the only way to save the company. A. H. Robins follows a similar strategy after a long controversy surrounding the Dalkon Shield.[6]

6. As more women enter the work force, companies adopt strict policies on sexual harassment. The U.S. Supreme Court rules that workers have a right to a working atmosphere free from sexual harassment.[7]

7. The competitive position of a number of U.S. industries declines as markets become global and as new players such as Japan and Korea target key sectors of the economy to develop. The results are loss of jobs, devastation of communities, renewed calls for trade protectionism, and diversification of some companies to other industries.[8]

8. Corporate restructuring has led many major companies to "downsize" their middle management. Estimates at companies such as AT&T are that 30,000 managers will eventually lose their jobs. The results at some companies are increased levels of stress for employees and more pressure to perform. Corporate loyalty has been radically altered.[9]

You quickly get the idea. There are multiple conflicts in the business world, and most of them arise because there are different values at work. These are clearly "business" issues, since the well-being of firms and individuals depends on how they are resolved. Just as clearly, they are "ethical" issues, since they allocate harms and benefits, and allow some to pursue their projects and prevent others from pursuing them.

Resolving the conflicts in these business decisions is difficult because the conflicts are about ethics and morality, concepts which are usually thought to be far from the minds of business executives. It is important to note that when we call a decision "a moral decision" we do not mean it is a morally correct decision. We mean that it is connected with moral issues, in much the same way that a financial decision is connected with financial issues. We mean that it is a decision of the moral kind. Strategic decisions are based on a set of values, and these values yield certain projects or purposes which key individuals or groups want to realize. If we want to understand the strategy, we must understand the values on which the decision was based. Let's look at some more examples in detail.

AT&T and Divestiture

On January 1, 1984, the largest corporation in the world ceased to exist.[10] AT&T was broken into eight separate multibillion-dollar companies. Early in 1982 the U.S. Department of Justice and AT&T agreed to a consent decree whereby the U.S. government would drop its antitrust suit against AT&T and allow it to compete in the relatively nonregulated computer business. In return, AT&T agreed to divest itself of its large distribution network and local telephone business, which embraced the wholly owned Bell System operating companies. During the months which preceded the divestiture, we can only imagine the tough decisions that AT&T managers had to make. Here was a strategic decision of the utmost importance. Billions of dollars rode on the outcome. The future of AT&T's business, and the way it was going to be defined, was up for grabs. But there were even more important issues at stake.

Over 1 million people worked for AT&T.[11] Many millions more, virtually everyone in the U.S. and many other countries, were customers of AT&T. A great many smaller firms made their livelihood by being suppliers to AT&T. AT&T had over 3 million shareholders. Local communities across the U.S. had AT&T facilities, and many had plants or offices on which the local economy partially depended. In short, the strategic decision to break up AT&T had effects on millions of citizens who had some stake in AT&T. Many had come to expect certain things from AT&T, from low-cost phone service to a job for life, and they felt that they were entitled to, or had a right to, these expectations. There was a virtual contract, perhaps a psychological one, for AT&T not to change overnight and break this string of stable expectations. The consequences of this decision and its effects on the lives of millions of people will not be fully known for a number of years.[12]

The important point is this: The strategic decision made by AT&T was essentially a moral decision. That is, the decision involved harmful or beneficial consequences to a number of human beings, and affected their rights, or their ability to pursue their own life projects the way that they had come to expect.

Corporate Pac-Man: Bendix, Martin Marietta, and Allied

In one of the most celebrated instances of corporate strategy, Bendix Corporation, a major supplier of automobile parts, attempted to enter the "high-tech" industries via acquisition.[13] In August of 1982, Bendix made a tender offer for Martin Marietta, an aerospace contractor. On the advice of its investment bankers and others, Martin Marietta made a counteroffer for Bendix, and each company began to line up financial backing in order to swallow the other: corporate Pac-Man was born. Both companies went heavily into debt, and the result was that Allied Corporation bought Bendix and that Martin Marietta was saddled with an enormous debt load.

This series of strategic decisions affected a number of groups that had a stake in these companies, from employees to customers to the U.S. government. Yet the decisions were made in relative isolation from those groups that had a stake in the firm.[14] These groups were not treated as if they were autonomous agents but rather as means to the ends of management of Bendix, Martin Marietta, and Allied. Should the stakeholders of these firms have a right to participate in decisions which substantially affect their well-being? Have they delegated their rights to participate to management? These are tricky ethical questions for which there are no easy answers, but which must be asked if we are to understand corporate strategy as it unfolds in the modern world.

The Excellent Companies

The last several years have seen a celebration of the management process at a number of companies deemed "excellent" on a number of dimensions.[15] At Milliken, Tupperware, Hewlett-Packard, Digital Equipment Corporation, the Tactical Air Force Command, and a host of other companies, we are told that work has meaning, and organizational members seem to have fun and enjoy what they do. We are all familiar with the stories and lore of the International Business Machines Corporation, and the unparalleled consistency of McDonald's around the world. Not coincidentally, these organizations are all high performers on almost any measure you want to take. As of early 1987, Peters and Waterman's book on the excellent companies had sold over 5 million copies worldwide, and had been on *The New York Times* best seller list for over 100 weeks.

The magic at these excellent companies is an understanding of human values and ethics, and how they fit into these firms' conceptions of where they are going, that is, their corporate strategy. The search for excellence is really a search for ethics.

We also have tales of Japanese companies where workers sing the company song, wear uniforms, and have an incredible dedication to their firms. Productivity increases, quality is unparalleled, and competition begins to fall all over the world. The secret is a close connection between values, ethics, and strategy.

So What?

In all of these examples, key business decisions are concerned with ethics. Almost all business decisions benefit some groups and individuals, while harming others. Almost all business decisions help some group to realize its purposes and projects, or cause some group to fail to realize its projects. The punch line is this: Ethics and business go together, and this book is about how to make them work together when we think about corporate strategy.

A BRIEF SUMMARY OF OUR VIEW

There has been a revolution in management thought and practice.[16] Like all revolutions, it has emerged over time and is not the sole province of one thinker or manager or corporation. The revolution in management has been brought to you by some fanatics: fanatics who believe in what they are doing and bring a real emotional passion to their work. Yet the "fanatics" who work in excellent companies are ordinary people, people like all of us. They happen to work in an environment which activates their values. Their work situation turns them on in a way that most would envy. We shall argue that the key to understanding the revolution in management is understanding values and ethics, and the role that they play in our organizations.

The revolution has taken place on two fronts that have been seen to be distinct and different, but are really quite closely related. And when we combine these two fronts we shall show that some new and extremely powerful ideas about the corporation are possible.

The two fronts of the revolution in management theory are these:

1. We have "discovered" that organizations consist of human beings.[17] And if you closely examine human beings, you find a complex network of values. Values are the ultimate reasons that we have for doing what we do. If we truly want to understand why organizations work the way they do, we must have a comprehensive understanding of human values. Therefore, managers are adopting "values management" techniques, "excellence programs," "culture management," "one-minute management," and so forth. Management theorists are busy trying to find a place for concepts like "symbolism," "myths," "culture," "individualism and collectivism," "strategy implementation," and "strategic human resource management," all in the name of better "people management."

2. We have "discovered" that organizations do not exist in a vacuum. In making choices—strategic choices—corporations find that there are other outside groups and individuals who have a stake in what they do.[18] These "stakeholders," such as customers, suppliers, communities, governments, owners, and employees, all make choices themselves, and all depend on organizations for accomplishing their projects. Likewise, organizations depend on them for their success. Managers are busy finding strategies to deal more effectively with government, activist groups, and so on, while management theorists write of "resource dependence," "population ecology," "corporate social responsiveness," and "stakeholder management," all in the name of improving the bottom line.

We can articulate these "discoveries" in two principles to which we shall constantly refer in the following chapters: the Values Principle and the Interdependence Principle.[19]

The Values Principle

Individual and organizational actions are caused in part by the values that individuals and organizations have.[20]

The Interdependence Principle

Organizational success is due in part to the choices and actions of those groups that have a stake in the organization.[21]

The powerful new conception of the corporation and of management theory is evident when we make the obvious linkage between the principles. *The first principle applies to those groups which the second principle says are important.* If the values of the corporation and its members are important in understanding corporate action, then so too are the values of key "stakeholders" important in understanding how they interact with the firm.

To understand why corporations choose to do what they do, we must understand the values at work in the actions of multiple stakeholders. Understanding corporate strategy means understanding the competing values claims of multiple stakeholders. Let us put it differently, again in the form of two axioms (or basic assumptions) which sum up the two fronts of the revolution in management.[22]

First Axiom of Corporate Strategy

Corporate strategy must reflect an understanding of the values of organizational members and stakeholders.

When different sets of values conflict (and even where they coincide), problems of ethics and morality emerge. Which values are going to win the day? How are we going to act? How *should* we act? Who is going to benefit and who is going to be harmed by our action? Who will be able to pursue their own projects, and who will be prevented from pursuing their projects, if we take this action? If there were no conflicts of values, no basic disagreements about how the world should be and how we should live our lives, then there would be no need for moral argument, no need for methods of resolving conflicts. Each person would go merrily about his or her own way. Ethics is important just because we do not always agree on what we should do, and because it makes sense to ask: Is this decision the very best one that could be made in these circumstances?[23]

This leads us to formulate a second axiom, or basic assumption, about corporate strategy:

The Second Axiom of Corporate Strategy

Corporate strategy must reflect an understanding of the ethical nature of strategic choice.

Almost all questions of corporate strategy are questions of ethics.[24] Furthermore, the role of ethics in corporate strategy has been, for the most part, systematically ignored in theory and in practice. We can easily summarize the real point of the revolution in management: *We must put ethics in its rightful place at the very center of discussions about corporate strategy.* Our argument is that the very best corporations can and should be managed in a way that is consistent with a strategy built on a foundation of ethics.

Once we return ethics to the center of corporate strategy, it becomes possible to articulate and defend a number of different theories or models of corporate strategy, each of which is based on a different conception of ethics. We believe that the best possible conception of corporate strategy is one that is based on the rights of individuals, both managers and stakeholders, to pursue their own projects without interference and coercion from others. Corporations are, in our view, to be seen as mere means toward the accomplishment of human goals. This contrasts sharply with the common view that corporations are ends in themselves, and that individual goals, wants, desires, values, and personal projects must be subordinated to those of the corporation.[25] We believe that this common view is in large part responsible for the current fashion of attacking the modern corporation. Let's look at some of the most recent rhetoric in more detail.

THE ATTACK ON THE CORPORATION

In part because ethics and values have little or no place in current conceptions of strategy, the corporation itself has come under increasing fire. This issue is well documented, and we shall mention it only briefly.[26] It is important to note that the attack on the large corporation has not filtered down to small business. Most of us still have the notion of the entrepreneur as the great American hero. This we believe because the entrepreneur clearly makes a statement about his or her values by deciding to become an entrepreneur. These value statements, exhibited through action, are what is missing in most corporate strategies.

Several charges have been leveled at the modern corporation in recent years. Each reflects an underlying concern with values and ethics.

1. *The corporation is too big and too powerful.* This sounds a familiar theme to those involved in trying to "democratize" the corporation or to restrict its power through structural means such as law. A U.S. Senate bill that was introduced repeatedly for several years would have put restrictions on the size of firms that would be allowed to merge. We often see comparisons of the sales and assets of General Motors, IBM, and others with the gross national products of many nations around the world. The argument is that since some corporations have become so large and so pervasive (they operate throughout the world), they have become virtually uncontrollable.

This particular attack on the corporation is obviously an ethical issue, at least to those who bring forth the attack. But why should executives be concerned with the ethics of growing to a certain size, through merger or just smart business? There are several answers. The first is that executives must understand why their critics see corporate size as a moral issue, and this requires applying the Values Principle to the strategy of the critics. Executives must find an answer to this question: What are the values which cause these critics to see the world this way?

The second answer is that while there is no logical connection between size and ethical or unethical behavior, there probably is a connection between size and the ability to respond quickly and effectively to those groups that depend on the corporation: its stakeholders. The very ability of the corporation to respond to its stakeholders is itself an ethical issue. If it cannot respond (let's leave aside the important question of its willingness to respond), then stakeholders will be harmed and some might find their rights violated. (If you don't like this argument, simply substitute "stockholder" for "stakeholder." It still holds true.) Thus, in growing to a certain size you need to examine your ability to be able to respond to the demands of your stakeholders. Now every executive worth his or her salt knows this basic business truth. But few see it as a moral issue—and to see it so gives it a renewed importance.

2. *The corporation in the U.S. has lost its ability to compete.* Again, this is obviously an ethical issue. But, so are the solutions that are proposed in response to this attack. Favorable government treatment toward some industries, in the form of import quotas and tariffs, tax credits, and the like, benefits or harms some groups in society, and it rides roughshod over the rights of some. The question is whether any of these "solutions" can be justified. The call for justification is a challenge to place these problem-solutions within the context of some moral theory.

Now, taking on the whole of moral theory is a pretty tall task to ask of anyone, and we certainly do not propose to solve all of the knotty problems of moral philosophy, but we do believe that if you really want to understand the problem of the ability of U.S. firms to compete in the world at large, you must at least be willing to address the ethical issues that are inherent in most views of corporate strategy. That is, corporate strategy must be built on a foundation of ethical reasoning. Such applied ethics must offer guidance on how to solve the problem of competition.

3. *The corporation is not "human." It is a nameless, faceless entity that simply does not care about human concerns.* The argument is not directed solely at the corporation but at bureaucracies in general. In recent times, two U.S. presidents have been elected because they gave the express promise to clean up the bureaucracy and to make government more responsive. The attack on the corporation is very much in line with what we have called the revolution in management: It is people that count, not corporations. All of the benefits of the corporation are benefits to some group of individuals—from customers and suppliers to owners and the local community—and without the individuals, there would literally be no corporation.

Once again we run squarely into the Values Principle and the Interdependence Principle. If we are to address this concern we must "discover" what it is to be human, and that entails an analysis of ethics and values. Likewise, if we are to formulate and implement strategies to make the corporation more responsive, we must understand the values issues and ethical issues of those groups that depend on the corporation. In short, we must link ethics and strategy. But there is another problem. In concert with the fashion of attacking the corporation, some critics have turned to the very concept of corporate strategy.

THE ATTACK ON CORPORATE STRATEGY

Corporate strategy and the hordes of MBAs who "think strategically" are the current targets of much scorn. However, we believe that the modern corporation cannot do without corporate strategy, even if the current versions are inadequate or irrelevant, and we shall argue that we need to infuse corporate strategy with an understanding of values and ethics. But first, let's try to understand the positions of the critics.[27] Consider the following stories as symbols of their attack:

> One *Fortune* 500 company has fired most of its strategic planners, and the CEO announced in a speech to the Harvard Business School that if you wanted to do strategic planning you ought to choose another company.
> Another *Fortune* 500 company (not alone) decided to stop hiring MBAs. It decided, rather, to train its own managers from within the firm.
> *Business Week* has renamed its "Corporate Strategy" column "The Corporation."
> Consulting firms are flocking toward the hot topics of "corporate culture" and "strategic human resources management," leaving strategic planning models on the drawing board.

On the theoretical front, books that deal with how to "manage people" have hit the best seller list. On the desk of every fast-track manager are the high-tech–high-touch world of *Megatrends*, the book *In Search of Excellence*, the latest on Japanese management, and the latest in psychological motivation as found in *The One Minute Manager* and *The One Minute Sales Person*.

The list is endless. Corporate strategy is out, and people are in. On the academic front, the hot topics are "strategy implementation," "corporate culture," "the symbolic nature of management," "population ecology," "corporate social responsiveness," and "strategic planning processes to create corporate futures."[28] The message in these incantations is clear: It doesn't make much difference what you decide to do, so long as you follow a process which gives people some sense of participation.

The reasons for the attack on corporate strategy are multiple, and some of them are quite valid:

1. *Corporate strategy has become the tail that wags the dog.* This objection states that while corporate strategy is important, it has led executives to ignore the main part of a business: its operational structure. Coinciding with the emergence of corporate strategy, we find the decline of manufacturing and operations as important. Manufacturing is only a part of strategy, and the overemphasis that most theories and models of strategy put on marketing and finance ignores the basics of producing some goods and services.

2. *Corporate strategy has become too analytical.* This argument states that managers have relied too much on the formal models of academics and consulting firms. What company has not had its portfolio plotted, does not understand the difference between dogs and cows, and does not know the relationship between market share and ROI, ROE, and ROTA? The emergence of a "strategy industry" has done more harm than good, say the critics, for in their drive to be "objective" and give "objective, hardheaded, numbers-oriented" advice, strategists have left out a crucial factor: managerial judgment. According to this critical perspective, strategy is really more an art than a science.

3. *Corporate strategy requires too much centralization.* The emergence of large planning staffs, filled with bright, well-scrubbed MBAs fresh from the B-schools, has led to control of business by staffers rather than line managers. To the extent that the concept of corporate strategy has meant "strategic planners," then it has led to endless layers of forms, reports, and overheads, all of which get in the way of operating managers.

4. *Corporate strategy has led executives to give short shrift to the people factor.* This is the main rallying cry for the revolution in management that we mentioned above. The critics argue that strategy treats people as factors of production, more or less capable of implementing any idea. In this view of strategy, people do not necessarily participate in the corporate strategy process, so they have no commitment to the strategy which is the outcome of that process. Hence, the critics emphasize the need to think more about people, implementation, and culture if this shortcoming is to be overcome.

While each of these criticisms has some validity, each ignores the fundamental mistake of most theories and models of corporate strategy. Individuals act as they do because of their values. The value sets of individuals provide strong reasons for action, and the most dear values are ones we call "moral values" or "ethical values." Corporate strategy which ignores the role of people in the organization simply ignores why organizational members act as they do. Corporate strategy must return to the individual values of corporate members, *before it is formulated.* It must be built on these values, rather than taking them as constraining forces.[29]

While we will have much more to say about values and ethics in later chapters, especially Chapters 3 and 4, it is important to note here that values are not slogans, nor are they necessarily shared among all organizational members. Addressing the problem as one of "implementation" or "culture" simply tries to fix (in vain) the wrong problem. It is no wonder that there is an "implementation gap" in most companies between the strategy and what people actually do. Strategy which is "good on paper" but "lousy on implementation" is simply bad strategy. Bad strategy makes for atrocious performance and calls into question the very legitimacy of the corporation.

The attack on corporate strategy is serious enough to warrant another look at the underlying nature of the concept of corporate strategy. While such an analysis is one of the leitmotifs of this book, the next section contains a general overview of our approach.

THE CONCEPT OF CORPORATE STRATEGY

The diversity of the modern corporation has led to an increased need for a framework or common language so that managers in a number of functions and business elements can talk to each other, and so that corporate-wide resource allocation decisions can be made. The manager of the timber business must be able to talk to the manager of the consumer products business. The top executives must be able to evaluate both businesses, when there are limited resources. And those same executives need to be able to talk to a variety of customers, employees, suppliers, and communities.

The concept of corporate strategy has evolved to deal with the complexities of modern business.[30] No longer can managers rely solely on "seat of the pants" common knowledge, nor can they rely solely on functional skills such as marketing, finance, or production to pull them through the complexities of today's global business environment. Corporate strategy provides a method and language to integrate multiple functions and businesses.

Corporate strategy has become a central metaphor for business.[31] Virtually every large and successful firm, like many small and unsuccessful ones as well, has a strategy, and most spend countless hours worrying whether or not it is effective.

During the last thirty years the concept of corporate strategy has gotten increasingly complex. From the tried and true pronouncements of consultants, to the case-study classrooms of the Harvard Business School, the study of corporate strategy has become a discipline in its own right, both in practice and in professional schools of management. The old methods of solemnly imploring "build on your strengths" have given way to computer simulation models such as Profit Impact of Market Strategies (PIMS), a plethora of analytical matrices, and complex theories.

Even though there are endless definitions and models of corporate strategy, we believe that corporate strategy is really very little understood. Standard views of corporate strategy describe it as a process which answers four essential questions:[32]

1. Where are we going?
2. How do we get there?
3. What is our blueprint for action?
4. How do we measure or control progress?

The usual narrative which justifies these questions runs something like the following:

> As the Cheshire Cat said to Alice, in Lewis Carroll's *Alice in Wonderland*, "If you don't know where you're going, then any road will take you there." It is the task of modern management to chart a course for corporations, and managers must ask the question "Where are we going?" Corporate strategy understood as helping to answer this question is simply inevitable.
>
> Equally important is the question of means: How do we achieve the desired direction? Without some thinking about how to get to where we want to go, a statement of corporate direction becomes just empty words. Alice's question to the Cat was the right one, given that she knew where she wanted to go.
>
> The third question is important because if executives can't articulate the connections between the desired path of the company and what individuals actually do on their jobs today, then strategy will not make much difference to the way the company actually runs. Connecting desired plans with the actual behavior of managers and other organizational members is a great challenge, one that is central to any effective conception of strategy.[33]
>
> Finally the issue of control, as stated by question 4, is important. If strategy is not to be just cheerleading or thinking great thoughts, then executives must have clear ideas about how to measure progress. Control of direction, pathways, and blueprints is necessary.[34]

Corporate strategy, articulated in the form of these four simple questions, is a powerful device for managing the large and multifaceted organization that today's corporation has become. It is hard to see how these questions can ever decrease in importance or become irrelevant. But we need to take a closer look at the very nature of the concept of corporate strategy. There is more to the concept, which a closer reading will unveil. The First and Second Axioms of Corporate Strategy force us to recognize that the question "Where are we going?" is ambiguous. The question assumes that the "we" is well understood, and that an answer, in terms of some corporate goal or purpose, is a straightforward matter. It is not.

Strategy As Purpose

A manager who approaches an important decision will likely ask: What is this situation really about? Who is taking action? Why are events unfolding in this way? In the back of that manager's mind is a set of related, but different, concerns: What are the appropriate responses? What will be required to take such steps? Eventually, if he or she determines that a response is warranted, the appropriate inquiry turns to: How can the effectiveness of these actions be determined? At the same time, managers in other organizations that are affected by this manager's decision are confronting the same set of questions.[35]

The Values and Interdependence Principles and the corporate strategy axioms imply that reasoning about the nature of strategy is equivalent to reasoning about the purposes of individuals and groups. We are going to try to convince you of this point by drawing on some everyday, common-sense examples, and on our practical understanding of what a purpose really is. There are obvious parallels and applications to the concept of strategy.

Having a purpose implies some continuity of action. To say that Jane has a purpose in buying the car is to say that her purchase is more than a mere fleeting desire or impulse. We tend to associate a person's overall competence and rationality with an ability to carry through on actions that are motivated by purposes.

This section addresses the meaning of purpose.[36] There are five key features of "purpose" which we want to explain. And we will argue that reasoning about strategy is the same thing as reasoning about purposes when we understand that:

1. Purposes are personal.
2. Purposes guide action.
3. Purposes require others.
4. Purposes are shaped by bargaining.
5. Purposes are the bottom line for performance.

1. *Purposes are personal.* Having a purpose is a capability that we commonly and uniquely attribute to a human being. Having a purpose distinguishes us from other living, sensing entities. Further, it is individuals, first and foremost, who have purposes. Our judgments about our own tastes, aspirations, and relationships lead us to an understanding of purpose as personal in three key respects.[37]

First, no one can experience the meaning of a particular purpose better than the person who has it. Empathizing with another person is as close as we can get to actually sharing his or her purpose. Second, the reasoning processes by which purposes are formed and realized are useful only if we can actually perform some actions. Each person, acting alone, uses his or her own knowledge and intuition in purposive action. Third, a purpose is subjective. The person who holds the purpose is the subject of it. Even if a person's purpose in life is to bring about social good, having that purpose is subjective.[38]

Strategy shares this idea of purpose as personal. Reasoning about strategy is not a mechanical affair. Production lines can be driven by technological wizardry. But corporate strategy is a creative endeavor that only an individual or a group can practice.[39]

The personal nature of strategy is clearly shown in the fact that the desirability of candidates for senior executive positions varies with the nature of prior managerial experience. Length and intensity of experience are presumed to reveal how well a person understands and acts upon the issue of corporate purpose. Some managers and theorists also believe that executive success varies with prior experience in similar settings. Hence, we should not be surprised to find Donald Trautlein, an accountant, at the helm of the financially troubled Bethlehem Steel Corporation. On this same reasoning, Peter Ueberroth's marketing skills at the 1984 Summer Olympics attracted major-league baseball owners in search of a CEO. In fact, this tale is told time and again as new firms begin to face broader strategic issues than those that were pressing during start-up. Howard Head at Head Ski, Steven Jobs at Apple Computer, and Seymour Cray at Cray Research moved aside when a different personal focus was needed.[40]

Despite the fact that it may seem to be just plain common sense, thinking of purpose as person-centered causes problems to our normal way of understanding both people and organizations. Purpose comes in many flavors. At any moment, we can be confused about our own purposes. Our sensory and reasoning capacities are limited and vary with natural endowment and development. Yet, none of these constraints means that we should give up the concept. Rather, we need to think more deeply about what purpose really means. In later chapters we will explain how purpose and a closely related idea, "values," are connected, and we will try to persuade you in Chapter 8 that taking seriously "purpose as personal" means a radical rethinking of our organizations. For now let's make things just a little more complicated.

2. *Purposes guide action.* People's purposes, along with their values and projects, give meaning to their lives. Meaning is distinctively human, and the search for meaning is in part a search for some purpose that realizes our deepest hopes and dreams. Purpose structures our attempt to find our way in the world. Purpose is about relationships, beliefs, and careers, not breakfast cereals and necktie styles.[41]

We need not see ourselves as complete existentialists to accept this truth about purpose and meaning. Few people, even existentialists, stop at every turn and probe whether their actions mesh in some coherent sense. Yet, most of us do so at certain points in our lives and in some form. Formulating and realizing our purposes depends on both action and reflection.

Having a purpose guides our actions in several ways. First, we try to make sense of the world, from our family and friends to the arms race, in terms of what we want to do, and how the world will affect our ability to carry through our projects. In asking "Does that situation apply to me?" we observe the world and compare it with the knowledge we have about ourselves. Hence, our purposes serve to interpret the external world. Second, we find alternative courses of action based on the particular purposes we have. We determine whether what we want to accomplish can continue in its present form. Finally, we use purpose in order to determine the resources that we need to acquire and develop. In asking "Can I accomplish this?" a person has to decide what skills and resources are appropriate. Reasoning about strategy encompasses purpose in each of these respects.

Why articulate a strategy at all? In the 1960's, some strategy theorists argued that in cases where industry change was negligible, nothing more than a "seat of the pants" approach was needed. In the decade that followed, some proponents of corporate strategy took a different stance. In their view, a strategy served an essential, simplifying function for a chief executive officer.[42] Faced with too much data and too little time to assimilate it, a CEO needs some help, and strategy fits the bill, by helping to pick out parts of the buzzing, blooming confusion as relevant. For example, we might expect that Donald Burr, CEO at People Express, uses a corporate strategy to study oil prices, but not cattle prices, in tracking the Federal Aviation Administration, but not the Federal Election Commission, policies.

Purpose can guide choices by helping managers to frame a distinctive competence for themselves and their organizations. We reflect upon our competence by examining our past accomplishments and seeing whether and how our hopes and dreams were realized. We probe our aspirations, at the highest level, by answering such questions as "What do I stand for?" In studying recent actions by the People Express management to acquire Frontier Airlines and Britt Airways, we want to ask: Were these decisions informed by People's purposes?[43]

Purpose guides action, too, when managers move from defining a distinctive competence to acting upon it. Pursuit of a purpose triggers a process of self-analysis about relevant strengths and weaknesses.[44] The current emphasis upon strategy implementation bears witness to the need for purposes to guide action. Returning to the merger activity at People Express, several examples of this point are clearly present. Until the Frontier acquisition, People had operated in a nonunion environment. But the acquisition of Frontier meant that management at People assumed responsibility for a set of collective bargaining contracts. Are People's managers competent with respect to labor contracts? The acquisition of Britt, based in Chicago, heightens People's presence in the already competitive Chicago market. Does People have the financial resources to withstand a competitive shakeout there? Finally, the proximate timing of the acquisitions raises the issue of People's competence in managing such a far-flung route network. In each instance, the level of competence at People is exposed as People uses purpose to guide action. Recent events surrounding the takeover of People Express by Continental may well show how an uncritical view of the basic purposes of an enterprise and its managers leads literally to organizational death, and great personal stress.

3. *Purposes require others.* If we are going to realize our purposes, then in all but the simplest cases we need the cooperation of others. The necessity for specialization and division of labor is reason enough, but the clincher for fulfilling purpose is the prospect for enduring exchange relationships. So, our definition of purpose needs further sophistication. Purpose is a personal guide for action, activated by agreements with others for mutual benefit.

This expanded conception begs an important question for strategy and ethics: How does cooperation endure in a world of persons more interested in their purposes than anyone else ever could be? Lest Thomas Hobbes's "war of all against all" occur, managers must find ways to ensure that agreements can be struck and honored. This strongly suggests that we look at the accomplishment of purpose in terms of bargaining among self-interested persons. At the very least, the bargainers will seek terms acceptable to each and will press for safeguards against the hazards inherent in fulfilling bargains over time.

Bargaining occurs across all levels of strategy. Carl Icahn moved to solidify his acquisition of TWA by negotiating new labor agreements with TWA's unions.[45] Apple Computer cofounder Steven Jobs and Apple management bargained to forestall growing acrimony surrounding Jobs's departure from Apple to start a new company.[46] Failure to consummate bargains can be equally significant. Lack of support from the parent labor union has significantly influenced the union local's strike tactics in the prolonged labor dispute at George A. Hormel and Company in Austin, Minnesota.[47] Finally, new forms of bargaining frequently emerge between suppliers and buyers. Many health-maintenance organizations and several major airlines are pursuing prepaid bargains with corporate customers for health services and business travel plans, respectively.[48]

4. *Purposes are shaped by bargaining.*[49] We compared appointment calendars in the midst of writing this chapter. Of course, the formal contract with the publisher commanded considerable blocks of time. No less insistent were obligations to our families and friends, not to mention commitments to teach, advise students, consult, and make progress on other scholarly papers in various stages of coherence. Since our purposes have a way of taking on multiple forms, managing them can become quite complicated. What we seek to avert is a "gridlock" situation in which we fulfill none of these obligations satisfactorily. We have various ways of dealing with the problem. Looking to purposes as guides, we set priorities. But, over a given time span, several obligations can command close attention simultaneously. We respond by interpreting (or reinterpreting)

our purposes in terms of acceptable thresholds of performance. For example, we may need to do what it takes to avert an insistent phone call from a university administrator on some project. As this example shows, knowing the terms of each bargain also help us set such thresholds. Furthermore, we attempt to subdivide tasks into pieces amenable to both available time and attention. Finally, we think about safeguards.[50] We require certain assurances from our partners so that we can satisfy our expectations. And they expect safeguards in return. Juggling multiple bargains is a fact of life for every competent person.

Maintaining a coherent purpose through multiple bargains is vividly depicted in the case of the corporate strategy necessary to manage a major-league baseball team.[51] In the months prior to the beginning of a playing season in April, the team's CEO will oversee contract negotiations for each of approximately forty players. While these bargains result in separate agreements for each playing employee, the individual bargains are not struck in isolation. Information costs have been reduced in recent years, so that one player—and his bargaining agent—can obtain insights into the terms of other players' bargains with the team. In this situation, the CEO has strong incentive to develop a set of working thresholds with regard to contract provisions. In baseball parlance, monetary limits are defended in order to "preserve integrity of the salary structure." This situation becomes all the more complicated for those CEOs who bid for the services of so-called free-agent players, who usually find their services in great demand and engage in concurrent bargaining for employment with several teams.

Within the major-league baseball industry, certain safeguards have been established. One is an arbitration process whereby a CEO and a player, through his agent, have incentive to converge on bargains before a third party is called upon to choose in favor of one over the other. Another is the use of incentive clauses, based upon individual performance, which can facilitate consummation of bargains uniquely suited to each player.

This is a simplified account, since the CEO and team management bargain with other suppliers, as well as with customers. Still, two points regarding team strategy become quite clear. First, the real purpose of a team is essentially defined by the pattern of contracts successfully negotiated, no matter what the owner happens to say in the press. Second, purpose emerges as a web of semiautonomous bargains, among individuals. Once you see the world in terms of persons and their purposes, it gets harder to draw a line between strategy formulation and implementation, especially because it is a distinctively organizational and impersonal idea.

5. *Purposes are the bottom line for performance.* Having a purpose serves its most important function as the test for performance. If we did not act upon a purpose we would be "fair game" for this question: Does that

purpose really exist for you? It is simply incoherent to claim that your purpose is to publish poetry and then evaluate performance on the basis of your handball skills. Yet, the tendency to reason in this way grows as people move farther from identifiable standards against which to check their progress.

Having a purpose can also be provisional, and some of our statements about purpose are clearly conditional. For example, a marketing strategy might be stated in this form: "We will use both direct sales and dealer distribution channels, unless dealer sales significantly impede relations with our most preferred customers." This statement provides for circumstances that are reasonably foreseeable. If the threshold in this strategy is crossed, a revised statement of purpose becomes necessary. Thus, managers who reason in this way move back and forth between purpose and actual cases, retesting a specific purpose on the basis of actual experience.

Purpose is also provisional in the sense that we become wiser over time. A manager who reflects upon a range of experiences will be more likely to pursue sophisticated actions in the future than will someone who is unreflective. Furthermore, the particular statement of purpose may take precisely the same form as before, but the reflective person will look upon the purpose with new appreciation. For example, one might have a purpose of being a loving and supportive parent. But the full richness of meaning in that purpose likely grows from year to year with one child, and from child to child in a growing family.

6. *Summary.* To say that we have a strategy but we have no purpose is a contradiction. Purpose is fundamental to any coherent account of strategy that recognizes the importance of choice. Purpose is complex, as each of the aspects above shows. Our argument has been a very simple appeal to the common-sense meaning of purpose, and its application to the everyday world of business. But the critique of the corporation and corporate strategy needs a simple response, not a complex one. Infuse the application of strategy with an understanding of purpose, and link it to ethics, and we can rehabilitate the whole idea. It is relatively easy to see that if all we attend to are variations of the four questions which most models of strategy ask, we will miss the rich explanatory power of a conception of strategy based on the concept of purpose. The very nature of "Where are we going?" assumes some purpose or other as an answer, and as we have shown, such answers are complex in and of themselves. To automatically assume an organizational level of analysis leaves out the interesting issues of how such a web of bargains emerges. If a particular conception of corporate strategy is built on an understanding of purpose, then it must be much more sophisticated. (In later chapters we will show you how the current theories or models or frameworks in corporate strategy have implicit assumptions about the importance of purpose.)

Corporate strategy is about purpose, and so is ethics. Purpose is a person-based justification for action, shaped through interdependent bargaining among multiple parties. Ethics not only parallels strategy, through a common concern with purpose, but also provides a framework for reasoning through the thornier aspects of strategy as purpose. By explicitly acknowledging this connection, we can make some real intellectual and practical progress in the study of corporate strategy.

THE PROBLEM: LINKING ETHICS AND STRATEGY

People whom we meet from all walks of life will typically ask us what we do for a living. We usually say that among other things we teach business ethics. They usually laugh, or snicker, or crack, "That's a contradiction, isn't it?" We don't like this state of affairs, and this book is in part our attempt to correct it. Business strategy must be linked to ethics if "business ethics" is to have any meaning beyond just so much pompous moralizing. And, if we can link ethics to strategy, we can revitalize the concept of corporate strategy. We will be able to address the most pressing management issues of the day in the very terms that they demand to be addressed in: ethical terms.

In a nutshell, our argument is this: Most, if not all, corporate strategies raise ethical issues. For the most part, managers and academics have not addressed these issues in ethical terms, and more than anything else we mean to rectify this situation.

How can we link ethics and strategy? It isn't easy, and you shouldn't look to this book (or anywhere else, for that matter) for a cookbook formula. Our purpose is to help you think about some difficult issues, but the best guide that you can have is your own behavior and the behavior of your corporation, but beware.

Ethics is a difficult and very personal subject. You will really understand the chapters that follow if you are willing to honestly address your own ethical beliefs, and especially to ask yourself some hard questions about what you really believe. Before we go further and show you how to link ethics and strategy, we have to meet a challenge of those who believe business ethics is a contradiction: the theory known as relativism.

★ ★ ★ ★ ★ ★ ★ ★ ★ **CHAPTER 2**

The Problem
of Relativism
When in Rome . . .

THE DANGLING CONVERSATIONS[1]

We have often heard businesspersons talk about how difficult it is to make ethical decisions. Since the Second Axiom of Corporate Strategy requires that strategy reflect the ethical nature of strategic choice, we need to answer the critics who would claim that you just can't make any progress in ethics because everything is relative. Some of their logic is reflected in the following conversations:[2]

Conversation 1: The Case of the Fake Résumé

    JONES: Did you hear about Peters? He's been with the company for two years and the personnel people finally got around to doing a routine check on his credentials. Seems that his resume wasn't exactly kosher. Good old Andy invented a Harvard MBA and dreamed up five years of experience in the computer industry, when in reality he was driving a cab for most of his life.

    SMITH: That's really too bad. I've worked with Andy on a project during the last year. He's made quite a contribution to the strategic planning process here. They fired him on the spot. I'm not sure how we'll replace him.

    JONES: Well, you have to admit that he deserved what he got. Lying never gets you anywhere.

SMITH: I don't see how you can say that. You or I may not have done what Andy did, but maybe he thought it was the only way he could get the job. And he did produce results. The way he did it may have been wrong for you or me, but I don't see how you can say it was wrong for Andy. He did what he had to do. Who are we to judge?

Conversation 2: The Case of the Reluctant Layoffs

(In this conversation, Topman is the chief executive officer of a manufacturing firm in financial trouble.)

TOPMAN: This has been a difficult time for me. Laying off those three thousand workers was the hardest decision I've had to make in thirty years of business. Where will they go, and what will they do? How will someone with twenty-five years of experience in our industry get another job? The whole industry is in trouble. I don't see how those people are going to make a living.

FRIEND: But, Jim, if it was such a tragic choice, why did you do it?

TOPMAN: I didn't want to. If it had been my personal decision I would have stuck with the plant and invested new money in it. But I have to put my personal feelings aside. As CEO I have a duty to do what's best for the shareholders. I can't let my own sense of right and wrong get in the way. This is a business decision, and as CEO I have to make it on business grounds.

Conversation 3: The Case of the Competitive Industry

JONES: Wasn't that awful news about Rath? Getting caught with his hand in the expense account, giving money to customers to get sales. I hear that the Flannel Company may prosecute him, really hang him out to dry. Just think! We've known him as a solid citizen in the community for all these years and now he may be a jailbird.

SMITH: Well, don't get me wrong. I wouldn't have done what Ben did, but the situation is pretty complex. His industry is a dog-eat-dog world. He had to get those sales or lose his job. Besides, from my information all of those things are accepted practice in the industry. Rath's problem was that he got caught and the company was forced to do something to save face. Our industry is different, and our salespeople are ethical. But I don't see how you can condemn Rath for doing his job the way it has always been done.

Conversation 4: The Case of South Africa

JONES: I think we should close our plant in South Africa. Aren't we supporting apartheid by staying there? Do you realize that our black workers aren't even allowed to live with their families?

SMITH: Now wait a minute. How are you so sure what's best for the South Africans? And why should we meddle in their affairs? Apartheid has a long and complex history, and there are lots of complicating factors. I personally detest apartheid, and I wouldn't accept a transfer to South Africa, but I can't judge their whole society.

JONES: But don't you think that apartheid is morally wrong?
SMITH: It's wrong given our U.S. morality, our culture, but not according to South African culture. We can't judge them by our rules.

THE PROBLEM OF RELATIVISM

The purpose of this chapter is to examine some widely held beliefs about the role of ethics in business decision making. The preceding conversations all illustrate a way of dealing with ethical questions that makes us believe that we just cannot decide matters of right and wrong, or good and evil. This doctrine is called "moral relativism" and claims that morality is relative to some personal, social, or cultural standard.[3]

There are many versions of moral relativism, and we find them to be quite common in business and in the literature on business. We want to demonstrate in this chapter how most versions of moral relativism are mistaken. And we will show how the seductive kernel of truth in relativism lends support to our main argument about the need to connect ethics and strategy.

There are two important consequences which seem to follow from moral relativism which are absolutely opposed to our approach in this book. Indeed, we believe that it is the uncritical acceptance of some version of relativism which gives business and business strategy a bad image, and leads people to say that "business ethics" is a contradiction.

The first consequence of moral relativism seems to be that since what is right and wrong is relative to the individual making the decision, there are no answers to questions like "Should Topman lay off 3,000 employees?" Ultimately it will be up to Topman to decide, and his answer will be "right for him." So, why should people like Topman bother to engage in a painful process of looking for absolutes?[4]

The second consequence of moral relativism is related. Moral relativism bars the door on constructive argument. Smith will do what is right for her, and Jones will do what is right for him. Each shouldn't judge the other. Each may agonize over the decision, but there is no method for deciding whether one decision is better than another, from a moral point of view.

In the following sections, we want to make two points. The first is that there are good reasons for rejecting most forms of relativism. However, if we don't convince you of that, we want to show you how neither of the two consequences above follow from relativism. Even if you ultimately believe some form of relativism (our efforts to the contrary), we want to show you how you still need to learn to reason about moral principles and their connection to actual business strategy decisions.[5] We will analyze four separate types of relativism as depicted in the earlier conversations, setting the stage for the next chapter, where we show you how the methods of ethics can be applied in a more positive fashion.[6]

NAIVE RELATIVISM

In the first conversation above, Smith seems to believe that matters of right and wrong are to be settled in terms of what each individual believes. Each person is to be the standard by which his or her actions are judged. What is right for one person may not be right for another person. This theory or set of beliefs is known as "Naive Relativism" (NR).[7] Let's try to understand the enormous appeal of this view.

Naive Relativism is based on three basic ideas about matters of morality. The first is that *moral decisions are deeply personal*. When we make them, we do not do so lightly or frivolously; and ultimately, we are each responsible for the consequences of our actions, and, hence, responsible for the choices that we make. We each have to reason in the best way we know how and respond with our best choice, as imperfect as it may be. The Naive Relativist argues that since each is ultimately responsible for his or her actions, we must let each make those decisions according to his or her standards.

NR would tell us that in conversation 1, Peters is ultimately responsible for the consequences of his action. It is Peters who must look himself in the mirror each morning and face the music for faking a résumé. By NR, if he can stand the consequences, who are we to judge?

The second appealing notion of Naive Relativism is that *moral decisions are very serious*. To call a decision a moral decision is to single it out as the most important kind of decision that we can make. Moral decisions are different from routine everyday decisions like what kind of suit to wear, what to have for breakfast, good manners, or courtesy on the road. They concern harms and benefits, rights and privileges for ourselves and others. Therefore questioning someone's moral judgment or ability to reason about morality is also a serious allegation. It is decidedly unlike questioning the person's ability to do discounted cash flow correctly, or conduct an accurate market survey, or ferret out the fine print in annual reports. Notice the difference between "Smith showed bad financial judgment in investing in ABC" and "Smith showed bad moral judgment in investing in ABC." In the first case we are claiming that Smith needs some more tools or better financial skills, while in the second we are questioning Smith's character and integrity. When we criticize people's moral judgment, we call into question their character and integrity, and indeed, their very worth as human beings. So, we are hesitant to judge others, or at least NR says we should be hesitant. In our Western society with its tradition of individualism, we want to be sure to respect an individual's beliefs and the right to run his or her own life.

According to the Naive Relativist, it is difficult to question Peters' right to run his own life. We don't know that he is a bad sort of fellow. In fact, from his performance we may have evidence that he is someone of the highest integrity. We all make mistakes, says NR, and we must be tolerant in a way that questioning the character of others prevents.

The third appealing idea behind Naive Relativism comes from the fact that *moral decisions are complex*. Situations are complicated, with many actors affected in a variety of ways. It is not always crystal-clear what the consequences of a decision will be, and often as not, many unintended consequences appear as a result of a quite ordinary decision. We find that reasonable, sane, and well-meaning people often disagree about what is the morally correct thing to do, and in quite similar situations we see different individuals making different choices. The Naive Relativist says that we must allow each person to interpret the situation and act on his or her own moral beliefs.

We can easily tell a story that may get Peters off the hook. Imagine that he has two very ill parents in dire need of financial support, or some sick children, or that he is sending his salary to starving children in the Third World. If the situation is that complex, says NR, perhaps what Peters did is not so bad after all. NR tells us that we shouldn't judge, because the situational aspects of moral decisions are complex beyond our abilities.

Having boosted the Naive Relativist's position with these three appealing ideas—moral decisions are personal, they are serious, and they are complex—all of which are absolutely correct, we now want to show how the doctrine of Naive Relativism is not a very good one. We want you to see how you can still believe that moral decisions are personal, serious, and complex without believing that each person must be left alone to set the standards for moral decisions.

A Critique of Naive Relativism[8]

It is a fact about our lives that once we accept the legitimacy of adopting an ethical point of view, we have accepted something that is deeply personal. Ethics is important because we seek to justify our life and the pursuit of our projects to ourselves and to others. We need to see how "things hang together" (in the largest sense of the phrase). In deciding to adopt an ethical stance, as opposed to a random, unjustified stance, you are engaging in a deeply personal action, not to be taken lightly, for each of us is responsible for the consequences of his or her actions.

The Naive Relativist concludes from this personal and serious nature of ethics, and the fact of our responsibility for our actions, that each person is the sole judge of what actions are morally correct. The Naive Relativist may well engage in a process of reasoning, but need not. To the Naive Relativist, we are each the sole judge, so we may well simply follow the dictates of conscience, our gods, or our hearts without engaging in reasoning at all. Individuals are each responsible for making the deeply personal and serious choices which confront them. Naive Relativists reason that since they are responsible first and foremost to themselves to justify their choices, if a particular action is "right for them," then no one else has the right to judge. But this logic is faulty.

1. *The problem of justification.* It doesn't follow from the personal and serious nature of morality that we can't reason about moral issues. Indeed, the opposite is true. Because morality is so vital in the way that we choose to live our lives, it is imperative that we do our very best thinking here. If other areas of our lives are any indication, we need the help and support of others engaged in a similar project of reasoning about their moral beliefs. If my moral beliefs don't have to stand up to your critical eye, how will I ever get better about finding out what I really do believe?

Surely, we must each justify our choices to ourselves. That much is a base-line condition for adopting any ethical point of view, the need to see how one's life hangs together and makes sense. But moral reasoning doesn't end here. Acting in a vacuum is relatively easy, but many of our choices affect others. We want to know how to act when the pursuit of our individual goals and dreams affects the similar pursuits of others. It is not that Peters can't run his own life and make his own choices, even unethical choices, but rather that his choice to fake a résumé affects others, and he needs some way to reason about this choice in terms of the interests and rights of these others and how far his own interests should be taken.

It is precisely here that "morality" and "moral reasoning" are helpful, at least in the common, everyday sense of these words. Moral principles, or at least the process of engaging others in a critical reflection about the effects of our actions on others, are supposed to help us decide what to do about these deeply serious and personal matters. While there may be many possible courses of action for Peters, or at least several ways to justify his actions, the point against NR is that Peters' actions call for some justification or other. If NR is correct, it is pointless to engage in such theorizing and reasoning, for we can never legitimately judge the moral beliefs of others or ourselves. There is no vantage point from which to say "that decision wasn't very good," since each person is his or her own judge in every circumstance. (Note that this is not the view that the interests of individuals win the day in every case, but rather that their sincerely held beliefs win the day, no matter what these beliefs happen to be.) So, we can never be confident of "getting it right," even though matters of morality are of the utmost importance. There is no standard for when a particular decision is better or worse than another decision.

Here the Naive Relativist's position becomes even stranger, for he or she must believe at the same time that "morality is deeply personal and serious" and that "we can never make decisions which are better or worse than previous decisions." But, if any decision will do, what do we gain by calling morality personal and serious?

Naive Relativists often take as good reasons for their view that matters of morality are hopelessly complex, and that reasonable people disagree over the proper course of action. Indeed, we sometimes find that rational and sane people make different choices in seemingly similar circumstances. But again, this logic is faulty.

2. *The basis for moral reasoning.* There are lots of ways to disagree.[9] We can disagree about the facts of the case, or we can disagree about how to use certain concepts, or we can even disagree about which principles are applicable. Take for instance our conversation about Peters' faking a résumé. Jones and Smith may well be disagreeing over the facts. Jones claims that lying is wrong, and Smith seems to disagree. But Smith, in saying ". . . maybe he thought it was the only way he could get the job," is not claiming that lying is never wrong, but perhaps means that there are some cases where the duty to tell the truth is overridden by other duties, and that the facts may be that Peters finds himself in such a situation. Jones and Smith may well be disagreeing over the nature of the case, the factual circumstances in which Peters finds himself.

Alternatively, we can imagine another, similar case where Peters merely stretched the truth about his credentials and Smith might claim that what Peters did wasn't really lying. Here Smith and Jones would be disagreeing over the application of concepts. They might agree, once again, that lying is wrong, but disagree over whether this is a case of lying. It is sometimes helpful to think of the abortion debate. No one disagrees that murder is wrong, except perhaps for a Naive Relativist, but both sides disagree over whether the aborting of a fetus is murder. This is a conceptual disagreement. It is not a factual one, nor is it a disagreement in principle.

Alternatively still, Smith and Jones may well be disagreeing about whether Peters or anyone else has the obligation to tell the truth. But if that is the issue, it, too, needs to be couched in larger terms. How, for instance, would communication take place if we could never be sure whether natural speakers of a language usually intend their asserted sentences to be true? How could we make agreements with each other, or how could business be conducted in contractual terms, for example, without a general presumption of truth telling? There are alternative answers to these questions, but they must be given in ways that hang together, not as a piecemeal response to a particular case.

3. *The problem of tolerance.* Because there are many ways to disagree over moral issues, a healthy dose of tolerance is necessary.[10] But, the Naive Relativist takes tolerance to the extreme, and asks us to be tolerant of all people regardless of how their actions affect us. Many times there is conflict about the proper course of action. Indeed, there is often conflict at the level of two competing moral theories. But we cannot conclude from the existence of rival explanations for action that there is no explanation, or that one explanation is just as good as any other. Rather, we

must continue to use our reason to try to sort things out. If we stop before this point, we, along with the Naive Relativist, have admitted defeat in coming to terms with our own lives.

In fact, the extreme tolerance practiced by the Naive Relativist is another good reason for rejecting this view. NR cautions us that morality is personal, serious, and complex, and that since there is a large amount of disagreement, we should be hesitant to adopt a particular moral theory or moral imperative. Judgment is left up to each individual. But, in articulating this view of tolerance in the extreme, NR makes a crucial mistake. Extreme tolerance is in fact not a relative matter. It is a perfectly absolute theory. We might turn the logical tables on the Naive Relativist and ask: What makes you so sure that Naive Relativism is always correct? Isn't the injunction "Always be tolerant" in fact a moral view, and aren't you arguing against absolute moral views? So, there is a contradiction at the heart of Naive Relativism strictly interpreted.[11]

4. *The need for moral debate.* There is an even more compelling line of argument against the Naive Relativist position. For the Naive Relativist the test of whether or not an action is morally correct is whether or not the agent *believed* it to be correct. So, we need not check on the content of a particular action; rather, we need only focus on whether the agent in fact had a belief and authentically acted on that belief. NR entails no difference between "Peters believed that faking the résumé was morally justifiable" and "faking the résumé was morally justifiable." If we want to settle the matter, according to NR, we need not worry about whether or not faking résumés is right or wrong; we need only worry about what Peters believed. The Naive Relativist focuses our moral talk solely on what each person believes and not the content of that belief. Discussions about abortion, infanticide, just wars, civil liberties, capital punishment, bribery, pollution, and power struggles are all a lot of hot air, according to NR, for we can only focus on whether or not someone has a particular belief about these matters.[12]

Here we come to the real weakness of the Naive Relativist: Naive Relativism is the lazy way out. Rather than marshall facts, construct theories, and do the difficult intellectual work required, the Naive Relativist is content to focus on the fact of belief, rather than the content of belief. To do so, we give up hope of coping with the world better than we do now. We give up hope of becoming better human beings. For the Naive Relativist the proper questions would not be "How do we cope better with the world?" but "How do we have the belief that we are coping better with the world?"; not "How do I become a better human being?" but "How do I believe that I am a better human being?" The irony is strong here, for the Naive Relativist shows us that if all we have is authenticity, an ability to act on our beliefs, we will ultimately engage in self-deception, for we will have no way of judging the adequacy of those beliefs, or of deciding which are authentic and which are not, which deserve action and which deserve setting aside. Thus, the Naive Relativist ultimately defeats his or her own position.[13]

We hope that we have said enough to convince you that Naive Relativism is not a useful idea. But, even if we haven't, please notice that the attractiveness of Naive Relativism, that morality is personal, serious, and complex, implies that each of us can stand to gain by reasoning about moral beliefs and principles. It surely follows from these features of morality that we have the greatest need to engage in constructive conversation.

We recommend that you take Naive Relativism as a caution flag that guards against jumping to absolute theories and conclusions. Take it also as a reminder that since moral decisions are personal, serious, and complex, we should adopt a healthy measure of tolerance and skepticism as we try to understand the connection between ethics and strategy. Naive Relativism alerts us to these issues, even if it is an incoherent theory.

ROLE RELATIVISM

Let us now consider the position which Topman articulates when he bemoans the fact that in his role as CEO he is forced to lay off 3,000 employees "against his personal wishes." This kind of relativism stems from the belief that the social roles which we adopt carry certain moral obligations with them. The CEO must put aside his personal beliefs and do what his CEO role requires, that is, acting in the best interests of his company. It is not a question of whether Topman's personal views or his views from the standpoint of a CEO are correct; rather, it is Topman's obligation to perform his role.[14]

Role Relativism is prominent in our highly specialized society. There are many professional groups such as doctors, lawyers, teachers, and nurses, and the move to "professionalism" in our society is well documented. Many members of social groups aspire to a "profession" as a method of climbing the socioeconomic ladder.

If we think of our society as a set of social roles[15] or functions which must be occupied by individuals who will "do their jobs" if society is to work, then morality and moral reasoning become a matter of properly defining these roles and the obligations that are attached to them. To the question "What should I do?" the Role Relativist responds, "Whatever is required by your role."

The intuitive appeal of Role Relativism is apparent when we think about the role of physicians.[16] None of us want our doctor to act solely on the basis of beliefs, but rather we want a doctor to act in the interests of his or her patients as required by the role of doctor. Suppose, for instance, that a doctor truly believed that all business people were "greedy capitalist bastards" and the main cause of evil and injustice in the world, and therefore should be eliminated. Most of us would agree that this personal belief is irrelevant to the practice of medicine and that the doctor's duty is to look after the health of the patient and not to cure the world of injustice. Furthermore, we want to assure ourselves that doctors won't act on such beliefs. We want this so much that we support long and arduous training and socialization programs for doctors. The physician qua physician should act in the patient's interest.

There are parallel arguments for lawyers acting in the interests of clients, teachers acting in the interests of students, and politicians acting in the interests of voters. There is also a parallel argument for managers acting in the interest of stockholders. It goes like this: Regardless of his or her personal beliefs, a manager qua manager has an obligation to act in the interests of stockholders, as their agent. Managers must set aside a concern for personal gain, and even a concern for others, in carrying out their fiduciary (moral) duty to the owners of the business. The trump card is always the role of managers and its duty to stockholders.

A Critique of Role Relativism

The first problem with Role Relativism is that we need some way to determine the obligations which are attached to each role.[17] If we must do what our roles require, how do we know what our roles in fact require? It is here that the Role Relativist must appeal to some moral theory or other to justify a particular role. If the moral obligations of a role are to be justified by appeal to a moral theory, then we have no quarrel with the role theory. In fact "Role Relativism" would then be a misnomer, for there need be nothing relative about a moral theory. But notice how this undercuts the argument given by Topman.

If Topman's action of laying off 3,000 employees can be justified by a moral theory, then Topman ought to do it. (Recall the seriousness of moral matters.) If he bemoans the fact that he, personally, wouldn't do it, then he is saying that he, personally, subscribes to a different moral theory or no moral theory, or else that he personally wouldn't fulfill an obligation. Either Topman doesn't really buy the moral theory in which the layoff is grounded, and therefore he acts in bad faith, or Topman's own interests outweigh the moral reasons he now has for the layoffs. Topman is in trouble either way.

If role obligations are justified by appeal to a moral theory, then that same moral theory makes those role obligations personal ones. Either we buy the moral theory and are committed to acting on it, or we don't, in which case the role obligations are suspect. Topman's reasoning is wrongheaded, because he wants to pretend that he is not to blame, or that he is not required to reason about the layoff because of his role. But either he is responsible, because he believes that he has a moral duty to do what the role of CEO requires, or he doesn't believe it and so needs another course of action. He cannot have it both ways.

1. *Roles in conflict.* This logical problem becomes more apparent when we consider the fact that in many cases we have more than one role. Topman is undoubtedly a citizen of the community. He is also likely to be a father, board member, and church deacon. Many times, roles conflict. If Topman's moral principle is "do what your role requires," then often he will be like Buridan's ass starving to death as he ponders two equally attractive haystacks, unable to decide which to attack first.

How do we solve role conflicts? One answer is that an obligation to do what a role requires is a *prima facie* obligation, not an absolute obligation.[18] It is an obligation other things being equal. In other words, roles create presumptions of obligations, but not actual obligations. For example, to take an extreme case, Topman has an obligation as CEO to look after the interests of owners, but not at the expense of shooting customers who complain too much, even if he could get away with it. Most of our obligations come in the form of "I am obliged to do A unless. . . ."[19] It is how we spell out the "unless" clause that helps us to decide among conflicting obligations. We can spell out the "unless" clause only by engaging in a search for moral principles, and we shall show how to do this in the next chapter. Once again, the "relativism" in Role Relativism is on shaky ground.

2. *The concept of the person.* There is a deeper problem with Role Relativism, one which concerns the concept of the person or moral agent. Topman speaks as if it were not really he but his role that is acting. We are sure that if questioned, part of the reason he would give for his action is "I was only doing my job." We believe that there is a grave danger in this approach. There are striking studies in social psychology that tell us how easily people adapt to roles and how easily we do what is required by those roles.[20] The danger is that by "only doing our job," we never realize that each individual is responsible for whether or not he should adopt a certain role. "Follow role requirements" may be a good rule of thumb, but don't forget that roles are optional. They are human artifacts and must be justified.[21]

The view that the human person is a collection of roles is not a view that we share. It is too easy to assume that we can put on a role the way we put on our socks. We believe that individual purpose and values give substance to a person and the person can adopt roles only in the context of his or her own purposes and values. "I was only doing my job" is never a complete justification for an action, for we can always ask, "Yes, but why were you doing your job? Why did you choose to do it?" Hence, we need a more fundamental account of our action than the role theory can give us. We will turn to such an account in Chapter 8.

SOCIAL GROUP RELATIVISM

In the Case of the Competitive Industry (conversation 3), Rath gets caught fiddling with expense accounts in order to get more sales. In defending Rath, or at least in tolerating his action, Smith appeals to the fact that such shenanigans are accepted practice in Rath's industry and company. Implied in the conversation is that Rath's actions became known outside the company and industry and that the Flannel Company was forced to take action against him. In appealing to this set of extenuating circumstances, Smith is claiming that since what Rath did was accepted practice by his relevant social group, once again we should not judge his action to be morally wrong. We shall call this appeal to the norms of a social group "Social Group Relativism."[22]

Social Group Relativism (SGR) is a slightly more sophisticated version of Naive Relativism, since it moves justification away from the helter-skelter of individual differences to the enduring norms of social groups. Again, it recognizes the right of individuals to act for themselves within the context of their friends and fellows. By SGR, morality is simply a matter of following the norms that are accepted practice.

This version of relativism is especially prevalent in business, and the conversation about poor Rath is one that is all too often heard. Managers argue that conditions and circumstances vary from company to company and from industry to industry, and norms which work well and bode success in one environment may put others at a disadvantage. Hence, smart executives pay attention to situational factors. They often look to see whether or not a particular action is *accepted practice* before deciding what they should do. If an action is accepted practice, then it appears to have some legitimacy, since many persons, at least by their actions, are engaging in it. Sometimes company codes of conduct or industry standards or even laws are meant to codify accepted practice, serving as a guide to what kind of behavior is morally acceptable.

Union Carbide's response to the Bhopal tragedy is a case in point: Union Carbide executives claimed that their safety procedures were as good as or better than anyone else's in the industry.[23] Reports from executives accused of making illegal campaign contributions often stated that such things were accepted practice. Some companies are noted for treating employees well, while others are more like nineteenth-century sweatshops, and both approaches are often justified by accepted practice. Corporate takeover raiders often justify their actions on the basis of accepted practice in increasing shareholder wealth. The recent Texaco-Pennzoil-Getty "broken handshake" is a clear dispute over what is or is not accepted practice in the oil industry, and in the takeover market.[24]

In teaching business ethics cases to executives and MBA students, we often find them asking for data on whether a particular action is accepted practice. Are expense accounts routinely juggled? Are gifts routinely accepted? Are price breaks routinely given via shipping discounts? Are business promises made to be broken? Are employee dismissals accepted practice in times of tight budgets? Social Group Relativism—what is accepted practice—is a pervasive phenomenon in the day-to-day business world.[25]

A Critique of Social Group Relativism

Many of the arguments and caution flags we have raised with respect to Naive Relativism and Role Relativism apply equally well here. For instance, we cannot conclude from the presence of differing circumstances and conditions that no one answer to a moral question is any better than another. Rather, it is the very complexity of business situations which entails a need to search for principles which will guide us through the difficult moral maze that each of us faces. And the relevance of the existence of particular social groups toward moral reasoning, like that of roles, needs to be justified. We hope that at this point in our saga you are getting better at constructing your own arguments, so that you can see why Social Group Relativism is not a good theory or position to believe. Just in case this is still troublesome to grasp, let us give you a few additional reasons.

1. *The problem of pluralism.* The first reason for rejecting Social Group Relativism is that each of us belongs to a diversity of social groups.[26] Except in cases of relatively isolated communities, there might be a variety of conflicting social norms. If SGR is correct, there is no way to decide which norm rules the day. SGR gives us no way, in principle, of deciding what to do in a case of conflicting norms. For example, as a church member Rath might be required to treat all members alike, while as a salesman he might be required to give some customers better prices. In dealing with a customer who is also a fellow church member, which social group norms should apply? SGR is no help. However, we would sound a familiar theme: Rath needs some principles or rules or a theory or a guide which will help with just these sorts of conflicts.

2. *The problem of followership.* The second reason for rejecting Social Group Relativism is that it relies too much on the notion of "accepted practice." Accepted practice is an inherently conservative idea which looks to the status quo to judge what should be done. But it is possible to judge and evaluate accepted practice. (Note that there may well be nothing wrong with a particular practice.) We want our practices and policies to evolve so that they help us to cope better with the world. By focusing on the norms of the day, we never strike out in new directions. We never set new norms. Leadership in the moral realm becomes impossible.

For the Social Group Relativist, there are no moral heroes, only victims. There are no leaders who strike a new responsive chord in others, but only followers who either do what accepted practice requires or who are punished by those who criticize their actions from another viewpoint. This is a real issue for business persons. The public memory is full of robber barons from the past, to be quickly replaced by the latest TV news "rogue of the week" such as Dennis Levine or Ivan Boesky. Because we focus on accepted practice, there are few celebrations. (Lee Iacocca is an exception, but perhaps one based on an equal though positive media hype.) Heroes must, by their very nature, go against the grain of accepted practice. All one has to do is read the stories in the "excellence" books to realize that the champions are the ones who go against the grain.[27]

The very nature of those persons who choose to try to justify their life is to try to integrate conflicting social norms into a whole. They do not see themselves only as members of various social groups but as members of some community which is a totality. Their actions affect others in the community and vice versa. If moral principles are based in society at all they are based in communities, not in individual decision, social professional roles, or the norms of particular social groups. We now need to turn to the idea that morality is relative to the particular culture or "relevant community" in which we find ourselves. This is a case of SGR taken to its logical conclusion.

CULTURAL RELATIVISM

The Case of South Africa (conversation 4) is a lightning rod for a variety of views in business ethics.[28] We believe that the variety of responses proves our point that ethics and strategy are intimately related. Whether or not to do business in South Africa is clearly a question of business strategy. Just as clearly, it is an ethical issue, regardless of whether one believes (1) executives have an obligation to eradicate apartheid, (2) executives have an obligation to promote apartheid, or (3) executives have no obligation with respect to apartheid but do have an obligation to employees, or stockholders, or both.

Cultural Relativism (CR) claims that morality is relative to a particular culture, society, or community (broadly defined).[29] It says that there are no good standards for judging the morality of a particular culture, and the best that anyone can do is to understand the particular mores or moral codes of a given society. CR tells us to understand "South African morality" and "U.S. morality" and "Japanese morality," but do not judge among them. If the norms and customs are shared by members of a society, what right does some outsider have to say, "That action is morally wrong, even though it is within the bounds of your accepted customs"?

The implications of Cultural Relativism for business are vast. More and more today, corporations are operating in a global marketplace. Employees hold allegiances to nations, races, and creeds. Managers may have to be able to do business in such diverse places as Japan, Korea, Saudi Arabia, France, Mexico, China, and Brazil, for example. Indeed, managers face a diversity of cultural norms, from different table manners to different practices with respect to abortion and infanticide. Cultural Relativism is the single most important ethical issue for businesses operating in a global environment.

If Cultural Relativism is true, then managers must obey the local moral code in countries where they operate. Must American managers in Saudi Arabia treat women as the Saudis treat them? Must American managers in South Africa treat blacks as the white South Africans treat them? Must white South Africans treat blacks in the U.S. as U.S. managers treat them? Must Saudis in the U.S. treat women as U.S. managers treat them? CR says yes, on all counts. To the Cultural Relativist, every cultural setting is a veritable Rome, where each of us should be Romans.

Cultural Relativism implies two principles for the operation of corporations internationally:[30]

Principle of Leqal Relativism

If a corporation does business in Country X, then it is obliged to obey the laws of Country X.

Principle of Moral Relativism

If a corporation does business in Country X, then it is obliged to obey the moral code of Country X.

The first principle follows from the fact that the legal system and laws of a country are generally thought to be part of the culture, mores, and customs of a particular society. So, according to CR, if we decide to do business in Saudi Arabia we are subject to the laws and constraints of the legal system. We are obliged to obey them because not doing so would be tantamount to judging them to be unfit or inappropriate according to some external standard. Cultural Relativism says there is no such standard. Of course, we could engage in some sort of civil disobedience, but only within the confines of the particular legal system we are disobeying. To the extent that the legal system has provisions for change from within, businesses operating within a country are free to engage in such change. Indeed, such was the effect of the signing of the Sullivan principles, and several years of pressure by companies operating in South Africa for the current government to change its policies on apartheid.[31]

The second principle recognizes that sometimes morality and the moral code of a particular society differ from that society's legal norms. For instance, it would be true to the spirit of Cultural Relativism to claim that while apartheid is the law in South Africa, it is not part of the generally accepted moral code. Such an interpretation of CR holds that the moral code is that of the majority, not the ruling minority, and a majority of blacks do not in fact believe that apartheid is a morally acceptable situation. A similar case could be made for following the moral code of the majority in Hitler's Germany rather than the oppressive policies of the National Socialist state. The second principle can be thought of as a way for CR to escape oppressive legal regimes. But notice the implications.

It is surely possible for a U.S. corporation to do business in a country which has a radically different legal system and moral code from the U.S. The People's Republic of China is a good example. A corporation operating in China must support the denial of the same basic political freedoms, freedom of speech, press, and religion, that its executives resoundingly defend in the U.S. Yet if it is to do business in China, a U.S. company must obey the laws or the moral code, at least according to CR. Companies even find themselves in situations where one government says "Do X" and another government says "Don't do X." Such was the case of Dresser Industries. The French government commanded Dresser's French subsidiary to sell parts to the Soviet Union for the gas pipeline to Europe, and the U.S. government forbade Dresser or any of its subsidiaries to sell parts to the Soviet Union.[32]

Cultural Relativism poses a substantial challenge to our view that we must search for moral principles hand in hand with our search for strategy. For if Cultural Relativism is true, the search for ethics is over. We merely obey the local customs, codes, and laws. Fortunately there are several compelling reasons to reject Cultural Relativism. There is also a kernel of truth in this doctrine, and it is to a critical analysis of Cultural Relativism that we now turn.

A Critique of Cultural Relativism

Cultural Relativism says that the corporation must be "all things to all people," at least in its sphere of operation. It is a warning against moral imperialism, imposing one's morality on others, or judging them by standards which they do not accept. As a warning, and like Naive Relativism, it is useful, for we need constant reminders to be tolerant as we embark on a search for ethical principles to put at the core of our corporate strategies. However, there are three compelling arguments which prevent us from taking Cultural Relativism any more seriously than as a warning. CR is not a position which has sound logical support.

1. *The problem of conflict, again.* The first argument is really a restatement of the arguments against Naive Relativism. Where cultures and cultural norms conflict, we need some help. In the example cited above, Dresser must act. If we follow CR, then the advice is simply "Do whatever

you like, because you violate a cultural norm (the law) whatever you do," and then we have simply given up any hope of reasoning through a tough situation. CR tells us to admit defeat, that our reason and rationality will no longer serve us.

Once again, we believe that this is the lazy way out. Cultural Relativism, like its naive cousin, depends on whether or not an action is in fact in accordance with a cultural norm. And it focuses on "the fact of belief," in this case a society's belief, rather than on the actual content of the belief, or the resulting action. Finally, Cultural Relativism doesn't follow from the fact of differing cultures, or from the fact of disagreement among cultures, for the same reasons that Naive Relativism doesn't follow from interpersonal disagreement. These disagreements spell out the need for moral reasoning and a search for principles which resolve them, rather than simply throwing up our hands in hopelessness.

2. *The problem of tie-breakers.* The second argument for rejecting Cultural Relativism is related to our discussion of the principles of Legal Relativism and Moral Relativism. Exactly whose norms are to count as the prevailing cultural ones? Societies are by their nature heterogeneous, with many conflicting "cultures," ethnic groups, races, and norms. Societies with a clearly established moral code are the exception, rather than the rule. Of course, there are some common principles across many cultures, such as "Don't kill innocent persons" or "If it would cost you very little to do a great benefit to someone, then you ought to do it" or "In most cases, unless there are extenuating circumstances, you ought to obey the law." But these principles are precisely the kind that we believe can be established by reason. Such a "common morality" is one starting point for evaluating the differences among cultures. It is all too easy to simply accept as a cultural norm a belief held by the elites in a society. Many times the prevailing norms simply favor the group in power at the expense of other groups. Cultural Relativism as a theory cannot explain this fact. The proper reply to Smith in the Case of South Africa is, "Apartheid is not the prevailing moral code of South Africa; rather, it is a means of the strong to oppress the weak."

In taking this line of reply to CR, we illustrate again an important feature of moral reasoning and moral choice. It is optional and voluntary. If, in fact, a society freely chooses to live by a particular principle, imposes no cost on any group or segment of society that chooses not to participate in such a system, and imposes no real cost on others outside the society, then it is difficult to find an argument against such a principle. But this is rarely, if ever, the case. Such a community we would call "tightly structured" or "extremely homogeneous." Notice, however, that the reason we fail to find fault with such a community is that a principle of voluntary agreement has been satisfied. The existence of such a community would not be evidence for Cultural Relativism, but rather evidence for how strongly we believe the notion that a person or society has a right to make its own choices so long as it imposes no costs on others.

3. *Relativism and reason.* A final argument against Cultural Relativism is that it seems to be an open question: "How should society be structured?" or "What norms are justified?" It makes sense to question whether or not the norms of the Nazi society were in fact morally correct. If nothing else, we hark back to the notion that within limits we can choose the society that we live in. We can certainly choose the societies with which we trade and do business. If such a choice is to take into account the effect of our action on the projects of others, then we are in urgent need of a method of reasoning about these choices and how they affect others. Just as we can question the law and legal apparatus from a moral point of view, so can we question the particular social norms of a group or society from a moral point of view. "Is this law a just one?" is a well-formed question, where the person who asks such a question is engaging in a meaningful act, not speaking gobbledygook. Likewise for the person who asks, "Is this society's norm of X morally correct?"

THE KERNEL OF TRUTH IN RELATIVISM

By this point you must be weary of our endless argument against relativism in whatever guise. What is the point of this extended analysis? We believe that relativism represents an admission that our human reason can no longer be useful. We believe that relativism represents an admission that we must engage in other forms of human interactions such as deception, physical coercion, even war, rather than try to do the admittedly difficult job of resolving conflicting moral viewpoints. Such a position may ultimately be correct, but we believe that there is much more hard work to be done before we reach such a conclusion. Finally, we have taken this extended tour of relativism to show you that accepted practices of strategy are laced with appeals to relativistic reasoning.

Certainly in business, where "business decisions" are often divorced from "ethical decisions," the task of articulating consistent sets of moral principles which can be helpful in formulating and implementing organizational decisions has barely begun. If relativism wins the day, this task will never be attempted, much less completed.

Morality and moral reasoning are indeed personal, complex, and serious. We conclude from these facts about such decisions that we *must* judge others and their actions in terms of how they affect the projects and hopes of those around them. We must also show a large measure of tolerance, for ethics, like business, has no place for arrogance. Because of the difficulty and seriousness of the nature of the decisions facing corporate managers, we need more than ever to engage in the search for ethics.

Relativism warns us of the variety of the human species, of the existence not only of communities but of diverse individuals. The proper level of tolerance is a real virtue, but in the extreme it becomes an all too easy vice that excuses any action. If Topman were running XYZ Corporation and excused an egregious accounting blunder by "Well, he thought he was doing the right thing," no one would be impressed. So it goes for the ethical realm as well. Authenticity is a necessary but not sufficient condition for the moral point of view, simply because there is a broader community with which we must be concerned, namely, that community of actors and moral agents whose life projects our actions can affect. And here, in the interplay between individual and community, is the kernel of truth in relativism.[33]

The notion of a broad human community is an important one, for in fact it gives us the intuitions that make relativism attractive and the intuitions that defeat it as a theory. Human communities give rise to communication and to language. Without a community, language itself is impossible. In fact, we all communicate through some language, and to communicate we must literally speak the same language. To speak the same language is to share the same kinds of experience, to live together in some sense of solidarity. We must know the accepted and proper use of words, else we cannot communicate. If we share the same kinds of experience—for example, the experience of language learning, family ties, and meaningful work—we already have a common base from which to look for principles. If we have no basis for communication, then we have no reason for morality and moral principles except as a way of codifying our beliefs about what our obligations might be to "persons" or "things" with which we have no communication.

Suppose we encountered an alien society, and all attempts to communicate with this society failed. If we could infer that the aliens were sentient, then we might have some basis for continuing to attempt communication. But if we could make no such inference, then we would have very little, if anything, in common. There would be no basis for exchange. We would come to see the "aliens" much as we see rocks and trees. Morality would simply not apply. The very fact that we speak each other's language means we are tied together in a larger human community independent in our own sphere and interdependent as well. The existence of such a human community makes the search for principles to govern our interactions an extremely important one. In philosopher Richard Rorty's terms, we need to figure out how we can "cling together against the dark." The darkness impels us to practice tolerance of differing views as well as a willingness to engage in a conversation with other cultures and with our history.

Finally, we might take from the various theories of relativism the idea that two moral theories or two sets of consistent and coherent cultural norms and legal systems can be equally justified. Just as in science, we suppose that this can be the case. At one time scientists thought that the wave theory of light and the particle theory of light were equally supported by the evidence. But notice what happens when two scientists or two conflicting schools of thought have competing hypotheses: they propose experiments or further evidence or revisions in the theory to sort out the conflict, or they search for those mechanisms which would sort it out. They can either find a standard or principle or theoretical revision which allows both hypotheses, or they can give up working.

Moral theory works the same way. It is incomplete and fallible. There are many times when we get it wrong, are mistaken, need new theories, or are not sure of the judgment in a particular case. We only point out that this is an argument for doing more work rather than giving up.

We began this chapter with four case studies which are based on real business situations. We hope that you see that none of these cases are good reasons for relativism. Relativism tells us to be tolerant. Relativism tells us to understand that we live in a broad and diverse human community. But if we are to cling together in solidarity against the dark, acting authentically on the very best reasoned beliefs and values, we need to search for principles that will help us. We will find no absolutes. We will be able to formulate no magic bullets for business success. But we will be able to look ourselves in the mirror and know that we have given every effort to articulate the intimate connection between our moral views and our business decisions.

★ ★ ★ ★ ★ ★ ★ ★ ★ ★ CHAPTER **3**

Reasoning about Ethics

THE LANGUAGE OF ETHICS[1]

In the previous chapters we have argued that ethics and strategy are intimately connected. We have tried to debunk the myth of relativism, the view that one idea or theory of ethics is just as good as any other. So, we can get on with the business at hand: showing how the Axioms of Corporate Strategy can be applied to connect thinking in strategy with thinking in ethics. The purpose of this chapter is to introduce you to the power of ethical reasoning. This is a natural process in which we engage everyday. If our argument about the revolution in management is correct, we need to be explicit about it and work to improve it. If business is to escape the moral low ground where it now resides, it must address issues in ethical terms.[2] And if we are to convince you of our "personal projects view" of organizations, later in Chapter 8, we need to say some more about the key ethical concepts of harms and benefits, rights, good, values, moral values, common morality, and the method of ethics known as reflective equilibrium.

Let us return to the AT&T divestiture example of Chapter 1.[3] We claimed that the divestiture was a moral decision in the descriptive sense of "moral," because it distributed harms and benefits to various groups with a stake in the decision. Also, it gave priority to the projects of some

REASONING ABOUT ETHICS 45

groups over others. Let us suppose that Charles Brown, CEO of AT&T, decided to use the language of ethics in making the divestiture decision. (Later, in the next chapter, we will show you how to systematically connect strategy and ethics via the notion of Enterprise Strategy.) To keep things simple let us also suppose that Mr. Brown had only two alternatives: (1) to continue to fight the Department of Justice (DOJ) in court and (2) to agree to the divestiture. Regardless of the alternative that is finally chosen, many arrangements must be made to convert it into action. Some will involve the revision of ongoing working relationships with bankers, unions, operations managers, and other employees within the company, as well as the establishment of new contracts with customers and new "understandings" with competitors and government. Some bargains will have to be forged from scratch, especially if AT&T is divested.[4]

Mr. Brown is leading a process that is profoundly ethical in nature. Ethics is the inquiry concerned with the justification for persons' actions. Such justification is the search for a coherent set of rules or norms which guide our actions when they cause conflicts with others. Our actions cause conflicts with others when they result in important harms or benefits, or when they prevent others from carrying out their projects. We need such rules because our projects often conflict, and it is the hallmark of civilization to solve conflicts without resorting to violence.[5] Each of Mr. Brown's bargains is a moral matter—moral in its nature—because the action of one person, or a group of persons, has a significant bearing on the important projects of others. The language of ethics is the language of harms and benefits, and rights and rules. It is a language that each of us knows how to use, but because of the myth that business and ethics are unrelated, its application in actual business decisions is lagging.[6]

We will use "ethics" and "morals" interchangeably. But we must be precise about how we use the adjectives "ethical" and "moral." Again, a situation is moral or ethical in a *descriptive* sense if the actions of a person affect the important projects of another person. This is the sense in which we will employ the terms. The opposites of these meanings are "amoral" and "nonethical." "Moral" and "ethical" are also *evaluative* terms, applied in a statement about the propriety of a given action. Our intent in writing this book is to build a strong case that strategy is intrinsically a moral matter in the descriptive sense, laying the groundwork for making moral judgments in the evaluative sense.

What kinds of concerns will Mr. Brown surface as he decides to use the language of ethics?[7] By using ethical reasoning, he will be able to discern who is harmed and who is benefited by each alternative, whose rights are protected and whose violated, and he will find a panoply of decision rules to use. For starters he will have to answer some simple questions, and in doing so he will discover that he needs a deeper understanding of moral theory. We will use these questions as a starting point for reflection on such issues, and we recommend that you try to answer them for each strategic decision that you make.

1. *Who is affected by this decision?* Regardless of the alternative chosen, stockholders, employees, customers, government, suppliers, local communities, competitors, and many others will be either harmed or benefited. In fact, even this list is problematic, for it is a list of generic persons, not actual ones. (Recall our argument against role relativism.) Ethics is about the effects of our actions on identifiable individuals and groups. By dealing with faceless and nameless generic groups, we are tempted not to use ethics at all. Actually specifying who is concerned with a particular decision, or who are the *moral agents*, is a tough, nontrivial task.[8]

2. *How is each agent affected? What are the harms and benefits?* Each strategy alternative may yield different results. If AT&T continues to fight the DOJ, it is far from clear what will be the outcome. If AT&T prevails, then stockholders, employees, customers, suppliers, and local communities will experience "business as usual." To the extent that business as usual benefits or harms these groups, the current allocation of harms and benefits will continue. Obviously, the government will suffer a defeat and be harmed, as will competitors who stand to benefit if AT&T is divested (or so they believe at the time). However, if the DOJ prevails, AT&T will be forced to make drastic changes, including divesting Western Electric and possibly parts of the local companies, and it will probably be prevented from going into the computer business. Some stakeholders will be harmed, while others will derive benefits.

Before this kind of analysis can be taken further, we would need a detailed account of the needs, wants, desires, and values of each stakeholder group. Before calculating the harms and benefits to each group, we would need to know the *interests* of each group, its purposes and projects. In the following section, we propose the concept of a group or individual's *good* to further specify harms and benefits.

3. *Who has rights?* Calculating harms and benefits, and devising a single measure of net benefit, represents one way to "do ethics," but there is another tradition. The notion of *rights* is complex, and we'll give a more complete explanation later. For now, in the context of the AT&T example, think about rights as entitlements.[9] At issue is this question: Given the past history of AT&T, who is entitled to benefits or to participation in the decision to change the allocation of harms and benefits? There are many arguments.

First, we might argue, stockholders have rights. Because they have risked their capital they are entitled to some return. But what about employees? After all, being employed by AT&T was a virtual guarantee of lifetime employment. By specializing their skills with "the only game in town," the employees came to *expect* lifetime employment. Because these expectations were reinforced by all parties, employees became entitled to them, or at the very least they are entitled to participate in decisions which will make major changes in lifetime employment. But what about customers? Historically, the cost of telephone service has been quite low. Costs were capitalized over long periods of time to keep basic service at an affordable price. "Universal service" became generally accepted by all parties. Customers came to expect basic service at an affordable price. Similar arguments can be made for other groups.

Rights, understood as entitlements, evolve out of sets of expectations that are stable over time.[10] Behavior becomes predictable, and we begin to count on it and plan our lives accordingly.[11]

We can also understand rights in a slightly different way. Rights come about as a method of living together in a civilized manner. In the Western tradition, this means that each of us has the right to pursue his or her projects. Rights set the boundaries for how our projects are allowed to affect others. They serve as side constraints on our actions. If harms and benefits were the only moral concepts, and if the decision rules we used were a version of "maximize benefits to society," then we could easily justify sacrificing the well-being of some people for the benefits of others.[12] Slavery, racism, and other terrible human inventions have often been justified by appeal to harms and benefits. Rights, though difficult to deal with, are an important part of moral argument.

4. *What decision rule do we use?* Even if Mr. Brown has the very best information about harms and benefits, and has thought clearly and deeply about who has rights, he still needs to decide on an appropriate decision rule. He might begin by examining some rules that each stakeholder uses.

Traditionally, management has believed (or claimed to believe) that it ought to maximize stockholder wealth. So, Mr. Brown could examine each alternative from the standpoint of stockholder interests. He could make those interests the trump card.[13] Alternatively, he could view the situation from the standpoint of employees, or employees and customers, or from "the public interest." Oftentimes these viewpoints will conflict, and he needs to choose one.

Note that whichever rule Mr. Brown chooses, he automatically allocates harms and benefits to other stakeholders. To put it differently, each decision rule has an implicit set of rights assignments, and each decision rule is a moral rule. (We will have more to say about moral rules below.) If he uses the stockholder interest rule, the stockholders are guaranteed winners.[14] If he uses the employee rule, then employees are guaranteed winners. He needs a way to find a decision rule which is effective.

These four questions—(1) Who is affected? (2) What are the harms and benefits to each? (3) Who has rights? (4) What is the decision rule?— are a start at addressing business decisions in ethical terms. In the following sections we want to delve into ethical reasoning in more detail, so that in the next chapter we can show you a number of ways to systematically connect strategy and ethics. The First Axiom of Corporate Strategy says that we must understand "values" and their role in motivating action, while the second says that we must understand where values conflict, that is, the ethical nature of strategy. Specifically, we need to examine the concepts of the good, values, rights, common morality, and reflective equilibrium. But there is a caveat. There are no easy answers, and we will not give you a simple four-step procedure for being ethical. Our approach is to show you how some concepts work, and to encourage you to apply them, perhaps clumsily at first, to real issues that you face.

PURPOSE, SELF-INTEREST, AND A CONCEPTION OF THE GOOD

Jane is Treasurer of the Blue Mountain Company and is on the fast track to being named Chief Financial Officer. But she is restless with this awareness. Her aspirations have focused more and more on the CEO position. She has watched the career paths of her peers and notes the edge given to those with marketing experience. Jane is sufficiently conversant in marketing concepts to perform in her role as an officer, but she still sees a deficiency. Finally, after a major product development meeting, she announces to the CEO and senior marketing executives that she wants to be considered for a District Sales Manager opening. Further, she offers to take a six-month leave in order to serve as a sales trainee. The reactions to her statements are swift: "Why would you do something like that? That's irrational!" Making this decision was not easy for Jane, and this kind of response does nothing to boost her resolve in pursuing the new purpose. How can ethics help describe this hypothetical, but all too real, situation?

Jane and her colleagues and friends are interested in what is best for her to do. Ethics helps us focus on the matter of "best" through a concept known as *the good*. Jane, like all competent persons, has a conception of her own good, or "that which is good for her." For each of us, our good is given particular meaning by the best possible plans for our life that we individually envision. Note that Jane, like us all, can only act on her own good with the natural and developed skills that she has. But, the *goodness* of her efforts is determined in comparison to her good, and not some abstract model human being.[15] Since the act of reflecting upon one's own good involves reasoning about oneself, having a conception of the good and acting in accordance with it are characteristics we generally associate with a rational person. Of course, some persons are generally believed incapable of rational deliberation, and they are deprived of the opportunities to make choices about their own good. In this category, we might include young children, convicted criminals, the mentally retarded, and—as many management theorists seem to believe—all persons associated with the modern corporation.

Still, Jane is a competent person, and whether hers is an "irrational" decision turns on the particular sense of good that she entertains. We will say that Jane's decision appears to be a "good" one, insofar as it is consistent with her plans. There are several clear messages in this for corporate strategy. First, identifying one's own good, much less that envisioned by others, is a difficult task. Few persons wear their good on their sleeves. However, if we are truly to discern harms and benefits of our action on others, we need to understand their concept of "the good."[16] Second, we have said nothing about whether the good is the only important element of a person's self-interest. In fact, if we stopped with this discussion, one would rightly see ours as a description of pure egoism. We will fix this incomplete depiction of rational action shortly, but we must next attend to a third aspect of the good. Jane's good is inevitably a complex pattern of preferences and desired future outcomes. We can only understand Jane's good if we look to concepts of "purpose" and "values," as the First Axiom of Corporate Strategy and the Values Principle require.

Purposes and Values

Jane has succeeded beyond her own expectations, and three years later she is CEO at Blue Mountain Company and is facing a strategic decision. A proposal sits on her desk recommending immediate release of GF4, a major enhancement to the company's main product line. Blue Mountain's market researchers, as well as an outside consultant, project big things for the product. Several major customers have gone so far as to deliver letters of intent for the largest individual orders in company history. The revenues would be welcome to Blue Mountain stockholders; profit margins have been on a decline for five years.

But the GF4 report is not the only one on Jane's desk. Another comes from an independent testing laboratory. Under some rather likely operating conditions, the testers report, GF4 could cause serious injury and illness to users. Three design features are fingered as contributory to most of the test failures. Overall perfomance results meet standards set by the industry's trade association, but failures slightly exceed Blue Mountain's own, longstanding criteria.

Jane has summoned Peter, Senior Marketing Vice President, to tell him that she wants a complete engineering check on the product. She knows that this will delay market delivery for at least six months. His reaction is not surprising.

PETER: Why are we hurting ourselves when the market is eating out of our hands?

JANE: I see liability suits of major proportions every time I think about GF4. We would be devastated with our current margins and difficulties in buying coverage.

PETER: The risk is virtually nil. We meet industry standards. Besides, we're all set to go with GF4. The sales meeting last week was like nothing I've ever seen here. We'll lose our go-getters if we pull out now!

JANE: I'd rather endure all that pent-up energy than have a disaster on our hands. That problem is fixable.

PETER: Yes, but we heard three years ago that the redesign would be prohibitively expensive. Besides, I can't go back to our major customers now and ask for a higher price. I've already quoted a price estimate.

JANE: We'll cross that bridge when we get there. You know that prices are not set yet anyway. Look, I know you're disappointed, but it's not as easy as saying that our revenue problems are solved with releasing GF4. In good faith, I cannot agree to releasing it until we have more assurances.

Why was this hypothetical product withheld from the market? Some might be inclined to say that Jane had the power and Peter did not. But Jane had the power of her office to do many things, including approving the release and ignoring the other news. So, power may not explain the event very well.[17] Others might be inclined to say that the decision was made for the good of the corporation. While this may turn out to be true, the potential effects on Blue Mountain's viability are neither patently positive nor detrimental.

Ethics points to a different source for explanation, namely, *values.* When a person values something, he or she wants that thing, or wants that future state of affairs to come to pass. Values are relatively permanent desires, intrinsically worthwhile to a person.

Values are the answers to "why" questions.[18] If we ask you why you are reading this book, you might answer, "I want to learn about ethics and strategy." If we ask why learning about that is important, you might answer, "It will help me be a better manager." If we ask why that is important, you might claim, "I will get promoted sooner and make more money." If we push you here, you might say, "I'll be able to spend it on the Picasso that I want." These questions will go on until you reach the point where you have no answer: You will reply "Damn it, just because I want it!" At this point you will have arrived at a value.

Consider the values behind the discussion between Jane and Peter. Peter stated his preferences for: responding to the wants of major customers, avoiding the communication of bad news to his salespeople, proceeding on a "normal"—by some standards—level of risk and honoring a verbal commitment to a customer. Jane was acting upon preferences of her own: revenue is not reaped at any price; major customers' interests do not hold absolute sway, and failure to correct foreseeable problems is irresponsible. In the end, she appeared to act on this last value in concert with one overriding value: "I cannot condone, and claim to be guided by, an act that significantly violates my own standard." To do so would amount to acting in bad faith. Now all or perhaps only some of these values will be intrinsic, that is, will be things which are wanted for their own sake, rather than as a means to a more important end.[19] Regardless, we will eventually have to find these key values if we are to really understand Jane's and Peter's actions and their conceptions of their own good. Values aren't mysterious. They aren't little things inside our heads or our hearts. Rather, they are like electrons. If we are to explain certain things, we must believe that they exist. Philosophers call such things theoretical terms, and much confusion exists because we can't see them but only their effects. The effects of values are revealed in behavior. But that is the way that all sophisticated scientific theories work, from particle physics to economics.

Values explain action.[20] When Jane, like all of us, acts intentionally, she has a reason for acting. In broad terms, that reason is the belief that performing an action will have a desirable result. Thus, we may say that an intentional action is the product of a certain belief and a certain value. Together, these two entities cause the action. Jane valued the preemption of a series of harmful product failures and believed that her action in denying the product release would have the effect of preventing harm. Values can certainly conflict. In cases such as the one just described, it is not possible to act according to all of one's values. Some will override others. From this, we can infer, as we saw in Chapter 2, that values often come with riders in the form of "unless" clauses. Jane may value responding to Big Customer Z, unless circumstances such as the product's test results intervene.

We should also understand what values are not. They are not mere dreams, espoused but never called into action. This is not to say that persons always act in accordance with their values. We sometimes act against the grain of our values while under pressure, and we can be confused about our values at times.

Furthermore, values are not mere slogans or folklore. Much has been made about "values management."[21] For a value to incite intentional action, it must be clear and salient enough to guide the person among alternative choices. The value "We do things as a team," for example, begs the question about the range of its applicability. Similarly, a value such as "The customer always comes first" does not provide much guidance for Jane and Peter in the GF4 example. In fact, we could logically justify contradictory actions on the basis of such a motto.

Values are central to strategy.[22] The whole point of corporate strategy is to act intentionally in the name of some collective, the corporation. The alternative to corporate strategy is to act randomly or according to the dictates of an outsider. It follows that acting strategically is a matter of acting according to certain values. The values that support a corporate strategy are the most important purposes that we are able to admit to ourselves, or discover by questioning others. They are embodied in our most important projects, which will take them to fruition.

Purpose, Rights, and Duties

Let's elaborate on the conception of purpose from Chapter 1 in the context of interdependent action and of the notions of "the good of a person" and of his or her values. At this juncture, ethics provides a crucial, broader perspective that mere consideration of purpose and strategy does not. What is it that enables persons to believe in the first place that they can act on their values and toward their own ends? And what limits prevent the pursuits of self-interested individuals or corporations from becoming pure anarchy? We need some concepts and some rules or principles which adjudicate the disputes that naturally arise because individuals each try to realize conflicting ideas of their own good.

Ethics provides the fundamental concepts of *rights* and *duties* as the bases for answering these questions.[23] A right is a claim that entitles a person to "room" in which to take action. In more formal terms, we might call this a person's "sphere of autonomy." Rights, like values, are rarely absolute. Rather, we commonly think of the exercise of a right as being conditioned by the potential interference with other persons' rights. For example, a person has a right to freely speak his or her mind, unless that action inhibits someone else's right to choose a job, as might be the case if the words were slanderous. Rights are also provisional in the sense that we need not act upon a right in order to retain it. Each of us, for example, can refrain from making a comment. In short, the reason why persons have any confidence that they can pursue unique life plans, tailored by values of their choosing, is that they possess certain rights to do so.

But rights are bounded. In the vocabulary of ethics, *rights are correlated with duties*. That is, whenever someone possesses a right, someone else has a duty to respect that right. A duty is, quite simply, an obligation to take specific steps. Rights and duties, thus, provide a full framework in which persons can take action of their own accord. With these twin concepts, we can also finally define a *moral agent* as a person competent to both understand the idea of "the good," both for him or herself and others, and to have a sense of duty in interaction with others.[24]

Now, all this may appear far removed from the day-to-day problems of corporate strategy, but this is not the case. Take the problem in Chapter 1, where we asked you to think of corporate strategy as intimately concerned with bargains in the marketplace. The very notion of a bargain presupposes that a bargainer has the right to seek an agreement in the first place. The notion of bargain also depends upon assurances among bargaining parties that the terms of an agreement will be honored. The duty to honor one's freely given commitments is fundamental to any claim that corporate strategy is even possible. Duties come in two basic varieties. Some duties apply to us because we enter into specific agreements with others. Other obligations exist in a more general sense among all competent persons in a society. Let's look at an example to see how all of this works, and to introduce one more ethical concept.

Apple Computer cofounder and Chairman Steven Jobs, as we might expect of a successful entrepreneur, grew tired of his association with Apple.[25] His ideas and those of Apple's operating executives seemed to go in different directions. Stripped of all day-to-day duties at the company, Jobs started his own company, Next, Inc., and hired away eleven of Apple's finest engineers.

Apple's managers could hardly be indifferent to what Jobs was doing. His track record was impressive. Moreover, Apple products had been under intense competitive pressure since IBM entered the personal computer market several years earlier. Add to this the suspicion that Apple was, in effect, supplying Jobs with basic R&D support when the eleven engineers walked away. Strategy and ethics were clearly enmeshed as values came into sharp conflict. The lines were drawn, and Apple filed suit.

In linking strategy and ethics, we now need another concept: *moral rules*.[26] Recall earlier that Mr. Brown of AT&T needed some rule to adjudicate the conflict of interest among a variety of stakeholders. Moral rules guide persons through situations where competing interests collide. We can think of moral rules as "tie breakers," guidelines to which persons appeal when agreements are at an impasse. They are rules for behavior, which often become internalized into *moral values*.

These rules have several characteristics which distinguish them from other rules for behavior. First, moral rules prescribe a certain action. "I should not lie, unless . . ." is clearly imperative about a certain behavior. Second, for moral rules to have the most extensive coverage possible, such statements must be generalizable to many situations. People who are serious about moral rules must be willing to have that rule applied to them in all similar cases. We have already encountered appeals to particular moral rules elsewhere in this chapter. Jane, our hypothetical CEO, decided to withhold GF4 on the basis of this moral rule: One should not contribute to the harm of others when one can take steps to prevent that harm. And, for the reasons discussed in the context of the AT&T divestiture above, a moral rule is expressed in the common performance criterion: We should maximize stockholder wealth, unless financial viability of the company is threatened.

These two examples reveal two additional characteristics of moral rules. First, such statements are usually not absolute, but instead are conditioned on some type of event—that is, the relevant circumstances for application of the rule. Finally, moral rules produce an allocation of harms and benefits and rights. Following moral rules solves the problem of conflict for which they were intended.

Jobs and John Sculley, CEO of Apple, reached a settlement in January 1986. Their agreement, as publically reported, is instructive about purposes, duties, and moral rules in two important ways. First, the case provides us some clues about what moral rules were used. Though we cannot be sure, there are several possibilities. Apple executives appeared most interested in seeing their proprietary rights to certain ideas protected. Further, they wanted to protect their investment in highly skilled engineers. Third, they wanted to avert an all-out outbreak of raiding for talent among firms in the Silicon Valley. Jobs sought to get his product on the market with a minimum of impediments, including lengthy legal proceedings. Next's financial position was probably not sufficient to withstand stepped-up hiring raids. In the settlement, Jobs agreed to permit Apple engineers to inspect a prototype of Next's product, and promised to delay deliveries until mid-1987. In return, Apple agreed to conduct the check for proprietary infringement within thirty days and to drop the suit. Jobs also consented not to hire Apple employees for six months.

From these sketchy details, we can infer the moral rules that led the parties to their agreement. Note that none of the parties must necessarily use these exact words in justifying their actions. In order to claim that certain moral rules were "at work," we need to reason from action to a broader principle behind that action. There may, in fact, be several such principles in a given case. In agreeing to the thirty-day provision, Sculley may have been acting on a principle such as this:

> We should not interfere with another party's business ventures, unless we have reason to believe that our rights to use proprietary technology are willfully violated.

On the matter of Jobs and other Apple employees moving to Next, the following principle may have been activated:

> We should not interfere with former employees' pursuits after leaving Apple unless they accrue material benefits for their new venture at Apple's expense.

On Jobs' part, his consent to the six months' hiring truce implies a rule constructed something like this:

> We should not interfere with an active employment relationship, unless all parties voluntarily agree to a termination of the relationship.

Each of these possible rules displays the characteristics noted above. Each mandates an action (the "should" is a hint). Each is stated in relatively general form. Each is conditioned upon certain possible events.

And each produces a result which gives priority to some party, or distributes harms and benefits in a certain way.

There is another instructive aspect of the Jobs-Apple settlement. It is the very existence of a bargain grounded in rules. To say that strategy and ethics are linked does not imply that the respective parties must completely deny their individual good. Indeed, any meaningful connection must take the good of each party into account. Jobs and Apple management did not share identical values, but found the terms sufficient to justify their coming to agreement.

Moral agents, individuals or corporations, need some assurance that the webs of bargains to which they are parties will be supported more generally. They are interested not only in the fair execution of specific agreements, but also in their ability to consummate new agreements.

Moral theory is complex. Actually working out all of the puzzling aspects of concepts such as "rights" and "harms and benefits" as they apply to business takes time. Where do we start, and how?

COMMON MORALITY AND THE METHODS OF ETHICS

We propose a concept from philosophy known as "common morality."[27] It is really very simple. Common morality is that body of rules which covers a large part of the ethical situations in which we find ourselves. Common morality is that set of rules that most of us live by most of the time. If we start with common morality, we can equip ourselves to deal with new situations. Let's briefly examine some basic principles of common morality and see how they work. In the following section we will describe the method of common morality which turns it from a sterile application of rules to a dynamic ethic which shapes our lives as human beings living together.

Some Principles of Common Morality

Most persons want some assurance that others will, on the whole, do what they say. We want to know that people keep their promises. Without the simple convention of promise keeping, social interaction would grind to a halt. Business would be impossible. How could people pursue their projects in life if whenever they made a deal with someone, the deal was likely to fail? Every moral theory that we have encountered holds some version of the following principle:

Principle of Promise Keeping

Most persons should keep most of their promises most of the time.

In keeping with our earlier discussions of "unless" clauses, we surely want to allow for complex circumstances, but all things being equal, the Principle of Promise Keeping is pretty basic.[28]

Earlier in this chapter we alluded to the concept of rights as a way to avoid the violent outcome of conflicts of interest. If we had to constantly worry about physical safety, our wants and desires would have a decidedly different flavor. We can capture this basic feature of most moral theories in the following principle:

The Principle of Nonmalevolence

Most persons, most of the time, should not inflict physical harm on others.

Once again there are clear exceptions. We allow and even obligate police to use force to subdue criminals in certain cases. We countenance wars that we believe are "just." And we permit persons to defend themselves when attacked unjustifiably. But on the whole there is a general moral prohibition against physical force and violence. Indeed, the very nature of morality, in whatever guise, is the attempt to escape the use of violence to solve disputes. Violence is always available, when moral reasoning fails.

Morality and moral codes exist in human communities among persons who jointly and separately pursue their interests. Most community members want to be assured of truth telling and physical well-being. But only a part of physical well-being stems from being free from attacks. We also want to know that our fellow citizens are going to help us, if the cost to them is not very great. So, we get the following principle:

The Principle of Mutual Aid

Individuals should help others in need if the cost to themselves is not very great.

Obviously, our set of moral principles need not require that we give away our wealth to the poor (though some particular theories might recommend it), or undergo great sacrifice for other community members (families may be an exception). However, the Principle of Mutual Aid is really a "good Samaritan" approach that can be seen as investing in the commonality of the community. Without the ability to get help from others, it is highly improbable that stable bargaining can occur, for sometimes bargaining agents need to give in to the needs of others even at some cost to themselves.

Principles like promise keeping, nonmalevolence, and mutual aid for the bedrock of social intercourse. They aren't absolute, but it would be enormously difficult to do anything if most persons didn't follow them. Obviously, there are other aspects of common morality; and very briefly, here are two, which we will discuss at more length in Chapter 8.

Principle of Respect for Persons

Most persons most of the time should treat each other as ends in themselves rather than as mere means to the ends of others.

Principle of Respect for Property

Most persons most of the time should gain the consent of others before using their property.

While these two principles are more controversial than the preceding ones, they are the cornerstone of our Western society. Treating persons as ends rather than as mere means involves treating them seriously, giving them reasons in terms of their own good for actions rather than persuading them, and making their projects important simply because they are their projects. Respect for property is a corollary if you think of a person as owning his or her own body, or if you think of property as an extension of the rights that people have to use those things which are theirs. Property rights are more complex than we can explore here, but suffice it to say that any workable analysis of property rights has to dissolve into a discussion of the right to enter into agreements.

Common morality has direct relevance for corporate strategy because this code is not the only institution which provides guidance in our social interactions. The emergence of the modern corporation presents special problems for ethical reasoning, because the moral rules implied by corporate action can conflict with those of common morality. For example, invoking the Principle of Mutual Aid to assist a person in need of help might draw sneers from corporate managers, if the distressed party were a competitor. So, before we go much further, we need to show you how the language of ethics fits together, and, in particular, how to apply the concept of common morality to business situations. This involves understanding the most fundamental methods of moral theory.

The Process of Common Morality: Reflective Equilibrium[29]

Common morality is about rules. If rules are to help us, they must give us guidance in our actions. The process of reasoning about rules and common morality is no different from the process of reasoning about other human endeavors. We begin with our judgments about some actions or decisions. Because ethics is designed to solve conflicts, and because in our Western civilization we believe that each individual has some basic rights, we want to be sure that the process of rule making is free from individual bias. In other words, the rules should apply to everyone, not only for a particular situation. So we take our judgments about a case, and check them for personal bias. We consider whether our judgment would be different if the actors were different, as opposed to their interests. (Clearly the interests of different actors may require different solutions.) We then try to formulate a rule which would cover other, analogous cases. A second case comes along, and we apply the rule. We check the answer with our considered judgment about the case, and we have two choices: revise our judgment, or revise the rule. There is no magic, until we examine a large number of cases. Let's see how this abstraction works in a simple, "everyday" example.

Lisa Yuppie, in a seemingly unprovoked attack, takes an ax to Michael Coworker. Michael's demise is immediate.

First we need to find out our considered judgment. Most of us would judge Lisa's action to be wrong. Perhaps we have a value that makes human life extremely important. Perhaps we have evolved a moral value not to violate the rights of others. (Note that there will always be some deviants—indeed, healthy society requires them—so our judgment won't be unanimous. Note also that Lisa may herself believe that she is doing nothing wrong, or even something good.) We look at the facts: Michael is innocent, and made no menacing moves that we know of toward Lisa. Michael's rights have been violated, if rights have any meaning at all. The benefits to Lisa don't seem to outweigh the rather sudden and final harm to Michael. Any way you cut it, Lisa's actions are wrong. And if the tables were turned and Michael had axed Lisa, our judgment would be the same. And if "I" were involved instead of Michael and Lisa, my judgment would be the same. Our (my) considered judgment is that Lisa's action was wrong.

Next, we search for a rule that will help us in similar cases. We immediately find: Killing coworkers is wrong.

Next, we come upon some new cases. Over at Acme Tool and Die, Beth Yuppie has taken an ax to coworker Herbert Scum. Our immediate judgment is that Beth's action is wrong, using our rule. But suppose the circumstances are different. Suppose that Herbert has threatened Beth with physical violence unless she agrees to stop smoking in the office, and suppose Beth sees Herbert oiling his handgun with a glint in his eye. Perhaps our judgment might be for Beth, and we might need to revise our rule to "Killing *innocent* coworkers is wrong." Killing others in self defense is permissible."

We have carried on this farfetched story long enough. You quickly get the idea of how it works. We revise our considered judgments and principles in a process of mutual adjustment until we have a coherent set. This set of principles is in some kind of equilibrium. They can be revised, but usually we feel comfortable enough with them that we use them as guides for making judgments. They adequately describe our view of "the person," and they depict the workings of a set of just social institutions. Notice that the very same process works in finance or accounting or marketing, where we have certain principles that we have deduced from cases. We use these principles to solve other cases, occasionally revising the principles or, more usually, revising our intuitions about what is a good decision. Most reasoning works this way. The only difference in ethics is that we use "harms," "benefits," "rights," "values," "moral rules," and such language to formulate and apply principles.

We don't have to start from scratch in moral reasoning, since we already have common morality. There are cases which will cause us to revise the principles of promise keeping, nonmalevolence and the like, perhaps even give them up, but we can use them as a starting point. Another way to look at this point is that the process of reasoning about moral principles helps us to see the exceptions and spell out the details of the "unless" clauses.

Likewise, we don't have to start from scratch in business ethics. There are lots of principles from which to choose, and lots of cases to compare. Since most business decisions are ethical in nature, we use some implicit principles all the time. Finance theory has implicit ethical principles. (Can you pick them out?) Marketing theory has implicit ethical principles. Business policy has implicit ethical assumptions. Indeed, in some of the very first business policy texts, ethics was thought to be quite important. And organizational behavior, with its "theories of the person," certainly has ethical assumptions. Most of the parts of "business theory" simply hold their ethical assumptions fixed. It is the job of business ethics to question these assumptions, and to show how new cases may lead to revisions. Business ethics is concerned with cases that cannot be easily handled with the current theory or the models that we have in each of the functional disciplines. Therefore, it searches for new principles that can create new ways of making decisions.

Here are a few principles that should be familiar to you:

P1. Always tell the truth to customers in your advertising.
P2. Act to maximize the well-being of stockholders within the confines of the law.
P3. Balance the interests of stakeholders.
P4. Bring about the most social good that you can.
P5. Follow standard business practice most of the time.
P6. Fulfill your contractual and promissory obligations.
P7. Try to achieve personal success and wealth.
P8. Treat employees with dignity and respect.

The problem is not that we have no rules; it is that the rules we have often conflict. The common morality of business is up for grabs in lots of cases. Dennis Levine and Ivan Boesky have violated accepted practice and broken the law; however, their actions have caused a renewal of the debate about whether there really is anything wrong with insider trading from several points of view. Their actions also failed to fulfill their promise not to engage in insider trading, and part of the current outrage among business people may signal that the doctrine of sanctity of contract is pretty important.

Corporations which have restructured in an attempt to fulfill principle P2 have not fulfilled principles P3 and P4. Are these good rules? Which ones should we choose? Pretty clearly, this set of principles is not in reflective equilibrium.

Where Do We Go From Here?

The real point of connecting ethics and strategy is for you to decide which principles you really believe are good ones to follow, and to reason about them in real-life cases. The only way to do this is to look at case after case after case, and by applying our concepts of harms, benefits, rights and rules. Can we do that systematically so that eventually we find a set of principles in reflective equilibrium?

We have taken much care to show that ethics is no mere adjunct of, and no mere afterthought to, corporate strategy. Strategy, as purpose, relies upon the precedent of ethical reasoning. By converging on the matter and meaning of purpose, we have given the first glimpses of how ethics provides a meaningful framework for corporate strategy. Much remains to be said on this, but one issue must be addressed before moving ahead. Students commonly object, at this point in the discussion, to an implication that ethics is concerned with everything about purposive action. But there are definite boundaries to the reach of ethics. We can identify these limits by observing several misconceptions about ethics and its application to strategy.

Ethics, first, is neither merely having good intentions nor feeling sensitive. As our many examples show, ethics is about action in association with others. It is true that social interaction is enhanced by virtues such as honesty, but these qualities must be translated into action to have any moral force. Ethical behavior, second, is not substantiated by comparing one's virtues with those of another. The test for our sense of propriety is only administered in the context of the duties that apply to us as others demand that their rights be honored. Ethics, third, is not identical to philanthropic activity. A person who has a duty to honor a contract to repay a loan does not merit moral praise for reneging on the promise and then giving a small fortune to the arts or charity. Duties are duties. Most persons, nevertheless, would look favorably upon philanthropy. The point is that duties cannot be traded, or offset. Furthermore, as the Jobs-Sculley case demonstrates, two parties can meet their moral obligations without acting benevolently. Finally, ethics is not merely a tool for deriving greater profitability or greater employee commitment to a given strategic program. A moral duty to respect a right must be fulfilled simply because the right has intrinsic worth. If financial benefit ensues from acting dutifully, the benefit is coincidental to the right, not justification for honoring it.

In the next chapter we will try to show you seven different alternatives for systematically connecting ethics and strategy, each of which will have its own set of implicit rules, or common morality. Then, after a tour of current models of corporate strategy, and an examination of their implicit ethical assumptions, we will return, in Chapter 8, to our attempt to find a corporate strategy based on a set of principles in reflective equilibrium: our answer to the search for ethics in corporate strategy.

★ ★ ★ ★ ★ ★ ★ ★ ★ ★   CHAPTER **4**

Enterprise Strategy: Making Ethics and Strategy Work Together

LINKING ETHICS AND STRATEGY

In the previous chapters we have established that ethics and strategy are connected. Most issues that require strategic thinking also require ethical thinking. We argued that by thinking about our common, ordinary notion of "purpose," we could begin to see how both strategy and ethics are concerned with the development and realization of our purposes. We also showed how the language of ethics, values, rights and duties, harms and benefits, rules and common morality, and such was also useful in thinking about corporate strategy. In this chapter we want to look more concretely at a way to make ethics and strategy work together. We will introduce a concept called "enterprise strategy," which lets you combine the best of ethical and strategic thinking into an answer to the question "What do you stand for?" To show you how this works, let's go back to the cases in Chapter 1 where we claimed that ethics and strategy were connected.

AT&T and Divestiture[1]

In Chapter 3 we argued that Charles Brown, CEO of AT&T at the time of divestiture, had the option of using the language of ethics in deciding what strategic decision to make. We showed how he might have approached his decision if he had used our four questions: (1) Who is affected? (2) How is each harmed or benefited? (3) Who has rights? (4) What decision rule should be used? Let's approach the same problem from the standpoint of justification. A justification, in this case, is the best answer to the question "Why did AT&T decide to divest its operating subsidiaries, the Bell operating companies?"

There are many possible answers to this question, and managers and scholars alike will no doubt devote many hours and books to its answer. The first thing to notice about the question, however, is the kind of answer that we are likely to give.

When the divestiture decision was announced, the immediate response was to analyze the impact of the decision on the industries affected, such as telecommunications and computers.[2] The reasons that AT&T and many others gave to the question "Why divestiture?" was in terms of the basic business strategy of AT&T. Mr. Brown, Chairman and CEO of AT&T, claimed that AT&T could have a clearer definition of its business, free from regulation and the uncertainty of the judicial process.[3] Obviously, the computer and telecommunications industry were merging because of the microchip revolution, and it just didn't make any business sense to arbitrarily split them. In divesting, AT&T saw the opportunity to plunge into the computer business with full force.

But, as complex as this answer is, there is another point to the question. Imagine a critic of the decision who says, "Yes, I understand the business logic, but I want to know what the reasons really were.[4] Given that for years AT&T symbolized public service and a commitment to building the best telephone system in the world, why did AT&T decide to divest? Given that the divestiture of AT&T required a radical departure from the expectations of employees, customers, suppliers, and others about how AT&T must behave, why did AT&T decide to divest? Did AT&T decide to change the things that it stood for? And, if so, why?"

The explanation that the critic calls for is one in terms of the basic values of AT&T and its executives, and those other groups affected by divestiture—that is, in terms of the very purpose of the enterprise and its members.[5] "We thought we knew what it meant to be a customer of AT&T, or an employee of AT&T, or even a regulator of AT&T, and now these very definitions seem to have changed. What are the values of AT&T? What does it stand for?" The executives of AT&T, as well as the other architects of divestiture, would surely respond to this line of questioning with "It was the best thing to do," but this won't satisfy the critic, nor will it address the point of these questions. How is "best" to be conceived? The critic wants to know for whom it was the best thing to do. Let's see what some answers to this set of questions would look like.

1. *Divestiture was in the stockholders' interest.*[6] This answer assumes that the uncertainty surrounding a continuance of the status quo—the antitrust suit, regulation, and so forth—would have brought down the price of AT&T stock over the long term and adversely affected its ability to

earn profits and generate cash. Stockholders would be harmed, or they would be forced to take their investment dollars elsewhere, leaving AT&T to pay higher costs for financing, thereby harming stockholders. Indeed, this answer is a familiar theme to anyone interested enough in business to read annual reports, newspapers, or elementary business textbooks.[7]

But our critic wants to know more: Why is it "stockholders" who count? Why should stockholders' interests be the "trump card" in the decision to break up Bell? These questions are really questions for an appeal to a moral obligation. They are requests for some "ought-judgments," which themselves are the best answers we could give. For instance, the questions could be answered if we believed that managers, including AT&T managers, have a moral obligation to stockholders to increase their well-being as much as possible. It would make sense to ask then, "How does this obligation come about?" but such a question is a request for a general theory that goes beyond the AT&T case.[8]

Answer 1, above, is a good answer to the critic only if it is embedded in a theory, or set of beliefs, that managers have moral obligations to stockholders. The theory would then have to be justified, that is, shown to be in reflective equilibrium with our other considered judgments about cases. And we would have to work long and hard, in reaching an important decision like divestiture, to really examine whether or not it was in the best interest of our stockholders (here is where the initial answer above about AT&T's business is relevant).

Notice that it just doesn't make sense for our critic to now say, "I know that AT&T had a moral obligation to stockholders, and I know that divestiture was in the best interests of these stockholders, and I know that the executives of AT&T took their moral obligations seriously, but I still don't understand why they decided to divest." The appeal to morality gives us the best possible reason for our actions.[9] This is why morality and reasoning about morality are so serious. Morality represents, or should represent, the end product of our reasoning, the very best answers to questions of "Why did you do that?" Let's look at some other possible answers.

2. *Divestiture was in society's interest.* This answer claims that a net positive gain to society will be the result of AT&T's divestiture. If it is carefully worked out, it would need to describe the effects on the whole society of allowing AT&T to compete in the computer business, and it would have to balance those with any harm done to stockholders, customers, employees, managers, and other stakeholders.[10]

Notice that it may well be the case that answers 1 and 2 are both true. But it is important to see that either one may be capable of standing alone. It can easily be argued that it is society's interest which counts, even if stockholders are harmed, just as some would hold that stockholders' claims have priority even though society may be harmed. There are several other plausible reasons that could be given, and we will address some of them later in this chapter.

The important point, for our purposes in this chapter, is to notice that by appealing to society's interests we are appealing to morality and ethics to justify a "business" decision. Furthermore, if we can establish some good logic for the moral and ethical claims that we make, we will have given the best answer that we could have given to our critic.

The question "Why did AT&T divest?" fundamentally raises moral and ethical questions. As we saw in Chapter 3, it is a request for the language of ethics. It is an appeal for the values and moral rules that the corporation and its executives hold. There are many possible answers, even in terms of ethics. We need to look at some more examples before we try to generalize about the connection. However, notice that if we can link this appeal to ethics with the business strategy of a company it will be possible to fomulate strategy on the basis of ethics.

Corporate Pac-Man

Why did Bendix try to buy Martin Marietta, setting off the chain reaction of each trying to gobble up the other? This question is probably more difficult than the previous one, but it illustrates a different aspect of the problem of linking ethics and strategy. It is usually not enough to reason in terms of consequences. We have to also understand what the intention of management really is. Part of the answer to the AT&T case was undoubtedly that AT&T believed that stockholders, employees, customers, or society, or some subset of these groups were being served. We can criticize whether or not divestiture was really in the interest of the groups that AT&T executives believed it was. Did they get the facts right? Or we can criticize whether or not AT&T management really believed that they had an obligation, for example, to stockholders, customers, and employees. Were they acting merely out of concern for keeping their managerial prerogatives? This comes out more clearly in the Bendix case.

If popular accounts in the press are to be believed, the senior management teams at Bendix, Martin Marietta, Allied, and United Technologies, and even the advisers of these companies were really concerned with growth and the accumulation of power. Perhaps the outcomes of this concern were also in the stockholders' and society's interest, but it is plausible to believe that the motive behind their actions, the basic value, was simply to gain control over more resources.[11] After all, why should any company want to buy another one? Stockholders of the acquiring company can buy the stock themselves in the capital markets. And resources can also be procured in the factor markets. Without further evidence, we can formulate a "managerial supremacy" theory that links ethics and strategy this way (we should note that the Bendix case is much more complex than its simple statement here):

> Management has a moral obligation to exercise its prerogative to manage
> and to gain control over as many resources as possible.

You might think that this statement is rather selfish, and is unworthy of the label "moral." However, it is closely tied to a whole tradition of moral theory called "egoism."[12] Also, it is worth noticing that if management is permitted to act to further its position, the effects on others may well be positive. After all, the stockholders of Bendix did do rather well in the resulting deal with Allied. We can't dismiss this connection between ethics and strategy lightly. Indeed, we need to develop it further.

The striking fact about the Bendix case is the tangled web that was woven by all of the actors involved. We are sure that at some point, literally no one knew what would happen if certain events took place. For instance, what would happen if Bendix had bought Martin Marietta, and what if Martin Marietta had bought Bendix? What were the roles of the investment advisers of each? What happened to the interests of employees and the community? What was the role of the government? The point is simple yet powerful.

Just as complicated strategic problems have to deal with a host of interests and issues, so do moral problems have to adjudicate the conflicting claims of multiple parties. By trying to base strategic thinking on ethical thinking, we are seeking to find some ways of establishing certain interests as "trumps." The "stockholder theory" which will emerge out of our earlier analysis says that stockholder interests are trumps. The "society theory" will make a similar claim about the interests of society. The "managerial supremacy theory" will claim that it is management's interests which should rule the day.

These conflicts are difficult. They are not just conflicts over how to conduct business, and therefore are not purely business issues. They are conflicts over how the world *should* be. All of the actors in the case wanted their own preferred outcomes to be actualized. Each wanted his or her values to win the day. While the resulting conflicts are about different views of the world, they are incredibly important, since they motivate action. The conflicts are fundamentally about ethics and values. They are about the set of moral rules we are going to adopt and which will guide our lives.

The Excellent Companies

In *In Search of Excellence* and *A Passion for Excellence*, Tom Peters has uncovered some phenomenal stories.[13] These stories have a striking similarity. The heroes are acting on the basis of deep-seated beliefs and values. In "In Search of" Peters finds people acting out of concern for customers, employees, profits, service, and a multitude of other values. In "Passion," he's looked closer and found that customer service and quality are really the key variables.

Now Peters goes to great length to show us that customer service and quality yield great profits.[14] He wants to take pains to show that this is not another bunch of "soft mushy stuff," but some real "hard-headed" business. No one who has read the books or seen Peters' presentations, or experienced the phenomenon himself, can have failed to be moved by the very dynamism that is depicted. But it is extremely unclear exactly what the driving force really is.

We don't believe that Peters has found a bunch of maniacs who really care about profits. While profits are necessary, the accomplishments are so great and the commitment so genuine that it is tempting to say that the basic value of stockholder well-being is the exception rather than the rule. In many cases customer service and quality are ends in themselves. Profits are a by-product, and an important one, but these heroes no more live for profits than each of us lives in order to produce more blood, as important as blood is to us.

We need to probe deeper and ask how customer service and quality are ends in themselves. We believe that the answer is simple. If managers start with the Principle of Respect for Persons, then those individuals with whom they interact every day will get respect. What does such a high-minded phrase as "respect for persons" really mean? It means, in part, seeing individual customers and employees as whole and complete, functioning persons, capable of making choices, listening to reason, enjoying the work that they do, feeling happy, sad, angry and joyous, and trying to find meaning in their lives. Most important for business, it means seeing persons as capable of making voluntary choices, and having a high degree of autonomy.[15]

We believe that the basic ethic of the excellence revolution is the respect for the individual. It lies beneath the surface of the concern for customer and quality, and it is the key to understanding the incredible commitment and performance that are the results. But we must keep in mind that performance is a side benefit, not an end in itself, and this is the hardest thing for managers to swallow. The excellence revolution can easily be misused. Give respect to individuals, not because they are worthy of it, but because they will perform. These misuses of ethics are just as prevalent as its proper uses (perhaps more so), and we will have a lot to say about this "bad faith" and manipulation in the chapters that follow. The foregoing is very different from most explanations given for corporate strategy. In Chapters 5 to 7, we will contrast our way of reasoning about corporate strategy with others.

The Task of Management

In Chapter 3 we saw that the language of ethics is applicable to corporate strategy, but there was no clear consensus on a set of principles or common morality for business. Rather than set forth some principles which everyone should follow, we want to articulate seven ideal types of strategy each of which would have to be defended. We are less concerned with your believing our approach to strategy (detailed in Chapter 8) than with your working out your own connection between ethics and strategy.

With these cases in mind, we have enough material to be more general about the connection between ethics and strategy. It revolves around adding a question to the traditional theories of corporate strategy such as the four asked in Chapter 1: (1) Where are we going? (2) How do we get there? (3) What is our blueprint for action? and (4) How do we measure progress?

ENTERPRISE STRATEGY: WHAT DO WE STAND FOR?

Corporate strategy usually starts with the question "Where are we going?" or Peter Drucker's famous question, "What business are we in?" But if strategy is about purpose, and if the examples in the previous section are valid, then there is another, deeper, ultimately more important question for executives to answer. We propose the question "What do you stand for?" as one which must be answered alongside "What business are you in?" and as one which will link ethics and strategy. "What do you stand for?" is an explicit appeal for a purpose, and as such, it forms a direct link between ethical reasoning and strategic reasoning.

Ethics is necessary, in part, because we all want to justify the lives that we lead. We want to be able to stand back and evaluate our actions in terms of whether or not they form some coherent pattern of meaning. We want to believe that our lives are not in vain. At some time or another, all of us have asked, "What do I stand for in life?" And we have been led to examine our actions, past, present, and future, in terms of the answers that we give. If you know what you stand for, then whether or not you decide to do something should be in harmony with your basic values and ethics.[16]

All of us are familiar with this pattern of reasoning that we apply in our everyday lives. Our point is pretty simple: There is no fundamental difference in the corporate world. Corporations must ask and understand the answers to the question "What do we stand for?" just as each of us does in our daily lives. What business we are in will be constrained by what we stand for. Because most of us stand for a basic right to life, we are opposed to the practice of murder. Similarly, if we stand for opposing repression, whatever its form, we will not choose to do business in South Africa if we believe that the system of apartheid in fact oppresses people. We cannot connect ethics and strategy unless there is some point of intersection between the values and ethics that we hold and the business practices that exemplify these values and ethics. In order to build strategy on ethics and avoid a process that looks a lot like post hoc rationalization of what we actually did, we need to ask "What do we stand for?" in conjunction with our strategic decisions. We can't wait until later.

There is a complicating factor. It is far from easy to decide just who the "we" are in the case of the corporation. There are many separate questions, such as "What does the senior executive team stand for?" and "What does all management stand for?" and "What do all employees stand for?" and "What do all stakeholders of the corporation stand for?" However we decide the "who" question, the "what" question remains.

We propose the concept of "enterprise strategy" to denote the conjunction of ethical and strategic thinking.[17] "Enterprise strategy" as originally envisioned by Peter Drucker and others was to give a *raison d'être* for the firm, a way of conceptualizing the enterprise as a whole rather than as a group of discrete entities. The only meaningful way to refer to the enterprise as a whole is to look for some basic values and some ethical principles.

We believe that a company has a coherent enterprise strategy, or E-strategy, as we sometimes call it, if it exhibits a commitment to a set of purposes or values and ethical principles. This commitment must be shown in the way that the company acts, and not merely said in the annual report. It must literally define the businesses that the company is in, as well as the way that it conducts itself in these businesses. It must answer the questions "Whose interests do we serve?" and "What are the trump cards around here?"

Enterprise strategy is not easy to think about, just as corporate strategy is not always simple. It requires an uncompromising commitment to honesty. If you are not willing to really examine your actions as well as your words, then enterprise strategy will harm you and your company. If you state that you believe in one thing and your actions show that you believe in another, you place yourself in a position of bad faith with others and self-deception with yourself. The executive who mouths "stockholder supremacy" yet turns down proposal after proposal which would merge the company at a premium to stockholders is acting in bad faith. If the management then really believes that it is acting in the stockholders' interest, despite all evidence to the contrary, then it is deceiving itself. Enterprise strategy won't help such a company and its management.[18]

On the other hand, if you want to build strategy and do business based on what you really believe in, and are willing to submit these beliefs to careful scrutiny in order to gain some coherence and consistency, then enterprise strategy just might help. By making such a connection between values, ethical principles, and basic business logic, we can make our corporations the human institutions that they need to be, serving human purposes rather than subverting them.

The Flavors of Enterprise Strategy

Enterprise strategy (E-strategy, for short) starts by answering the question, "What do we stand for?" There are many possible answers to this question. We do not have one formula, or really any formula at all, even though in Chapter 8 we will try to defend one conception of E-strategy that we believe is desirable. For now, it is important to see the variety that is available.

From our experience, and our interpretations of the business world, we have identified at least seven different conceptions of enterprise strategy. Each of these seven "theories" assumes different moral views and gives different answers to questions of whom the corporation owes moral obligations and whose interests it should serve. We do not believe that all E-strategies are equally defensible, however; we shall concentrate on their statement rather than their defense. Each articulates fundamentally different corporate strategies, and different ways of life for corporate members and stakeholders. It is possible for a particular action to fall under many different E-strategies, but over time, different E-strategies will lead to different patterns of action, simply because they are based on different systems of ethical principles. Remember, as you read this list, that E-strategies are the basics. They are what you stand for. They symbolize your perceived moral obligations. Your actions may also be in the interests of others, outside the scope of your E-strategy, but that will not be the reason for the action. The E-strategy is the best possible reason (given that your E-strategy can be articulated and defended) for the actions you and your firm take.[19]

The seven flavors of enterprise strategy are:

1. Stockholder E-Strategy: The corporation should maximize the interests of stockholders.
2. Managerial Prerogative E-Strategy: The corporation should maximize the interests of management.
3. Restricted Stakeholder E-Strategy: The corporation should maximize the interests of a narrow set of stakeholders, such as customers, employees, and stockholders.
4. Unrestricted Stakeholder E-Strategy: The corporation should maximize the interest of all stakeholders.
5. Social Harmony E-Strategy: The corporation should maximize social harmony.
6. Rawlsian E-Strategy: The corporation should promote inequality among stakeholders only if inequality results in raising the level of the worst-off stakeholder.
7. Personal Projects E-Strategy: The corporation should maximize its ability to enable corporate members to carry out their personal projects.

In the following section we shall explain each kind of enterprise strategy and give some examples. An important caveat is in order. We have only begun to articulate these strategies. This is not a cookbook, and what follows is not a set of recipes. Formulating your own E-strategy is not as simple as choosing what to have for dinner. These seven proposals should be taken as food for thought, as a potential menu, once we have learned much, much more about how ethics and strategy go together. Our work is extremely exploratory, and we hope to stimulate you to do more.

Some Examples of Enterprise Strategy

What follows are brief sketches of some potential enterprise strategies. Each of them could well be the subject of a book in its own right. We shall merely try to show you what kinds of values and ethics each would hold, to assist you in beginning to formulate your own enterprise strategy.

1. *The Stockholder Enterprise Strategy.* Familiar to all managers, this strategy is the cornerstone of the U.S. business system. Stockholders are the owners of the firm. They have put up their capital and bear the risk of the firm, and therefore management must act as their loyal agents. Managers have a moral obligation to act in the stockholders' interests. Stockholders' claims are the trumps for the corporation.[20]

It is often thought that the stockholder E-strategy is to be counterposed with "ethics," that ethics requires managers to do something else in addition to acting in the stockholders' interest. Such is the argument in favor of corporate charity. However, clever defenders of the stockholder view such as Milton Friedman have propounded it as an ethical theory. They believe that managers who do not act in the stockholders' interest are behaving immorally.[21]

The fundamental ground of this theory is some notion of property rights and private property. It is because managers have been entrusted with the care of owners' property that they must act in their interest. This theory is often confused with a utilitarian notion that says that if managers maximize stockholders' interest, then the greatest good for society will emerge, but we shall treat that separately. The stockholder E-strategy says that the *raison d'être* of corporate action is that it furthers the interest of its owners, the stockholders. It is enough to know that a particular action is the best one for the stockholders in order to know that it must be done.

Are there any companies which really operate on this principle? There are certainly many who believe they do, or at least say that they do. But words and deeds are quite different. What would such a stockholder-oriented company look like?

First, management would have to always seek and entertain bids for the company which would give stockholders a premium. They would always look out for the best possible deal for the stockholders, even if it meant giving up their own positions. Second, they would have to run the company in a lean manner, insofar as management perks and salaries go. They would have to pay what the market demands to get the best management, but there could be absolutely no fat in the expense budget. Product and market choice would be determined solely by financial criteria. Products which do not produce would be dropped, and markets which are not profitable would be closed. No public contributions or community activity would be allowed except insofar as there is a direct relationship to profitability. No corporate jets would display company colors. Employees would be expected to perform to the limit in order to further the interests of stockholders. The company would be oriented to the short term, constantly worried about the returns to investors today.

You might want to stop us and complain here. Surely we have painted too stark a picture. Surely we need to take account of the long term and "long-term profitability."

We think that the answer to this objection is easy. If you really have the stockholders' interest at heart, you'll understand that if the company doesn't earn up to the level of market returns, then the stockholder who continues to hold the stock is just crazy. There is no long term for stockholders. The capital markets ensure that stockholders are short-term creatures.[22]

If you think that you stand for the interests of stockholders, and service to stockholders' goals, ask yourself the hard question about the long term: Is the long term merely a rationalization for my keeping my position? Stockholders want quarter after quarter of increases in the value of the firm. Short-term excellence naturally blends into long-term excellence.

We think that there are fewer companies that actually follow a stockholder E-strategy than there are companies that believe that they do. We would take as evidence for our view the recent spate of proposals for poison pills, golden parachutes, and corporate restructurings as a way to prevent the capital markets from effecting even more takeovers.[23]

The strength of this strategy is that there is a whole body of theory in economics and finance that usually accompanies it. We know, or at least think we know, what a firm run in the interests of stockholders would look like. It fits nicely with our economic theories about markets, and at least explains the words, if not the deeds, of a great many corporate executives. It also fits nicely with our intuitions about the sanctity of private property, and the responsibility of someone's agents to respect his or her property.

The weaknesses of this view are many. First of all, we need to ask whether owning shares of stock is like owning a chair and a table. Is corporate property like other forms of property? The answer is not simple. Second, what happens to the claims of other groups that are affected by the use of this property? Normally, we are not permitted to use our property however we want to, and we are responsible for the consequences of its use. Are stockholders responsible for the use of corporate property? The whole notion of limited liability says that they are responsible only for the amount of their investment, and this doesn't seem right from a common-sense moral point of view.

We shall have more to say about this E-strategy in later chapters, especially Chapter 6, where we examine the moral assumptions of the economics of corporate strategy and the marketplace. Suffice it to say that the debate rages about its worthiness, and it is quite difficult to follow in practice, though easy to put into words.

2. *The Managerial Prerogative Enterprise Strategy.* This E-strategy claims that management's interests are the supreme claims. Management must act in its own interests. In serving its own interest, management is best able to act, for it is simply human nature for us to act in our own self-interest. Why should we expect anything more of corporate managers than we do of most people? Usually, those who believe that the managerial E-strategy is desirable also believe that stockholders, society, or some other group will also be served, but this is a side benefit and not the motivating force behind adoption of the strategy.

Berle and Means's classic statement of the separation of management from control of the corporation and the ensuing debate in the academic literature during the last fifty years predicted that management would begin to follow this strategy, if it was left uncontrolled by government or other methods.[24]

Why have we chosen to call this a connection between ethics and strategy when it is often said to be an example of how ethics and strategy differ? Simply because to believe the managerial E-strategy is to make some claims about the connection between ethics and strategy. We see no need to rule it out by definition. A defense of it would have to be made in terms of ethical egoism.[25] That moral theory is not totally discredited. For instance, it could be argued that if managers pursue their own interests, and if others in society do so as well, then checks and balances may occur and the resulting system will be a good one. If we want managers to do something that is not in their interest, the resulting dishonesty and deceit will erode the public's confidence in business as an institution. The outcome of such a process will be more and more regulation of business so that each of us is unable to pursue those purposes that require business as an institution.

What would life be like in a company run according to a Managerial Prerogative E-Strategy? First of all, there would be no pretensions that the interests of other parties counted, if advancing these interests did not simultaneously advance the interests of management. The dance around the question "Does this proposal maximize shareholder wealth?" could be made optional. The relevant question would be, "What do we have to do to keep shareholders happy so that we can continue to use the company to advance our own cause?"

Notice that management would still have to satisfy customers, suppliers, employees, and owners, since the firm would literally fail if these groups withdrew their support. But the *raison d'être* would be the interests of management. In a way, many owner-managed small businesses follow a Managerial Prerogative E-Strategy. These firms do not try to be all things to all people, and if certain actions aren't in the interest of the entrepreneur, then they just aren't continued. Perhaps such an E-strategy is more pervasive than we think.

More important, it seems to us that many corporations are actually run on the basis of the managerial prerogative E-strategy, regardless of whether or not anyone would admit it.[26] The overwhelming evidence of the prevalence of the managerial prerogative view is reason enough to try to state such a view. Maybe it can't be defended, but let's try, so that we can put aside the issue of bad faith, espousing "good" things like public service, stockholders, and so on, while really being driven by the egoistic values that underlie the managerial strategy.

In the rush to formulate principles for governing the corporation, either in the law or just in theory, we often forget that management should also count as persons. Managers have a real claim to a stake in the corporation, perhaps in addition to the claims of others. Understanding the values that are behind this particular claim is crucial if we are to really link ethics and strategy.[27]

We shall have more to say about this E-strategy in our discussion in later chapters of the moral assumptions behind current models of strategic management. Suffice it to say that while this strategy is pretty easy to follow in practice, it is difficult to follow in words. We have yet to see a statement of it appearing in an annual report or in *The Wall Street Journal*, or an academic treatise recommending it as desirable for management to follow.

3. *The Restricted Stakeholder Enterprise Strategy.* This strategy is a more general version of the earlier two, and so much of what we have said applies here. The Restricted Stakeholder E-Strategy says that some narrow set of stakeholder interests are what management stands for. It is customers and employees and stockholders that are important, for example, and our role as managers is to serve these groups.

Why would you believe that you have an obligation to serve these groups? Well, it may be that you believe that each depends on the corporation, and therefore on you, for its success, or its well-being, and that by the nature of its relationship with the corporation each has some claim which needs to be honored. Therefore, it is your obligation as trustee for the corporation to honor its claims and contracts.

This E-strategy broadens the notion of the purpose of the corporation, and it is becoming more and more prevalent today. A company run in this manner pays attention to the claims and needs of those groups who are in the "restricted set." Thus, if customers are there, management must be "close to the customer." If suppliers are there, then "fair dealing with suppliers" must be paramount. Ultimately, this E-strategy forces you to decide questions of how much participation each group should have in decisions which affect it.

Since there are many possible versions of this strategy, let's pick one for further analysis: the Employee-Stockholder-Customer E-Strategy (ESC).[28] In an ESC company, the interests of these groups would be the trumps. Many of the stories told by Tom Peters make sense only if the companies involved believe in customer service, employee participation, and making money.[29] These organizations are built to be responsive to the needs of these groups. Any activity which did not advance the interests of these groups would be peripheral. Thus, in an ESC company, we would expect relatively little time and attention to be paid to community service, lobbying and government affairs, trade associations, media relations, and fancy dinners with suppliers.

When the obvious conflicts of interests arose, they would have to be balanced. For instance, suppose that an ESC needed some employees to work long, arduous hours in order to fill customer orders. If such demands were routinely made and the employee had little choice other than accepting the demands or being dismissed, we would claim that such a story is evidence that employee interests are not being balanced. A more likely scenario for an ESC would be for all employees to be willing to sacrifice some of the time in return for higher wages, or more vacation, or some other benefit that is in their interest.

Rather than say more about the ESC strategy, we urge you to read Peters' books, and to ask yourself: What fundamental purposes are being enacted by the stories that he tells? What are the real values at work? What do the companies, and their heroes, really stand for?

The problem with this strategy is straightforward: How to pick a set of stakeholders to serve. What principle can you use to single out, for instance, employees, customers, and stockholders? What about the community? Or suppliers? One answer may be that ESC really advances the interest of society, but then notice that ESC is a means to an end, rather than a fundamental end, and the point of E-strategy is to find ends. A second answer is that employees, stockholders, and customers have more at stake. They stand to gain and lose more than other stakeholders. The moral principle underlying such an argument is something like this: Collectives or organizations should be run in the interests of those who have the most to gain or lose. But it is hard to defend such a principle, if it involves trampling on the rights of some who have only a little to gain or lose but who may still be disadvantaged. However, we also know that these problems are going to be there for almost any E-strategy, so we believe that the Restricted Stakeholder E-Strategy can be a viable one from a moral point of view.

4. *The Unrestricted Stakeholder Enterprise Strategy.* Once again much of what we have said above applies here. Companies that adopt this strategy of serving all of those groups that have a stake in the firm usually do so because it is an operationalization of "serving the public interest." "Public interest" is general and vague, while "stakeholder" denotes a definite set of groups and individuals.[30] After all, if all of those groups that have a stake in the firm are satisfied, then what is left over for "the public?" If "the public" has a stake, then by definition it will be included; however, if it does not, it is not affected and should not be served. Typical groups that have a stake include, in addition to those discussed above, media, protest groups, government, and communities.

Of course, the interests of these groups conflict, but this strategy says that it is management's job to sort out and solve the conflicts of interest. The usual basis for this strategy is an ethical theory known as "utilitarianism." It appeals to our intuitions that we ought to seek to bring about the greatest good that we can, at least if we are going to act in a morally commendable way.[31] If management takes these "public service" values seriously, then it will adopt a version of the Unrestricted Stakeholder E-strategy.[32]

We might also note that management may find that it really does further the interest of all groups by acting in the interest of one group: the stockholders. Here is the proper place for Adam Smith's Invisible Hand to work. It would remain a gargantuan task to convince the other stakeholders that the Invisible Hand should be allowed to work, especially when some of them may well be feeling the back of the hand. Management's failure in this regard could well be one of the reasons for the distrust of large corporations that we see today.

We often confuse the Stockholder E-Strategy with the Unrestricted Stakeholder E-Strategy. The whole point of E-strategy is to reach some end-point of justification. E-strategy offers an answer to the question "Why did you do that?" If the answer is "Because it is in the stockholders' interest, and acting in the stockholders' interests brings about the greatest good for the greatest number," then the appeal is to the Unrestricted E-Strategy. If the answer is "Because it is in the stockholders' interest and they own the firm," then the appeal is to the Stockholder E-Strategy. This distinction is important, because if a particular action happens to be in the interest of most stakeholders but not in the interest of stockholders, the Stockholder E-Strategy forbids the action, while the Unrestricted Stakeholder E-Strategy may allow it. (Remember that stockholder interests also count here, but not as much as in the Stockholder E-Strategy, where they are the trump card.)

Historically, we think that AT&T's development of a principle of "universal service," to literally ensure that everyone who wanted a phone could afford one, is a good example of this E-strategy. If most accounts are to be believed, AT&T acted out of a sense of public service, and spent time and money in understanding the needs of various constituencies in society.[33] The very purpose of AT&T was to provide universal service. If a particular issue came up which affected various stakeholders, the trump card was nearly always universal service. Thus, in the 1960's in New York City, when there was a severe service shortage, the company adopted a mode of crisis management until the problem was fixed, and embarked on an engineering program to ensure that it didn't happen again.[34] Now, some may argue that AT&T has always been quite profitable, the darling of the "little old person in tennis shoes" investor, but accounts of life at AT&T by those who spent their careers there claim that the financial health is a by-product of the attention to public service. The result of this singular attention to universal service (as a proxy for the public interest) was the best telephone system in the world. Of course, "the public interest" was defined by AT&T, in a manner that may have become out of date as technology and markets changed, necessitating a need for radical change. But at least part of the furor around the AT&T divestiture can be explained as a shift from the purpose of universal service. And changing an E-strategy is not easy.

The difficulty with this E-strategy is again reflected in the AT&T story. How, exactly, is the common interest of all stakeholders to be defined? It will be a complex task of management to continually balance the competing claims of all stakeholders. If a very general notion of "stakeholder" is used to include media, corporate critics, competitors, government, foreign groups, and the like, this strategy implies that, at least over time, the corporation has to be all things to all people.[35] Such an institution could well end up being not valuable to anyone. Hence, it is easier to defend this strategy if you believe that acting in the interest of a narrow set of groups actually promotes the welfare of a larger set of groups. The difficulty here is that your obligation is to the larger set of groups, and if you find that acting, for example, in the interests of stockholders does not over time promote the interests of other groups, and in fact systematically harms some group, you are obliged, under this E-strategy, to refrain from such actions.

5. *Social Harmony Enterprise Strategy.* This strategy says that the key value for corporate executives and their companies is the promotion of social harmony. "Social harmony" can be defined in lots of ways, but it must include the promotion of eventual consensus on policies among all aspects of society, and a minimization of conflict about the ends of a society. While this strategy sounds foreign to those of us who are used to the pluralism of the United States, this is not so in other societies, where individuals put a high value on fitting in and collectivism.

Richard Pascale and Anthony Athos discuss the pressure on executives at Matsushita to conform, and the attempts by the company to promote social harmony.[36] Consensus is the operative concept inside such a company, and conflict is to be minimized. The purpose of the corporation is to fit into the general society and into the value system of the community.

Life in a Social Harmony E-Strategy company is best depicted by some Japanese students of ours. When questioned about how to deal with corporate critics in Japan, they answered that the only approach was to meet with them and to reach an accommodation. When asked what happens if no accommodation is possible, they answered that they would continue meeting until an accommodation was reached. These executives did not have the concept of prolonged conflict within a community defined as "those who have a stake in the firm."

A second example of the Social Harmony E-Strategy could well be the proverbial "company towns." Here the corporation is intimately involved in promoting harmony and consensus among members of the community. (Of course, some company towns may exist because of a Stockholder E-Strategy or even because of exploitation, but this need not always be the case.) The interests of company and community become identified with each other, and the most important point is that such identification continue. Workers must come to see the company as acting in their interest, and the company must come to see the workers as acting in its interest.

The major problem with this E-strategy is that it values consensus over all else. There is no room for other values, and such a social group becomes a closed system, not open for change. Social Harmony E-Strategy companies will have a difficult time if they decide to venture outside their social groups. They will be tempted to exploit the interests of "foreigners" for the sake of "insiders," those defined as worthy of harmony, causing resentment among the foreigners. Nonetheless, we know too little about this E-strategy, since our own society places such a high priority on individualism and pluralism. Given the rise of Eastern nations in the business world, and the long traditions of collectivism in these societies, we need to understand this strategy better.

6. *The Rawlsian Enterprise Strategy.* This strategy is named after the philosopher John Rawls, who has written about the role of social institutions in promoting justice.[37] Justice, for Rawls, is concerned with two principles. The first says that an institution, such as the corporation, is just if it promotes the greatest amount of basic liberty which is compatible with a "like liberty for all." The second principle says that inequalities among society's members are permissible only if these inequalities raise the level of the least well-off members of society, and if the offices and privileges of the institutions which promote inequality are open to everyone.

Translating this view to our notion of E-strategy is difficult, but not impossible. On this account, corporations should promote a maximum amount of liberty, such as freedom of speech, freedom of religion, freedom to participate in those important decisions that affect those groups that have a stake in the corporation. If some groups have more wealth or other basic goods than others, then the corporation and its managers have an obligation to raise the level of the least well-off stakeholder group. And the corporation must take great care to see that its offices and privileges are truly open to everyone, regardless of race, sex, and other morally irrelevant indicators.

Obviously, this is a complex theory, but there may be instances of corporations trying to act on it. We are reminded of William Norris at Control Data Corporation and his commitment to helping alleviate the problem of unemployment and a lack of training in depressed areas.[38] Norris attempted to spend resources to help inner-city neighborhoods address problems of job training, to tackle the most difficult social problems. Of course, he also expected to profit from these enterprises, but our reading of his actions is Rawlsian. He sought to redress the inequities in the world by raising the level of the worst-off stakeholders of Control Data, while increasing the size of the pie for others. Control Data has suffered through a difficult period recently, and many critics have blamed Norris's "social programs." The company has moved to sell off some ventures and close down others. The jury is still out on whether Norris was a visionary or someone who wasted shareholder resources, and the final answer will depend on whether or not you believe that something like a Rawlsian E-Strategy is appropriate for a company.

Another apparent example of a Rawlsian E-Strategy emerged late in 1986 after an IBM decision to close a parts distribution center in Greencastle, Indiana. Nearly 1,000 employees—in a town of 8,400 residents—were directly affected. Many more stood to suffer serious harm, since IBM paid nearly $800,000 annually in local property taxes. From published accounts, it appears that IBM managers singled out two groups as "least well-off": employees, and local merchants who supplied IBM. Employees were offered a variety of compensatory terms, such as early retirement premiums, transfer opportunities, retraining, and commuting subsidies for those employees who chose to leave IBM. To local business interests, IBM responded by offering to donate the facility to the town, by granting over $1 million for local business development, and by assigning a full-time employee to assist in business development.

As with the Control Data case, the evidence is still sketchy as to whether this can be considered a Rawlsian E-Strategy. It is possible that IBM management ignored those still worse off than employees and local merchants, and it is possible that the compensation programs will harm others. Still, the program has some prima facie appearances of a Rawlsian E-Strategy.[39]

All of these issues are complex, and more needs to be said about what the corporation would be like if it followed such an E-strategy, but once again we see no reason for ruling this one out. At least it seems to be a candidate for further study and thought.

7. *The Personal Projects Enterprise Strategy.* Since this strategy is the subject of Chapter 8, we shall be quite brief for now. The main value behind this strategy is the worth of the individual and his or her autonomy. This strategy says that personal autonomy, operationalized in the projects that each of us wants to pursue, should be the guiding force behind what corporations do. Corporations should be means for individuals' achievement and flourishing, and not collective ends in themselves where individuals have to subordinate their own goals to those of the corporation.

We believe that this view of E-strategy is the very best one from the standpoint of linking ethics and strategy, but making the case for our view is a long story. Indeed, it is what the rest of the book is about. We don't know of many instances of large corporations that have put these principles into practice, though there are some, so it is incumbent on us to describe briefly what such a world would be like.[40]

The principle of individual autonomy says that each individual has a basic right to pursue his or her own projects in a manner that is free from coercion and interference from others. If these projects affect others, then it is a different story, but even so, conflicts must be solved in a manner which respects the autonomy of each individual. A corporation which followed these principles would value each and every individual employee, customer, supplier, and so forth, for his or her own sake. Individuals are ends, and never mere means to someone else's ends. We imagine that a corporation so constructed would look quite different from those of today (perhaps not too different from some of the ones that Tom Peters has found), but the level of commitment from its members would be incredibly high, for the company would be a place for the achievement of individual purposes. And that, to us at least, is a vision worthy of further study.

THE PROCESS OF ENTERPRISE STRATEGY

Each of these E-strategies has implications for the whole of management theory and practice. The purpose of the previous, and extremely brief, descriptions of the different flavors of enterprise strategy was to examine how the decision-making principles, and hence the decisions actually made, would differ from the standard view of corporate strategy. It is also relevant to ask the managerial question, "How do we decide what E-strategy to pursue?"[41]

There is no foolproof process for deciding on enterprise strategy. Many impostors abound, as consultants and academics have jumped on the "values and culture" bandwagon. But E-strategy is really more than the current understanding of values and culture. Often these accounts are really about slogans, or the corporate regimen, or just plain socialization.[42]

E-strategy appeals to reason. Specifically, it asks managers, for starters (since they are most in control), to reason about purpose. What really is the purpose of the firm? The process of enterprise strategy starts, but doesn't end, with management's taking a good hard look at its own purposes, and whether or not they are the ones espoused in the annual report, press releases, employee communications, and daily operation of the business. Without such a fundamental process of reasoning, E-strategy can and should go no further.

The second step, in line with the Values Principle, is to see how far away from the fundamental purposes of employees the current thinking of management is. Now obviously, we do not recommend a large, 1,000-person T-group, or rows of couches and shrinks; we just think that some honest conversation about what you stand for will help to begin the thinking about enterprise strategy.

The third step, in line with the Interdependence Principle, is to have the same conversation with key stakeholder groups. Which stakeholders do you contact? The internal probing of management and employees will give a preliminary answer.

Once a preliminary E-strategy is formulated, it should be subjected to rigorous criticism by all concerned. E-strategy will emerge, not be formulated and implemented. Companies will create their own, but they must not try to move quickly, for this is no "one-minute" gimmick.

A general caution is in order. There is no standard process for E-strategy. E-strategy is just good reasoning, good logic, and a careful analysis of what you really believe in, using ideas about values, the good, moral rules, common morality, and reflective equilibrium. The steps that you use to come to some decision obviously matter, but process does not hold the answer. Any magic that is to be found in a process is because of a "critical approach." What we mean by "critical approach" is not self-flagellation, but a skeptical attitude toward easy solutions. Values, purposes, and ethical principles often lie beneath the surface.[43] And if our search for ethics is to be meaningful, we have to be willing to probe into painful areas. Without the atmosphere that warrants such self-criticism, enterprise strategy is better left alone.

The first hurdle to overcome is the standard business thinking that questions of ethics, values, and morality are so soft and squishy that any answer will do. We believe that this is mistaken, and that our arguments in Chapter 2 should cause you to put relativism aside.

The second hurdle to overcome is to give those involved the skills and tools to routinely reason about matters of ethics. That is, all managers must take harms and benefits, rights and rules, and values into account in their decision making. Without such concrete skills, E-strategy will become another task force, another binder, some more grand words and ringing speeches, and a big waste of time and money. Our arguments in Chapter 3 should give you at least a start on this project.

Some Pitfalls and Cautions

Before we discuss some more of the critical issues that face us as we try to connect ethics and strategy, we want to once again caution you about the whole concept of E-strategy.

1. *This is serious stuff.* We believe that connecting ethics and strategy is as serious as it gets. The very use of words like "ethics" and "morality" signals that matters of the highest importance are being discussed. We are not just talking about another kind of slogan, or set of rules that we sometimes follow, but rather the very nature of your corporation. Trying to understand your own values is hard work. Many people can't do it alone and require years of professional help. Enterprise strategy is just as difficult. It would be a mistake of the gravest sort to think that you could settle the question of enterprise strategy quickly, and once and for all.[44]

2. *You need to muddle through for a while.* A second pitfall would be to believe that you could simply announce your company's E-strategy and settle the matter. Since E-strategy requires an analysis of the values of the key actors, they must participate, in some sense, in the process of formulating an E-strategy. How can you decide that you really stand for being a servant of stockholder's interests when you haven't talked to any stockholders, so that you know what their interests actually are? Impossible. But managers spout such nonsense daily. (We also note that academics are just as guilty, especially when it comes to the interests of students.) E-strategy requires participation because it deals with important and personal issues. These issues are relevant for all corporate members. Some E-strategies require different forms of participation from that required by others. Obviously, the managerial supremacy strategy requires different participation from what an unrestricted stakeholder strategy requires. The point is clear: It is okay, even necessary, to muddle through. Better to muddle through, and to have a process with some basic integrity, than to shove something regarding ethics down the throats of corporate members.

3. *Actions and words are important.* Like good corporate strategy, E-strategy is about action. Talk is cheap, but action is dear. The vision of the company must be not only articulated but acted upon. Where moral matters are concerned, it is no excuse that "we can't afford to do it this year." Morality requires us to act, and if you aren't willing to act on your principles, then you just don't really believe in what you say. If you won't act on what you stand for, then for our money, you are engaging in self-deception.

4. *Process and content are important.* While we have argued that the process of participation is important, so too is the content of what is decided. As far as morality and ethics are concerned (and we believe that strategy fits here, too), what you do is at least as important as, and often more important than, how you decide to do it. We are not advocating a corporation-wide touchy-feely T-group. We are advocating understanding what you really believe, and trying to justify those beliefs in terms of building a corporate strategy to act on them.

5. *Authenticity and criticism: Without them, don't try it.* One of our colleagues once remarked of our concept of E-strategy, "Is it really worth the trouble? Aren't you just telling executives to go through a lot of soul-searching and uncover a lot of stuff that they are better off not knowing, or even screwing around with?" Our colleague was right on the mark in her analysis of how difficult E-strategy really is. She pointed out to us how hard it is for each of us to be authentic, to really act on what we believe, and how difficult true self-criticism is. However, we know of no other way to link strategy and ethics in an honest way. If you don't have the stomach for authenticity and criticism—and most people don't—realize that you also are giving up your right to complain about how others unfairly compare business and ethics, as if they were totally divorced.

SUMMARY

We've covered a lot of ground in this chapter. We began with an analysis of some cases and claimed that if you really want to understand why AT&T divested, or why Bendix embarked on its Pac-Man strategy, or even why some companies are "excellent" and some are not, you must enter the thicket of issues surrounding ethics and morality. We proposed a concept known as "enterprise strategy" as a way of stating seven, out of many, ways of connecting ethics and strategy. We hope you took these seven different "theories" as they were intended, to help you begin, and only begin, to assess where you and your company stand on the connection between your corporate strategy and your views on ethics. We realize that they represent a very different way of understanding strategy.

At this point you have the very best tools to tackle the issue of connecting ethics and strategy. There is a lot more that could be said about all of the ideas in these last four chapters, and if you want to read further, go back and examine the endnotes for a list of the ideas of others on these issues. We're now going to show you, in the next chapter, how ethics and strategy have been explicitly connected, via the notion of corporate social responsibility. In Chapters 6 and 7, we are going to show how common models of corporate strategy have implicit ethical assumptions. Throughout these chapters we are going to make use of the language of ethics and our conception of strategy as purpose. If you're not interested in how others have thought about ethics and strategy, you can move to Chapter 8, where we defend our own theory of E-strategy: the Personal Projects Enterprise Strategy.

★ ★ ★ ★ ★ ★ ★ ★ ★ ★ CHAPTER **5**

Disconnecting Ethics and Strategy: The Case of Corporate Social Responsibility

INTRODUCTION

The purpose of this chapter, is to take a look at one recent attempt to link corporate strategy and ethics: the concept of corporate social responsibility. We believe that this concept, as it has been operationalized by both managers and theorists, simply doesn't do the job. Either it calls on managers and corporations to be generic "good citizens," or it simply asks them to be "responsive" to social changes. It does not require that the very essence of a business be built on ethical foundations.

CORPORATE STRATEGY AND CORPORATE SOCIAL RESPONSIBILITY

We explained in an earlier chapter how "strategy" and "strategic management" had become a dominant metaphor for the large corporation of today. Concurrently with the development of strategic management models, the concern with "corporate social responsibility" appeared. Rooted in the post–World War II social environment, particularly the social movements in the 1960's, models of corporate social responsibility were developed to enable managers to understand the societal obligations incurred by their firms.

The basic idea of corporate social responsibility is simple. Firms are social entities, and so they should play a role in the social issues of the day. They should take seriously their "obligations to society" and actively try to fulfill them. From 1950 to 1980, many treatises on corporate social responsibility were written, and various approaches were proposed. Most urged executives and their companies to be good citizens and not to ignore their role in society. Milton Friedman sounded the drum on the other side, by publishing an essay condemning executives who undertook any projects other than maximizing the interests of stockholders. Published in *The New York Times*, Friedman's essay sparked a debate that continues today.[1] In Friedman's view, if corporate social responsibility required giving profits to charity or using them in a way without a direct benefit to stockholders, it was tantamount to stealing from stockholders. On the other hand, Friedman argued, if corporate social responsibility was just good public relations, and investing in communities actually produced greater profits in some future economic period, then it was hard to see how any noneconomic responsibility had been fulfilled.

The debate over the meaning of corporate social responsibility was brought into sharp focus with the formation of Campaign GM, by Ralph Nader and others. The purpose of the campaign was to make General Motors "socially responsible." The group bought stock in General Motors and proceeded to wage a proxy fight to force GM to adopt stricter safety testing and environmental standards, and to put women and representatives from minority groups on its board of directors.

Executives reacted to the pressure to be socially responsible in a variety of ways, from simply ignoring the issue to eventually agreeing to the demands of the critics. At GM, women and minority representatives were eventually named to the board of directors. Some corporations gave to charity and to the arts. Some got involved in politics, and many of them created special offices to deal with "public affairs" and "social responsibility."[2] However, there were problems.

Practically speaking, what happened was that executives were increasingly drawn into interactions with critics, and a lot of negotiation or at least jockeying for position in order to satisfy the critics, or to make them go away. These experiences were not lost on researchers worried about the meaning of corporate social responsibility.

Theoretically, the concept of "corporate social responsibility" as "fulfilling the firm's societal obligations" led scholars to question how management could even, in principle, determine what its social obligations were. On the other hand, it was easy to see how to respond to critics, and it was just good management technique to ensure that there weren't lots of folks who hated the company or were out to boycott its products. But how could management know whether it should help the poor or open a new plant or give to the United Way? Taking a page from

Friedman, was it even management's job to do so? In the larger society, shouldn't these decisions be left to government?

So, rather than return to an ethical analysis, and the difficult job of understanding the values at work and all of the tools and concepts from moral philosophy, researchers and managers alike latched onto a new idea.[3] A revision from "corporate social responsibility" to "corporate social responsiveness" transpired. The argument was made that as long as the firm was "responsive" to the demands of society and tried to anticipate and meet these demands, issues of responsibility could be left for the debate among philosophers.[4]

The point of "responsiveness" should be pretty obvious by this point in our journey toward linking ethics and strategy. You merely have to respond to others, not build strategy based on your own moral principles. Remember that a moral principle deals with others, by definition. Therefore, the appeal of merely responding amounts to an admission that the interests and values of others need not really count. In this way the idea of corporate social responsiveness embraces a form of relativism which counsels managers to take the path of least resistance. The idea is that values and ethics are relative, and so who should decide ethical issues? Not corporations, for they are in business. By being responsive, managers could keep things quiet, appear to be ethical, and get on with business. Being responsive was good business, argued many, and corporate social responsiveness was thought to be about as good a concept as there was, without launching into some impossible philosophical problems.[5]

Over the years a consensus emerged over what kinds of actions were socially responsive. The basic idea is that management spots some social problem which affects the firm and does something about it before it festers into a crisis. Standard examples include: (1) withdrawing certain products voluntarily, rather than being forced to do so by regulatory agencies; (2) giving to charities which promote the welfare of certain customer groups; and (3) adopting a cooperative posture toward critics. Sometimes being responsive meant forgoing profits. It was thought that in the long run the profits would be regained through reputational effects of responsive behavior, but the ensuing debate about the social performance of corporations has failed to demonstrate this to be fact.[6] Examples of being "unresponsive" are just as numerous; they include the Ford Pinto's exploding gas tank, the Firestone 500 tire, Nestlé's marketing of infant formula in the Third World, and in general, continuing to do battle with government and with critics.[7] Ethics and strategy are connected, in this view, but in a loose way, because ethical analysis is seen to be incidental. The main principle at work is to be responsive to those who can affect you, not from any sense of obligation to them, but because they can cause you potential harm. So, if you are going to look after the stockholders' interest in the long term, being responsive pays.

In order to show how the whole idea of "corporate social responsiveness" rests on just the mistakes that we have warned you about, we need to take a brief detour. We need to look again at how to operationalize the two principles of Chapter 1: the Values Principle and the Interdependence Principle. We turn to some elementary game theory to do the trick.

THE USE OF SIMPLE GAME THEORY

Corporate strategy can be readily understood as a series of interdependent choices made by interested parties. Our First and Second Axioms of Corporate Strategy (Chapter 1) guarantee that this is so. To understand corporate strategy in this way is to engage in reasoning that is essentially game-theoretic. Game theory deals with "vicarious problem solving," that is, literally putting yourself in the place of the other stakeholders affected by corporate strategy and trying to see the world through their eyes.[8] When you engage in vicarious problem solving, it is important to try to understand the values of each player, or else you just won't understand how each really sees the world.

Diologic?

If we understand corporate strategy in this way, a basic proposition, a Third Axiom, for effective corporate strategy follows:

Third Axiom of Corporate Strategy

Effective strategy will be formulated and implemented if and only if each player successfully puts himself or herself in the place of other players and endeavors to see the situation from the others' perceptions.

The analytical framework of game theory is a powerfully efficient tool, the potential of which has only begun to be tapped in strategic analysis. For the most part the development of game theory has proceeded along mathematical lines, and the applicability of game-theoretic models has been confined to "operations research" problems. Recent advances in applied game theory have demonstrated how theorists can capture the essence of the game-theoretic method without encountering its traditional, imposing measurement limitations.[9]

Game theory analysts make some assumptions that are familiar to us, given our discussion in Chapter 1 about strategy as purpose. They assume that people are self-interested, in the sense that each has a set of preferences and values. Game theorists assume that people are rational, in the sense that they are interested in actualizing their preferences and values. In short, they assume what we have argued to be true in Chapter 3, that values cause our actions. The three Axioms of Corporate Strategy together with the Values and Interdependence Principles really describe game-theoretic reasoning pretty well. The point is simple. Each of us has values, and the outcomes of our interactions will be a function of what each of us expects the other to do, and how we respond accordingly.[10]

It is difficult to understand why game theory has not been readily applied to strategic management. A sufficient condition for a game to exist is that the interests of multiple actors must be interdependent, with each player's decisions influencing the outcome for all players. What complicates strategic choice is the firm's dependence upon the interests of customers, suppliers, employees, and other stakeholders, all of whom are exercising their respective strategic choices. Failure to recognize the Interdependence Principle and failure to elevate it to a preeminent position in strategic management led both managers and researchers to overlook the very reasons that compel organizations to act as they do. These reasons are grounded in individual and corporate preferences, which, in turn, are grounded in values. Game theory affords a framework within which to investigate the activating role of values.[11]

Having introduced you to the simple idea of game theory, we are ready to return from this detour to the main point of this chapter, showing how the very idea of "corporate social responsiveness" rests on a mistake. We use game-theoretic reasoning to make our case.

PROCTER AND GAMBLE'S REMOVAL OF THE RELY TAMPON

The toxic shock syndrome (TSS) controversy of 1980 represents a classic and instructive game situation. Medical researchers investigating the increasing frequency of TSS in the late 1970's began to find evidence of correlation between TSS and the use of tampons and, in particular, use of the Rely brand marketed by P&G. Procter and Gamble, a major supplier of household products, had entered the tampon market in 1972, and in just eight years had gained a preeminent market position.[12] At the time of the Rely game, P&G had wrested a 20 percent market share in the face of stiff competition from Johnson and Johnson, Kimberly-Clark and Playtex. During this same period, Congress had vested in the FDA a broader charter of regulatory responsibility, covering such products as tampons.

The Rely tampon game comes into sharp focus in September 1980, with release of the most convincing evidence to date linking Rely with TSS. The next move, the first strategic play in this game, belongs to P&G. For our purposes here, we will refer to P&G managers and FDA officials with the shorthand labels "P&G" and "FDA," respectively. We do this for simplicity's sake in presenting the analysis. We realize that within "P&G" and "FDA" there were multiple conflicting sets of purposes and values.

In the simplest construction of the Rely game, P&G and the FDA each have two primary strategic alternatives. P&G can voluntarily recall Rely from the market, or it can take no action. The FDA can issue a recall order or seek P&G's signature on a consent decree, which is tantamount to no overt action. These respective strategic sets are summarized in Table 1. This analysis of P&G and FDA strategies should be considered an illustration of "how to do game theory," rather than an illustration of a "correct" strategy. If new facts are uncovered, a more definitive account of the Rely game may well differ from that developed here. Indeed, game theory is powerful precisely because it points analysts toward the *relevant facts* for settling conflicting theoretical explanations.

TABLE 5.1   The Rely Game: Overview

Players	Procter and Gamble (P&G)
	Food and Drug Administration (FDA)
Strategic Sets	P&G
	1. Remove Rely from the market. (R)
	2. Do not remove Rely from the market. (NR)
	FDA
	1. Issue ban; recall Rely from the market. (B)
	2. Issue no ban; take no action. (NB)
Game Situation	1. Toxic shock syndrome (TSS) has been tentatively associated with tampon use and use of the Rely brand in particular.
	2. The FDA is prepared to act; the latest research report confirms earlier findings about Rely.
	3. P&G has the next move.

The Game Payoffs

On the basis of the facts of the case, it is apparent that the actions taken by P&G will have a direct bearing on the FDA's position, and vice versa. To initiate a game-theoretic analysis, the analyst needs to identify the possible consequences of P&G–FDA interaction. These *game payoffs* are summarized in matrix form in Table 2. Though it is a simplified account of the results of interdependent moves, this background provides a substantial basis upon which to specify the strategic postures that P&G and the FDA could pursue.

TABLE 5.2   The Rely Game: The Outcome Matrix

P&G	FOOD AND DRUG ADMINISTRATION
B	NB
R P&G proactive. FDA ban late and punitive. P&G action helpful in civil proceedings.	P&G loses market. FDA threat seen as effective.
NR P&G is "bad guy." P&G faces huge civil damage-suit costs. FDA is consumers' champion.	Rely sales continue. FDA perceived as weak and comes under political pressure. Some civil actions against P&G.

1. *The Remove–Ban Payoff.* One outcome of the Rely game finds P&G removing Rely from the market while the FDA issues a recall order. Several payoffs result from this play. First, P&G emerges as a proactive firm by taking action of its own accord in a difficult situation. A second, and related, payoff for P&G is the likelihood that the firms's voluntary behavior can carry over and influence the severity of any civil penalties that P&G might incur as a result of the TSS-related suits.[13] Third, an FDA recall order coinciding with P&G's decision would be perceived by the FDA's stakeholders as an *ex post*, needless, and punitive action.

2. *The Remove–No Ban Payoff.* In another strategic scenario, P&G removes Rely from the market and the FDA takes no overt action. P&G has conceded its place in the highly competitive tampon market, possibly never to retrieve its share. The FDA, while not taking any overt action, has achieved its desired outcome in light of the agency's chartered mission.

3. *The Not Remove–No Ban Payoff.* P&G also has the strategic opportunity to ignore Rely's suspected association with the TSS controversy. Should the FDA decide not to issue a recall order—the lower right-hand quadrant in Table 2—P&G's tampon sales will proceed, although the company may still be confronted with civil actions. The FDA's reluctance to pursue the matter will improve the company's chances of emerging from litigation relatively unscathed. The FDA, in taking no action, comes under increasing pressure from Congress, the media, the Office of Management and Budget, consumer advocate groups, and other stakeholder groups, all of which perceive an inactive FDA as either unwilling to act, incapable of acting, or both.

4. *The Not Remove–Ban Payoff.* Finally, an FDA ban on Rely sales, given a P&G decision to ignore the controversy, clearly casts the latter in a villainous role. P&G becomes vulnerable to not only pressure from the media and consumer advocate groups, but also to considerable litigation. By issuing a recall order, the FDA reaffirms its role as responsible for product safety in the food and drug industries.

The Original Account

With the game payoffs specified, the game theory analyst need only add an account of the players' preference sets in order to activate the game. These preferences, and their rankings, are crucial, because they provide operational meaning to the *interdependence* between the two game players in the Rely example.

In the actual Rely game, P&G removed Rely from the market and the FDA issued no recall order. (A consent decree was eventually signed.) The next step in the present analysis is to reconstruct an account of the Rely game based upon the payoffs discussed above. The analysis will then proceed to compare the original account with alternative explanations of the game. There are many places to start.

One explanation already given in the literature is that P&G acted in a "socially responsive" manner in removing Rely from the market without any overt action by the FDA.[14] Accepting this conclusion as the basis for our original account, the payoffs, or outcomes, shown in Table 2 can be used to interpret a "Social-Responsiveness" strategic posture for P&G and a "Fight If Need Be" strategic posture for the FDA. *Strategic postures* reflect the preference rankings held by a game player, in the context of the game's outcomes matrix. While there are a great number of different valuations of the outcomes, any set of valuations must have some underlying coherence. This must be the case if players have some purposes which motivate their actions. The strategic posture of a game player is a mediating construct to give this coherence. Strategic postures, in fact, plausibly reflect the preferences derived from a player's simultaneous participation in multiple games.

With this as background, the strategic postures which activate the original account can be reasoned as follows.

1. *P&G Social-Responsiveness Strategy.* P&G most prefers to remove Rely from the market in the absence of FDA action. In this context, P&G is acting voluntarily to concede its self-interest in a lucrative market. Further, the company's choice can be expected to cast a favorable light upon its conscientiousness. P&G least prefers to ignore the TSS-Rely problem and receive a recall order from the FDA. To ignore the controversy and incur the government's wrath is antithetical to social responsiveness, as commonly defined.[15] P&G's "next-best" preference is for the entire matter to blow over; that is, to not remove Rely from the market and to have the FDA sit on its hands. This posture reflects the juxtaposition of P&G's profit-seeking objectives and social responsiveness valuations.

2. *FDA's "Fight If Need Be" strategy.* "Fight If Need Be" depicts an FDA strategy of calculated activism. P&G's voluntary removal of Rely best serves the agency's interests. The public interest is served. The agency has not had to expend a significant amount of resources. And most

important, the voluntary removal confirms to the tampon industry, industry and commerce in general, and the media that FDA threats carry clout. The worst outcome for the agency when playing such a pragmatic posture is the "no action" alternative in the face of P&G's retention of Rely on the market. For the FDA to create the perception of an inactive regulatory agency, powerless—by implication, at least—in the face of industry maneuvering, is clearly not in its self-interest. The FDA's "next best" strategic move is the issuance of a recall order to a recalcitrant P&G. The activist FDA, flexing its authority when compelled to do so, is perceived as capable of acting effectively to protect the interests of the consuming public. This preference, along with the remainder of the FDA's rankings, as well as the suggested P&G strategic rankings, is shown in Table 3. The numbers shown in brackets indicate the *ordinal rankings* of each alternative strategic outcome, with a 4 indicating a most preferred outcome. By game theory convention, the first player's (P&G's) preferences are listed first in the brackets.

TABLE 5.3   The Rely Game: The Original Account

P&G plays Social-Responsiveness strategy. FDA plays "Fight If Need Be" strategy.

GAME IN 2 × 2 FORM			
		FDA	
		B	NB
P&G	R	(2, 2)	(4, 4)
	NR	(1, 3)	(3, 1)

GAME IN 2 × 4 FORM				
		FDA		
		B/B B/NB	NB/B NB/NB	
P&G	R	(2, 2) (2, 2)	(4, 4) (4, 4)	
	NR	(1, 3) (3, 1)	(1, 3) (3, 1)	

Solution (underlined): P&G removes Rely; FDA takes no action.

Note: The first number in each bracket indicates P&G's ordinal preference for that outcome, and the second number indicates the FDA's preference. The ordinal rankings range from 4 (most preferred) to 1 (least preferred). The game solution is read from the intersection of the two players's preferred strategies.

A two by two form for the Rely game is an unrealistic representation, in the sense that a simultaneous-choice situation is implied. In reality, interdependence between P&G and the FDA does not preclude sequential strategic decisions made by each player with knowledge of the other's actions. In order to more accurately account for this feature of games, a two by four form can be readily derived from the two by two form, as shown in the lower portion of Table 3. Interpretation of this format is quite straightforward. All that has changed is the form for specifying the form of the FDA's responses to P&G's behavior.[16]

The FDA can:

1. Ban Rely, regardless of P&G's behavior. (B/B)
2. Not ban Rely, regardless of P&G's behavior. (NB/NB)
3. Play "tat for tit": ban Rely if it is removed, not ban Rely if it is not removed from the market. (B/NB)
4. Play "tit for tat": not ban Rely if it is removed, ban Rely if it is not removed from the market. (NB/B)

This completely specifies the FDA's range of action in this account of the Rely game.

In game-theoretic terms, P&G's Social-Responsiveness strategic posture is a mixed situation. That is, for some, but not all, alternatives available to the FDA, P&G prefers to remove Rely from the market. The FDA, on the other hand, prefers "tit for tat"—the third column—to all other moves. This is called a "dominant strategy."[17] Given that the FDA has a dominant strategy, P&G makes the best (best for its interests) available choice and elects to remove Rely from the market. This solution to the game is underlined in Table 3. Again, this reconstruction of the game represents *one* interpretation of the actual game.[18] The task ahead is to explore other plausible explanations for the rational moves of P&G and FDA in the Rely game. The intent is to demonstrate that the original account is not a unique account of the Rely game, and hence that corporate social responsiveness is an inadequate explanation.

In order to conduct this sensitivity analysis, three representative generic strategic postures will be assumed for P&G: Social-Responsiveness, Moral-Responsibility, and Profit Maximization. Likewise, the three generic postures available to the FDA will be assumed to be: "Fight If Need Be," the Fighting Activist, and the Pure Inactivist. The sensitivity analysis, thus, is perfomed on the nine possible pairings of strategic postures for this simplified game account.

Alternative Interpretations

1. *"Fight If Need Be" FDA and Profit-Maximizing P&G.* For the next two game interpretations to be analyzed, the FDA's calculating activism strategy is assumed to hold, an assumption which will be relaxed later. Susan Foote has argued that P&G could be seen as responding to a complex legal and regulatory environment in a purely profit-maximizing mode.[19] Accepting this interpretation for now, a Profit-Maximizing strategic posture for P&G can be derived to indicate P&G's greatest preference for the Not Removed–No Ban outcome of the Rely game (Table 2: upper

right-hand quadrant). First, Rely remains on the market. In the absence of any conclusive evidence concerning the Rely-TSS link, sales continue. The FDA's reluctance to "throw the book" at P&G supports the prospects for reasonably healthy sales, because no implication of guilt on P&G's part is forthcoming. Second, P&G recognizes the likelihood of litigation in civil damage actions, but assumes that, in the absence of FDA action, the storm can be weathered without serious harm to profits.

The worst outcome for P&G in this context is the Not Remove–Ban result. As if the expected flurry of litigation would not be enough, trends in the frequency and magnitude of punitive-damages awards do not bode well for P&G if the FDA issues a recall.[20] Both remaining preferences facing P&G involve voluntary removal of Rely from store shelves. The lesser of two evils here appears to be the removal of Rely without incurring FDA action, on the premise that steering clear of the government regulation is most conducive, now and in the future, to profit maximization. P&G's preferences clearly indicate a dominant preference for FDA inaction. The solution to this game is shown in Table 4.

TABLE 5.4 The Rely Game

P&G plays Profit-Maximization strategy. FDA plays "Fight If Need Be" strategy.

GAME IN 2 × 2 FORM			
		FDA	
		B	NB
P&G	R	(2, 2)	(3, 4)
	NR	(1, 3)	(4, 1)

GAME IN 2 × 4 FORM				
		FDA		
		B/B	B/NB	NB/B	NB/NB
P&G	R	(2, 2)	(2, 2)	(3, 4)	(3, 4)
	NR	(1, 3)	(4, 1)	(1, 3)	(4, 1)

Solution (underlined): P&G removes Rely; FDA takes no action.

2. *"Fight If Need Be" FDA and "Moral Responsibility" P&G.* A Moral-Responsibility strategy places stricter conditions on P&G than does its Social-Responsiveness counterpart. In playing this strategy, P&G always prefers removing Rely from the market. By definition of "moral responsibility," P&G is sensitive above all else to the injury that its actions in marketing Rely can cause for any of its stakeholders.

As with the Social-Responsiveness approach, voluntary removal of

Rely without FDA action is most preferred by P&G management. This same move in the context of an impending FDA ban is next-preferred. A self-directed moral response is valued by P&G management more than the same response prompted by FDA's action. Least favored by P&G is the decision to retain Rely in the market in the absence of any FDA action. Again, the implication is that such behavior is not as self-constraining as it could be. Note that P&G prefers the outcome where the FDA bans Rely, if P&G does not remove it, to the outcome where Rely is not removed. Such is the meaning of "moral responsibility." P&G, if acting in a morally responsible way, prefers that Rely be off the shelf regardless of the economic consequences to the firm. When these respective rankings are brought together in Table 5, a now familiar account appears: P&G voluntarily removes Rely without FDA action.

TABLE 5.5 The Rely Game

P&G plays Moral-Responsibility strategy. FDA plays "Fight If Need Be" strategy.

GAME IN 2 × 2 FORM

		FDA B	FDA NB
P&G	R	(3, 2)	(4, 4)
	NR	(2, 3)	(1, 1)

GAME IN 2 × 4 FORM

		FDA B/B	B/NB	NB/B	NB/NB
P&G	R	(3, 2)	(3, 2)	(4, 4)	(4, 4)
	NR	(2, 3)	(1, 1)	(2, 3)	(1, 1)

Solution (underlined): P&G removes Rely; FDA takes no action.

3. *"The Fighting Activist" FDA.* The Fighting Activist prefers, above all, to take action by challenging P&G's stubbornness with a recall order. The "next-best" move is the voluntary removal of Rely without need for issuing any order. To the Fighting Activist, affimation of its power through mere threats is nearly as desirable as actually carrying out the threats. An *ex post* ban on Rely casts doubt upon the agency's timing. Hence, the Remove-Ban outcome is least preferred by the Fighting Activist. Table 6 depicts this strategic posture in ordinal-ranking form. The FDA's preferences are shown in the right-hand portion of each bracketed preference pair.

TABLE 5.6   The Rely Game

P&G plays Social-Responsiveness strategy. FDA plays Fighting Activist strategy.

GAME IN 2 × 2 FORM

		FDA	
		B	NB
P&G	R	(2, 2)	(4, 3)
	NR	(1, 4)	(3, 1)

GAME IN 2 × 4 FORM

		FDA			
		B/B	NB/B	B/NB	NB/NB
P&G	R	(2, 2)	(2, 2)	(4, 3)	(4, 3)
	NR	(1, 4)	(3, 1)	(1, 4)	(3, 1)

Solution (underlined): P&G removes Rely; FDA takes no action.

The analysis shows that, regardless of the strategic posture chosen by P&G, the intersections between a Fighting Activist FDA and P&G yield the same actual game account. Hence, if the FDA was, in fact, pursuing a Fighting Activist approach, none of the three imputed P&G strategic

TABLE 5.7   The Rely Game

P&G plays Profit-Maximization strategy. FDA plays Fighting Activist strategy.

GAME IN 2 × 2 FORM

		FDA	
		B	NB
P&G	R	(2, 2)	(3, 3)
	NR	(1, 4)	(4, 1)

GAME IN 2 × 4 FORM

		FDA			
		B/B	B/NB	NB/B	NB/NB
P&G	R	(2, 2)	(2, 2)	(3, 3)	(3, 3)
	NR	(1, 4)	(4, 1)	(1, 4)	(4, 1)

Solution (underlined): P&G removes Rely; FDA takes no action.

TABLE 5.8 The Rely Game

P&G plays Moral-Responsibility strategy. FDA plays Fighting Activist strategy.

GAME IN 2 × 2 FORM

		FDA	
		B	NB
P&G	R	(3, 2)	(4, 3)
	NR	(2, 4)	(1, 1)

GAME IN 2 × 4 FORM

		FDA			
		B/B	B/NB	NB/B	NB/NB
P&G	R	(3, 2)	(3, 2)	(4, 3)	(4, 3)
	NR	(2, 4)	(1, 1)	(2, 4)	(1, 1)

Solution (underlined): P&G removes Rely; FDA takes no action.

postures aid the researcher in determining why the game unfolded as it did. Tables 6, 7, and 8 provide the details for these three pairings.

4. *"Pure Inactivist"* FDA. At the other end of the FDA's strategic spectrum is a Pure Inactivist strategy. This may not reflect an ineffective agency, as the strategic label might imply. Realistically, the FDA participates in a number of games concurrently. These games involve other firms, Congress, and other government agencies, and these are internal games, besides. The FDA, like any organization facing decisions of resource allocation, decides to "starve" certain efforts as unimportant relative to the remainder of its agenda.

A Pure Inactivist operates on the principle that no action is preferred to any action. This is not to say that an inactive FDA is insensitive. Rather, the Pure Inactivist FDA prefers most the voluntary withdrawal of Rely. Specifying the worst outcome for the inactive FDA is a tossup; the game solution is unaffected, as it turns out. The claim here is that the Pure Inactivist's action threshold is triggered by P&G's determination to maintain its market presence in the face of a recall order. Thus, the Not Remove–Ban alternative is preferred to issuing an *ex post* ban. Tables 9 and 10 depict the game solutions pairing the Pure Inactivist FDA with the Social-Responsiveness and Moral-Responsibility strategic postures available to P&G. Again, the actual Remove–No Ban result is replicated.

Only in the game interpreted as involving a Profit-Maximizing P&G and a Pure Inactivist FDA does any solution other than the Remove–No Ban one turn up. In that instance (not depicted here), the logical game solution is P&G's decision to take no action regarding Rely's distribution, in the face of no FDA action.

TABLE 5.9 The Rely Game

P&G plays Social-Responsiveness strategy. FDA plays Pure Inactivist strategy.

GAME IN 2 × 2 FORM

		FDA	
		B	NB
P&G	R	(2, 1)	(4, 4)
	NR	(1, 2)	(3, 3)

GAME IN 2 × 4 FORM

		FDA			
		B/B	B/NB	NB/B	NB/NB
P&G	R	(2, 1)	(2, 1)	(4, 4)	(4, 4)
	NR	(1, 2)	(3, 3)	(1, 2)	(3, 3)

Solution (underlined): P&G removes Rely; FDA takes no action.

TABLE 5.10 The Rely Game

P&G plays Moral-Responsibility strategy. FDA plays Pure Inactivist strategy.

GAME IN 2 × 2 FORM

		FDA	
		B	NB
P&G	R	(3, 1)	(4, 4)
	NR	(2, 2)	(1, 3)

GAME IN 2 × 4 FORM

		FDA			
		B/B	B/NB	NB/B	NB/NB
P&G	R	(3, 1)	(3, 1)	(4, 4)	(4, 4)
	NR	(2, 2)	(1, 3)	(2, 2)	(1, 3)

Solution (underlined): P&G removes Rely; FDA takes no action.

Summary of the P&G–FDA Games

Table 11 summarizes the sensitivity analysis process. Without exhausting the set of possible strategic interpretations for the Rely game,

TABLE 5.11   The Rely Game

Summary of Game-Theoretic Explanations

	FDA		
P&G	Fight If Need Be	Fighting Activist	Pure Inactivist
Social Responsiveness	R/NB	R/NB	R/NB
Moral Responsibility	R/NB	R/NB	R/NB
Profit Maximization	R/NB	R/NB	NR/NB

Note: The following summarizes the notation shown above:
R: P&G removes Rely.
NR: P&G does not remove Rely.
B: FDA bans Rely.
NB: FDA does not ban Rely.
R/NB: Game result whereby P&G removes Rely and the FDA takes no action.
NR/NB: Game result whereby P&G does not remove Rely and the FDA takes no action.

the original account and seven other different intersections among strategic postures were all found to "explain" the Rely game as it actually unfolded.

Using nothing more than logic and elementary game theory, an account of eight equally valid explanations for the Rely game outcome has been given. Hence, the analysis provides an *indeterminate* account of the Rely game. It is important to understand what such indeterminacy does and does not demonstrate.

First, the results cast doubt upon the sufficiency, for explanatory purposes, of such common, generic strategic postures as "maximization of profits" and, in particular, "corporate social responsiveness." P&G removed Rely from the market, in the absence of an FDA recall order. This result was explained in the context of a Profit-Maximizing P&G and a Fighting Activist FDA (Table 7). This result was also explained in the context of a Moral-Responsibility strategy imputed for P&G and an Pure Inactivist FDA (Table 10). The diversity of explanations begins to demonstrate—one case is but a start—the inadequacy of many common "explanations" for strategic behavior in the current models. If we rely simply on looking at outcomes and ignore the values that cause the outcomes, or if we rely only upon our own purposes and ignore those that drive others, then our strategies will be incomplete.

Second, the inadequacy criticism can be leveled specifically at the *corporate social responsiveness* explanation. "Corporate social responsiveness" has been found no more powerful in explaining the Rely game than any of the other strategic postures examined in this chapter.

The mistake is that corporate social responsiveness ignores the Values Principle, the Interdependence Principle, and each of the three Axioms of Corporate Strategy. From P&G's perspective, a Profit-Maximizing posture and a Moral-Responsibility posture indicate fundamentally different preferences for the outcome of the Rely game. Yet for these two imputed strategies, the same game result is explained in five of six cases (Table 11: rows 2 and 3). It is evident that P&G is not interacting with an anonymous "nature," but rather with at least one other preference-driven strategic actor, the FDA. The conclusion to be drawn from this is that corporate strategy models need to take greater account of the antecedents to strategic outcomes—namely, the values that drive the game's strategic actors to formulate and implement certain strategic postures. In short, an account based solely upon the responsiveness of P&G's management ignores both the First and Second Axioms of Corporate Strategy, and hence ignores the Third Axiom as well.

One claim that cannot be made here is that the analysis sheds light on the specific values which led to the observed Rely game results. Indeed, that is part of our point. You can't do corporate strategy unless you are willing to take a hard look at your values and the reasons that others have for acting jointly with you. You cannot simply focus on the outcomes and the results, nor can you "freeze" values into measurable aggregates and assume that you understand your interdependence with others in this way. If we are to link ethics and strategy, then we must be explicit about the role of values.

Rd   The whole point of the move from corporate social responsibility to corporate social responsiveness was to be pragmatic, and to get away from those mushy, philosophical issues of values and ethics. But we have seen that there is no free lunch. If you get away from values, the price you pay is systematic ambiguity. No one can say, from an analysis of outcomes alone, nor from an analysis of P&G alone, why P&G did what it did. And in evaluating its strategy from a moral point of view, we are simply lost. "Corporate social responsiveness" perverts the connection between ethics and strategy. In doing so, it represents a paradigm case of how not to do ethical reasoning. It is simple and easy, and wrongheaded.

There is another way to take our analysis here. Perhaps what we have shown is that each way to connect ethics and strategy makes some assumptions. Invariably, these assumptions point to morality, and what is and is not important in the eyes of those who use the particular theory or model. For example, corporate social responsiveness theorists, and managers who claim to be socially responsive, simply deny, by their actions, if not their words, the importance of open and honest criticism about values, relying on responsiveness instead. They do not believe it is necessary to build strategy on ethics from the ground up, but rather think they can rely on being "responsive," assuming one posture after another whenever it is convenient.

We need to look carefully at other theories of corporate strategy to determine the assumptions that each makes, for if we are right that corporate strategy is ultimately concerned with values and ethics, then no doubt other models of corporate strategy will slip moral assumptions through the back door. And we want to know what assumptions each makes, before we use it.

By this point in our endeavor, you should begin to get the picture that we need to put "morality" squarely into the center of our discussions of ethics and strategy. When strategic management is recast as a matter of values-activated, interdependent strategic choice, "corporate social responsivenes" needs to give way to "corporate moral responsibility," a concept which we have embedded in our notion of enterprise strategy. Interdependence breeds conflict among strategic actors, and conflict, in turn, breeds moral dilemmas facing strategic actors. An account of "corporate moral responsibility," includes rights and duties, consequences, and values, all of which refer to specific strategic actors. The test of any adequate theory of corporate strategy is the extent to which it gives or is capable of giving an account of corporate and individual behavior as fundamentally concerned with ethics. Corporate social responsiveness fails miserably.

★ ★ ★ ★ ★ ★ ★ ★ ★ ★   CHAPTER **6**

Economic Theories of Corporate Strategy

INTRODUCTION

The purpose of this chapter*, and the next, is to critically examine the existing theories of corporate strategy, and to evaluate them from the moral point of view. Do these models make hidden assumptions about the role of ethics and values? Do they assume one form or another of Enterprise Strategy? If executives follow these models of strategy, what will be the result in moral terms? Do they require that we violate certain accepted moral rules: those of "common morality"?

We argued in Chapter 3 that "common morality" is not mysterious. It represents the starting point of moral debate. Most any moral theory or model of ethics will have some rules like the principle of promise keeping or nonmalevolence. We also listed a number of business principles in Chapter 3 which gave conflicting advice to managers, and in Chapter 4 we showed how to pick one or a few of these principles and articulate an answer to "what do we stand for?" By looking at what principles are implicit in a theory of strategy or by looking at what behaviors are required if the theory is to be generally applicable, we can see whether current theories of corporate strategy conflict with common

*Portions of this chapter originally appeared in Daniel R. Gilbert, Jr., "Corporate Strategy and Ethics," *Journal of Business Ethics*, Vol. 5, No. 2, April 1986, pp. 137–150.

morality. An additional benefit of this line of argument will be to show how far from common morality some E-strategies, implied by current corporate strategy theories, really are.

THE IMPLICIT MORALITY OF AN INSTITUTION

The device which we will use throughout this chapter is known as "the implicit morality of an institution," and it works like this.[1] By describing the rules which members of an institution have to obey if the purpose of the institution is to be realized, we can see what behaviors will emerge from a general acceptance of the institution. The ground rules or implicit morality are important because they give institutional members good reasons for their actions. Because the implicit morality of an institution is dependent for its definition on the institution, notice that the institution itself can come under moral scrutiny from an external view such as our general notion of common morality. For example, the implicit morality of slavery would clearly violate any conceivable standard of common morality.[2]

Think of the implicit morality of an institution as the internal rules which must be followed if the institution is to be a good one of its kind. These rules are often implicit, because the explicit rules of an institution may well be the reason that the institution functions rather badly. Such might be the case with most governments, for example. Another way to think of the implicit morality of an institution is as the internal *logica* of the institution. Once this internal *logica* is clearly understood, we can evaluate its required behaviors against external standards.

For example, we might list the rules which members of a particular church must obey if the church is to carry out its mission. That set of rules, usually codified by the management of the church, could then be analyzed to see whether it required members to act against the Principle of Promise Keeping.

The logic of the implicit morality of an institution is quite simple. From the behaviors necessary to the proper functioning of an institution, we deduce the imperatives by which institution members are obliged to bring about and maintain the institution. Suppose that if the church is to be a functioning institution, then church members must give freely of their wealth to the church. It follows that church members have an obligation qua church member to freely give of their wealth. To believe otherwise would be self-defeating under such circumstances. Similarly, if there are to be perfect markets, there must be perfect information. It follows that some institutional actors are obliged to bring about the conditions for perfect information.

Now obviously, common morality and the implicit morality of an institution can conflict. Christopher McMahon has shown how the institution of the marketplace could conflict with several principles of common morality, and we shall look at this claim in more detail later.[3] An institution can require that we harm others, or refrain from helping them at little cost to ourselves, or it can require that we violate their rights, by treating them as mere means to our ends. But it is not enough just to show how common morality and institutional morality conflict. After all, sometimes we want to set aside the dictates of common morality. We let police use force, and forbid citizens to do so, in most cases. We encourage lawyers to be an advocate for their client, even when it means shading or hiding the truth. We permit parents to inflict physical punishment on their children, when a similar act by a stranger upon another generally violates the Principle of Nonmalevolence. There are many other such cases, and recently, a whole field of study known as "professional ethics" has emerged to address them.

In addition to whether or not there is a conflict between common morality and the implicit morality of a particular institution, we want to know what good is brought about by the institution. We need to evaluate just what kind of conflict there is, and whether it is outweighed by other factors. If common morality always wins the day, then we can rest assured that the process of reflective equilibrium has broken down. The resulting moral theory will reflect a conservative bias toward the current principles in force, and new circumstances will be ignored or the principles will be misapplied. It is the existence of new and different institutions and innovative individuals, the avant-garde, that challenges existing moral codes and ensures that moral principles are questioned constantly. To do otherwise is to accept the world as it is, necessarily.

In the following sections we are going to show you how these ideas work. We start with the marketplace of economic theory, and spell out the implicit morality of the marketplace in the form of "Ten Commandments of Capitalism." That is, if the purpose of capitalism is to be fulfilled, what imperatives should capitalists follow? We think you will be surprised. Now obviously, the capitalism of economists, depending as it does on perfect, frictionless markets, is rarely realized. Yet, it is often touted as a standard or ideal toward which we should aim, and one way to think about corporate strategy is that it helps us to approach the ideal of capitalism. We're going to show how two specific ways of thinking about corporate strategy compare with the implicit morality of the marketplace and how they compare with our principles of common morality such as Promise Keeping, Nonmalevolence, and Respect for Persons. The last step in the argument is to formulate an implicit morality of corporate strategy and to show once again how both the implicit morality of the marketplace and common morality are violated. Finally, we will argue that, as yet, corporate strategy yields no compelling reason to revise common morality. Furthermore, in Chapter 8, we will show how to rethink corporate strategy to make it more consistent with common morality.

PERFECT MARKETS AND THE IDEALS OF CAPITALISM

A quick review of freshman economics will set the stage. (For conven-ience' sake, capitalism, perfect competition, and free enterprise will be used interchangeably). Collective economic activity, we learned, will lead to the greatest aggregate social good through the automatic and efficient operation of the market price mechanism. This remarkable system works in the following manner.[4]

That which is produced—goods and services—is largely determined by consumers who act in accordance with their unique individual prefer-ences. Consumers "vote" their preferences in the market arena with their wealth resources. Repeated exercise of these choices, thus, informs pro-ducers what they should produce. The price mechanism acts to relay this information.

Producers, like consumers, are assumed to act in their individual self-interests. Taking the market information from prices, they focus upon how best—that is, most efficiently—to employ the factors of pro-duction at their disposal to produce what the market demands. The individual producer's goal is clear: to deliver his or her supply to the market in the cheapest possible manner. Producers, in other words, will strive for profits, but profit will only be awarded to a producer by the price mechanism if efficiency is achieved. Otherwise, the impersonal price mechanism will direct consumers to lower-cost competitors, and inef-ficient producers will be forced to leave that market.

This describes the process at work in output markets. Parallel to this market, and interconnected with it, runs the factor market. Input factors of production are similarly allocated through the efficient operation of a price mechanism. Together, general equilibrium will result, if all the rules of the game are simultaneously honored by all participants in the mar-kets.

The move from here to effective market operation is a straightfor-ward one. Individual economic actors, pursuing their own self-interests and seeking nothing else but personal gain, will then automatically con-tribute to the greatest aggregate social welfare. This, of course, is the work of free enterprise's Invisible Hand.

Taking this one step further, welfare economics theory postulates that if all the conditions for general equilibrium—such as output prices equaling marginal costs and factor prices equaling marginal products—are simultaneously present, then no improvement can be made in the aggregate welfare without at least one individual actor suffering eco-nomic injury. This is the Pareto optimality result.

Many Pareto optima can be obtained, which points up the inherently problematic nature of this concept in terms of the subsequent distribution of the aggregate welfare. In addition, the Pareto optima which are gener-ated are a function of the initial endowment of resources in society. The market simply impersonally and efficiently reallocates to capture all of the possible gains from trade. If the initial endowment of wealth is skewed, then assuming that members want more wealth rather than less, the resulting market allocation will be skewed. This problem is not to be minimized and is often misunderstood. But our argument can be made nonetheless.

The Implicit Morality of the Marketplace (IMM)

If the achievement of Pareto optimality depends upon the presence of certain general-equilibrium conditions, and if these conditions represent the work of individuals engaged in collective endeavors, then what steps should these individuals take? Economists assume that the general-equilibrium conditions are descriptive of the way the world has to be if the Pareto-efficient allocation is to be achieved. But we may well ask: How can individual capitalists bring about these conditions? If a morally desirable outcome is a result of certain conditions, then moral agents are required to seek the realization of these conditions. In short, we need to link economic theory with moral imperatives.

Christopher McMahon has proposed such a link by constructing the Implicit Morality of the Marketplace (IMM), consisting of ". . . hypothetical imperatives which are generated by economic theory when the achievement of economic efficiency is taken as an end."[5] These imperatives form a code of principles which must be wholly satisfied by each market participant, acting independently, for Pareto optimality to result.

McMahon gives an account of two such requirements, which are paraphrased here in advance of our elaboration of such a code. We advance these moral requirements in the form of commandments, or the Ten Commandments of Capitalism, because we believe they represent a test of how deeply one believes in the myths of capitalism. The two imperatives derived by McMahon are:

1. Perfect information: Thou shalt bring about perfect information.
2. Consultation: Thou shalt consult stockholders in cases of morally significant decisions.

The first commandment applies to all market actors in both output and factor markets, while the second is specifically addressed to managers acting as agents for owners of the firm.

For the market mechanism to ultimately be effective, all parties require access to that information necessary for each to make efficient choices. This requirement can go beyond a pledge not to interfere with the flow of information. It can actually include an imperative that an individual must act to amend incorrect information.[6] Thus, if a buyer is found to hold certain erroneous beliefs about a product's capabilities, a seller must take reasonable steps to correct those beliefs, lest the buyer make a suboptimal choice.

The second commandment is an interesting one, in part because it is less obviously linked to welfare economic theory, and in part because of its implications for the practice of corporate strategy, as will be developed later on. This imperative is based on the reasoning that in some instances, such as those where morally problematic decisions cannot be accounted for in the market mechanism, no justifiable separation of owner and management preferences can exist.[7] Separation of interests is an issue because economic theory has shown that owners, acting independently of management of the firm, can make rational, self-interested decisions under conditions of perfect capital markets.[8] The point is that, to the extent that owners are liable for the use of their capital entrusted to management, certain decisions of the firm cannot be separated. Further, by this commandment, management must not assume the universal applicability of this separation principle.

It might be objected that individual capitalists have no obligation to obey these and other commandments. But if it is true that the proper functioning of markets requires these conditions and if no individual has an obligation to bring them about, then the conditions of perfect markets will be realized only by accident. If, on the other hand, these commandments are treated as assumptions, then they must have implications for the way that market participants behave.[9]

From this beginning, and by developing the principle of the prohibition on monopoly, suggested by McMahon, we get an expanded set of commandments. Hence, we articulate a more complete IMM. Once again, IMM is the set of imperatives that any market actor must obey to ensure operation of free enterprise and, accordingly, the attainment of Pareto optimality.

3. Consumer sovereignty: Thou shalt respond to consumer preferences.

One central question for economic science concerns the actual array of goods and services that will be produced to satisfy individual wants and needs. General-equilibrium theory assumes that the choices made by individual consumers will dictate the nature and character of products in demand. Consumers' preferences, assumed to be rationally ordered to optimize scarce household resources, are communicated and confirmed through their market "votes" for one set of products over alternative sets.

Producing firms, in this context, acknowledge this preference information by focusing their efforts on how to provide the necessary supply most efficiently. Consumer preferences are not entirely deterministic, it should be noted, because the possibility exists that products demanded can fall outside the boundaries of a society's technological frontier. The realm of consumer sovereignty applies to factor markets, as well. A firm, in organizing to meet consumer demand in the output market, will vote its preferences in the labor markets, for example. Producers of such input factors as labor must, in turn, honor the sovereignty of firms that consume such inputs.

4. Price competition: Thou shalt compete solely on the basis of price.

Implicit in the efficiency conditions sufficient to lead a social system to Pareto optimality is the requirement that the method of conducting transactions is itself efficient. If this were not the case, an otherwise optimally efficient firm would presumably incur extra costs in obtaining market information and in negotiating the terms of each and every transaction. The institutional framework that mitigates such a costly search process is, of course, the perfectly competitive market. In an efficient market, supply and demand are just matched through the operation of the price mechanism. Thus, it is incumbent upon the participating firm to internalize all relevant production costs and endeavor to drive them to the minimum. The price system will do the rest.

5. Rent seeking: Thou shalt not be a rent seeker.

Having specified the imperatives of consumer sovereignty and price competition, an even stronger imperative can now be formulated. That is, market participants operate under a strict requirement to honor only consumer preferences and to compete only on the basis of price. The boundary of possible production, tempered by technological limits as already noted, will be entirely circumscribed by consumer preferences. A producer can choose to forgo participation in a given market, but the set of possible markets is defined through consumer action.

Likewise, faithful adherence to price competition is crucial for a system of free enterprise to operate optimally. Price plays the key informational role in this process, but that role can only be fulfilled if producers concentrate solely upon the costs of production. There is no room for nonprice competition, given the power of the price mechanism.

Statement of this imperative is not meant to imply that market participants cannot accrue economic rents. Temporary imperfections in a given market will likely yield short-run surpluses and deficits for market participants, a situation acknowledged in the theory of perfect competition. The salient point is that, for free enterprise to operate in the interests of the aggregate social good, economic actors cannot consciously seek such rents.

6. Mutual unconcern: Thou shalt not be concerned with thy neighbor or with thy neighbor's property.

A basic result of efficient market operation is that no one consumer or producer should be able to, by weight of his or her actions alone, influence the market's allocation of goods and services. Through the free flow of information, producers are apprised of consumer preferences. Prices guide all actors in this process toward making choices consistent with each party's self-interests. The point is that all actors must focus solely on the dynamics of the market itself, since all necessary information and economic satisfaction can be obtained there. For a firm to expend resources in an effort to learn what its competitors are doing, for example, is to inefficiently apply such resources.

By this logic, it remains possible for two firms to participate in a joint venture, if such an organizational arrangement will result in more efficient production. What may appear on the surface to be an overt manifestation of mutual concern is, in reality, a transaction taking place in another marketplace.

7. Externalities: Thou shalt not commit externalities.

A given producer, unconcerned with the activities of his or her competitors, will use both market information and knowledge of the firm's own capabilities to efficiently organize the necessary factors of production. When the residual effects—externalities, in other words—of some other individual or organization are perpetrated upon this producer, his or her ability to accurately make economic choices is impaired, since externalities impinge upon the cost function. Accordingly, the price mechanism's efficiency will be jeopardized.

In principle, it makes no difference whether these effects take the character of external economies—as in the case of a technological breakthrough—or external diseconomies—as in the case of acidic rainfall. To the extent that these benefits and costs cannot be fully entered into a producer's cost calculus, the efficiency of the price system becomes problematic. What is therefore required of all actors is the internalization of all costs, even if the resultant choice will mean ceasing an externality-producing activity.

8. Free entry: Thou shalt welcome new participants into the market.

Implicit in classical economic theory is the desirability of new participants' appearing in the market process. "Incumbent" firms should view such entry as being wholly consistent with their own self-interests, if market survival represents at least one element of those interests. The underlying conditions for market entry provide the link between self-interest and new entry.

A firm will seek to enter a market only if the prospects exist for profitable participation in some short-run period. To make a profit, as has been explicated already, efficient production must be demonstrated. The impersonal operation of the price mechanism will push self-interested market incumbents to maintain or enhance their individual levels of efficiency. This process, driven by new market entrants, thus serves the larger social interest.

9. Purpose: Thine actions must be purposive.

A concept underlying participation in a free enterprise system is the voluntary nature of such action. Once a choice to take part is made, the individual or firm must focus solely within the bounds of the market system. But this does not imply that the individual or firm of the obligation can act in a haphazard fashion; for example, not only must information be permitted to flow freely, but that information must be accurate and complete. Thus, the meaning of each actor's behavior is as important as his or her attention to the set of rules that structure the market process.

10. Model behavior: Thou shalt do all that is required to bring about perfect-market conditions.

Finally, participants in the free enterprise process must endeavor to satisfy simultaneously each of the preceding nine imperatives that make up the IMM, if Pareto optimality is to result. This is an issue of part-whole relationships; the whole of optimum aggregate social welfare can be achieved if and only if each of these conditions is met. To step outside these bounds of performance is to enter the problematic realm of "second-best," wherein coming close in satisfying the IMM imperatives provides no guarantee that the composite social result will approximate optimality.

McMahon argued that IMM violated common morality. In particular it required actors not to help those in trouble at little cost to themselves. Mutual unconcern under Commandment 6 requires a direct violation of the Principle of Mutual Aid. In addition, if consumer preferences are bizarre enough, other parts of common morality may be violated. Consider the market for pornography, which treats women or children or men as mere means, objects rather than subjects. Suppose that a consumer segment values lying, cheating, and breaking promises. IMM does not forbid transactions with such a group even if such transactions encourage, even necessitate, violations of common morality.

But all is not lost. Everyone knows that capitalism, understood as how perfect markets work, is an unrealizable ideal. It serves the purpose of the gods, as a way to compare mere mortals with an ideal, and as an ideal toward which to strive. The difficulty is that too often, we fail to realize how far the world really is from the ideal of capitalism.

The real issue is the alternative. If we conceive of the way the market actually works in its imperfect way, how close does it come to the ideal? Does it compensate for violations of common morality, or does it merely compound them? If corporations have strategies and if the results of those strategies represent the actual, as opposed to the ideal, workings of the market, then models of corporate strategy will serve as surrogates for perfect markets. To test this proposition we can evaluate corporate strategy in terms of IMM and in terms of common morality. But first, we need to say a few words about the concepts of "market imperfection" and "second-best."

Market Imperfections and the Second-Best

Two key questions are "Why do markets operate as they do?" and "What does it mean to say that a market is 'imperfect'?"

Capitalism, as we have seen, presumes that individuals act in accordance with predetermined preferences. But this is a rather sterile treatment of the individual actor, and seems to be distinctly nonhuman. The reality of the marketplace clearly relies upon human action. Consumers and producers voluntarily make choices in their respective, individual self-interests. But to what can we attribute the determination of such self-interest in the first place? Are market participants acting upon momentary preferences?

We have argued in Chapters 1 and 3 that people can be understood as trying to realize their purposes. Persons have values, which collect themselves into purposes and give rise to projects, which, in turn we try to realize through exchange with others. Projects are fundamentally concerned with commitments to certain ends which the individual perceives as being of value. Indeed, to describe an individual is to recognize the unique relationship between that person and his or her ends.[10]

Recall from Chapter 3 that rights enter the picture closely on the heels of acknowledging individual project pursuit. Because such action is predicated upon a project's holding significant value to its holder, then certain trade-offs are likely to be vigorously resisted, if pursuit of a project is potentially impaired. As we argued in Chapter 3, in a world made up of project pursuers, the potential for conflict is clear. The issue thus becomes a moral one, since the balancing of rights claims will enter the picture. Lomasky puts the point by saying ". . . a regime of rights entails minimal constraints demanding the forbearance of others such that individuals can pursue projects amidst a world of similar beings."[11]

Summarizing this line of reasoning, individuals can be identified and distinguished in terms of projects that they pursue. Since projects are chosen for their value to individuals, the potential for conflict necessitates a system of checks and balances; that is, morality. The claims that project pursuers make are human rights claims; that is, personally oriented, normatively necessary, moral requirements.[12] So, markets operate as they do because human beings each pursue projects, resulting in conflict and necessary means of adjudication.

This leads directly to our second question, of the meaning of market imperfection. Recall that, in a perfectly competitive market, an impersonal price mechanism is presumed to automatically and efficiently mediate supply and demand, for the greatest aggregate good. In effect, the price mechanism resolves all conflicts. But is this consistent with the claim that individual actors can be characterized in terms of their own projects? It seems not. If market operation, which after all is merely the sum of individual project pursuits, is impersonal, then people and their projects could be interchangeable, thus extinguishing, in Lomasky's words, the ". . . especially intimate relationship between a person and his ends."[13] To the degree that individuals value their own projects and ends, markets are imperfect because, at the very least, the impersonality condition for free enterprise is overridden. Persons and their projects simply are not interchangeable. The price mechanism is guaranteed to fail if there are some things, projects, which are *mine*, which have no price. Everyone is a monopolist about his own projects.

So, suppose the conditions for perfect markets are absent. What happens to the ability of market participants to realize their projects in a Pareto-efficient way? One argument is that the closer the market approximates perfect markets conditions, the closer the outcome of market activity will be to Pareto optimality. An individual actor, under this assumption, will endeavor to bring about the best possible results given those factors and choices under his or her control. This is the concept of "second-best."

Economic theorists have shown that the pursuit of second-best conditions does not necessarily guarantee approximately optimal welfare results. One peculiar result can occur when the ratio of price to marginal cost is equalized across all producers. Under such conditions, it is possible to achieve optimal economic results in a market populated by oligopolists.[14] More generally, it has been shown that when at least one free enterprise condition is constrained, an optimum can only be achieved by departing from all other Pareto-optimal conditions.[15] An important corollary to this states that nothing conclusive can be determined about the directional effect on aggregate welfare if more or fewer of the remaining conditions are present. Economic policies, public and private, targeted toward remedying any subset of purportedly significant market conditions will, therefore, be futile.

Economic analysis, thus, raises questions about the validity of a "second-best" solution for aggregate social welfare. But we might not stop with this conclusion. Corporate strategy as a second-best solution is doomed to violate IMM, but this does not mean that it must violate common morality, or that it is unacceptable from a moral point of view.

We shall first look at two particular views of strategy and then seek a more generalized account.[16]

PORTFOLIO APPROACHES TO STRATEGY AND ETHICS

John Sullivan is CEO of Diversified Conglomerate Incorporated (DCI). DCI is the leader in air compressors, basketball backboards, and coffee imports. In addition, DCI has a substantial presence in baby beds and innerspring mattresses. It has recently started ventures in biotechnology and retailing gourmet coffee, and others are planned. Also, there are fifteen other businesses in which DCI engages to varying degrees. In short, DCI is a company where there are many diverse and unrelated businesses, and many diverse people with different projects.

John Sullivan has a problem which is solely a function of DCI's diversification. He needs to be able to allocate resources across a wide range of businesses which do not have much in common. He must compare baby beds with air compressors, and he needs a language to make such comparisons.

With the rise of multiproduct, multidivisional firms, such as DCI, corporate strategy adopted the concept of "portfolio" from finance in order to be able to compare often unrelated businesses. Such "portfolio models of strategy" are especially adaptable to understanding and managing companies like DCI.

The General Idea

Portfolio models ask us to think of a company as similar to an investment portfolio.[17] Just as an investment portfolio is a collection of stocks, bonds, and other investments, so a company is a collection of individual businesses. Individual businesses, like investments, have clear, identifiable returns and risks. The goal of a company should be to maximize returns for a given level of risk.[18]

From a portfolio perspective, corporate executives are like smart investors. They should try to minimize the number of businesses that are losers and maximize the number of winners. The models imply that executives should freely buy and sell businesses on the basis of their evaluation.

Portfolio models are especially applicable to a company organized along the lines of a corporate holding company with some staff and a group of relatively autonomous business units.[19] Otherwise, it is difficult to allocate joint costs and evaluate a business on its own.[20] Typically a firm's businesses are plotted and compared on several dimensions, and each is given a particular strategic role, such as growth, income, or divestment. The role of corporate managers is to allocate resources and buy and sell businesses. The role of business unit managers is to concentrate on making winners out of their particular businesses by executing their strategic role.

There are a number of ways of putting meat on the bones of this general description. We will examine three ways, using DCI as an example of how these models work.

The BCG Approach and the GE-McKinsey Business Screen

There are several key ideas to the Boston Consulting Group (BCG) approach to strategy: the product life cycle, the experience curve, and the growth-share matrix.

The product life cycle is the remarkably simple, yet powerful, idea that products go through at least four phases: an introductory phase, a growth phase, a mature phase, and a phase of decline. What the Boston Consulting Group and its founder, Bruce Henderson, noticed was that when volume doubled all product costs dropped by one third. This effect, dubbed the "experience curve," was due to economies of scale, the learning curve, and other factors. Combining the two ideas, we see that if a company can quickly get to the high-growth phase of the product life cycle, its costs will drop, and it will be in a position to make substantial profits.

BCG developed the growth-share matrix as a way to summarize the main points of its approach. Each product or business can be arrayed in terms of the growth rate of its industry, and the amount of market share the product or company has. There are four possibilities. High-share–high-growth businesses are called "stars," because the prospects are good for their being leaders in the industry. High-share–low-growth businesses are called "cash cows," because they generate lots of cash. (They are reaping the benefits of the effect of the experience curve and are in the mature phase of the product life cycle.) High-growth–low-share businesses are "wildcats," because while the company position is not good, there are good possibilities in the industry. Finally, low-growth–low-share businesses are called "dogs," because there is little future.

The BCG model gives clear direction for each type of business. "Continue to grow" the stars. Stars may generate their own resources, or given the cycle of a business may need resources. "Harvest" the cash cows. (Milk them, in the vernacular.) Cows generate resources that can be used by other businesses with a future of higher growth. "Grow" the wildcats so that they can turn into stars or cows. "Sell" the dogs, for they are a drain on resources.

Returning to our example of DCI, let's assume that it has a dominant position in air compressors, basketball backboards, and coffee imports, none of which is a high-growth industry. So, the BCG model would classify these businesses as cash cows. Currently, baby beds are a booming business, and DCI's substantial presence would make it a star. Biotechnology and gourmet coffee retailing are obvious wildcats, while we can rest assured that some of the remaining fifteen businesses will fit other categories. DCI corporate managers plot the businesses, determine the strategic role of each business, and allocate resources in a coherent way. Managers in the cash cow businesses try to run their operations in a very efficient way, to earn as much cash as appropriate. Managers in wildcat businesses try to "get down" the experience curve as quickly as possible. Managers in star businesses try to maintain or grow their dominant positions. And managers in dog businesses do what they can to make the best of a bad situation.

Rather than focus on market share and growth, the McKinsey-GE business screen arrays businesses on an external dimension called "industry attractiveness" and an internal dimension called "competitive position." This represents a powerful generalization of the BCG approach. Various factors make up industry attractiveness, such as industry growth and the economic, technological, social, and political setting of the industry. Competitive position is a function of market share, but also profitability, human resources, and other factors. A similar set of strategic roles are assigned, and things proceed much as in the BCG case.

The differences for DCI managers is that they have much more room to make judgments, and the factors for success may well differ from industry to industry. Each business manager must think through the key success factors.

Porter's Approach to Strategy

George Russell is a division manager at DCI responsible for baby beds. He finds the business in a difficult position. The market for baby beds has been growing for the last few years, after years of flat sales, because baby-boom women are now starting families. However, an increasing share of DCI baby beds is going to K-Mart, Wal-Mart, and Sears, the large retailers. DCI manufactures the wooden parts of the beds and buys the brackets and other metal parts. Recently, one source of supply has gone out of business, leaving one U. S. firm and one Taiwanese firm that are capable of supplying the quantity that DCI needs. There are several new companies in the industry whose beds have more features than DCI's best bed and command premium prices. George Russell believes that the Taiwanese supplier is set to enter the U.S. market with two products that compete with his low-end beds. To ice the cake, a recent study questioned the use of baby beds or cribs, and touted a new idea— the infant sleep carrousel—as producing a happier baby.

In two powerful recent books, Harvard Business School Professor Michael Porter has articulated a view of strategy that will help managers such as George Russell.[21] Porter says that business success is due to five forces that shape an industry: (1) the amount of rivalry among competitors, (2) the bargaining power of customers, (3) the bargaining power of suppliers, (4) the threat of new entrants into the industry, and (5) the threat of substitute products.

Porter claims that the greater the aggregate impact of these forces, the lower the returns in a business. He goes on to formulate three generic strategies to adopt as a way of "defending" against the forces in an industry. "Focus" puts emphasis on doing a few things well, limiting either product line offerings or the customers served. "Differentiation" puts emphasis on having the customer perceive a product as unique and different. "Low cost" emphasizes cost reduction, efficient production, and minimum need for service. Porter goes on to give details on how to analyze and implement these generic strategies in detail, but that need not concern us here.

George Russell's high-end competitors have adopted a focus strategy by appealing to a particular market segment, those parents who want an expensive, brand-name baby bed. The Taiwanese competitor will enter the market on a low-cost basis. And George Russell must decide how to respond.

Portfolios, Porter, and Ethics

Portfolio approaches to strategy clearly violate IMM. The focus of BCG on gaining market share to gain a dominant position to force out competitors is a clear violation of the commandments against monopoly.

Just as plainly, each theory is the result of a Stockholder or Managerial-Prerogative E-Strategy. If a portfolio approach represents a true effort to act in the interests of stockholders, we must be suspicious. When diversification is unrelated, we have to ask why stockholders can't do so for themselves. Indeed, the large increase in mutual funds investments can be read as a vote of no confidence in the ability of managers to successfully diversify.

Portfolio theory makes the societal context of business decisions unimportant. While we argued in the last chapter that a concern for social responsibility, as a program of responsiveness, is not the proper way to connect ethics and strategy, neither is it completely irrelevant. Except for a brief "check-off" in the McKinsey-GE model, the externalities of a decision are ignored. Notice that this singular unconcern with externalities violates both IMM and common morality. The following true but disguised story is symptomatic.

XYZ Corporation had invented a container for soft drinks made of a substance that was lighter, cheaper, and more convenient than current materials. In accordance with current thinking, XYZ rushed to grab market share, "drive down the experience curve," and reap appropriate rewards. It decided to market the container before gaining FDA approval. The container was found to be carcinogenic and had to be withdrawn from the market at great cost to the company, not to mention the cost to any who were actually harmed. Portfolio approaches seem to imply that a concern with stockholder wealth allows pell-mell harm to others.

More important, there is a curious absence of persons in these theories. In thinking of DCI as a portfolio, John Sullivan treats employees as mere means. If importing gourmet coffee doesn't pan out, he ought (given the theory) to shut it down, and to do so without asking for the consent of those who would be radically affected. Treating others as mere tools to the achievement of corporate ends clearly violates common morality's injunction to treat persons as ends, though it may be consistent with IMM.

If George Russell thinks of DCI's baby bed division as responding to the external forces at work in the industry, he has two sets of choices. The first set of choices involves trying to prevent the competition from being successful. In short, he has to become a monopolist, erecting barriers to entry, or convincing government that there are barriers to exit for which DCI should be compensated. He might seek trade protection from the Taiwanese, or concessions from the work force. The point is that he will try to extract the costs of DCI's past action from those who must pay the price for the future. Rarely have we seen the George Russells of the world make an impassioned plea for stockholders to accept lower returns. Indeed, the very nature of the capital markets prevents such actions. These actions clearly violate IMM and common morality.

The second set of choices available to George is to realign the businesses so that the competitors are what Porter calls "good competitors." Each picks a particular niche and respects the niche of others. The Taiwanese take the low-cost segment. The specialty firms take the high-end market. And DCI becomes the differentiated producer that serves each segment in a different way. Such an arrangement, which would take place implicitly rather than overtly, clearly violates IMM, but, curiously enough, may not violate common morality.

By avoiding competition and focusing on the particular market where it can add value to suppliers, customers, and other stakeholders, DCI may well obey common morality. If such cases are the norm, Professor Porter has given us one of the great ironies of all times. His books entitled *Competitive Strategy* and *Competitive Advantage* rest on cooperation and would be better titled *Cooperative Strategy* and *Cooperative Advantage*. Such ideas would so clearly violate the laws of the land as to be ludicrous; however, we should be careful. The power of Porter's framework, in this interpretation, lies in its ironic twist. Ethics creeps in no matter the attempts to keep it out.

THE IMPLICIT MORALITY OF CORPORATE STRATEGY

Can we generalize the critique of the previous section? We can, to the extent that we can judge the concept against the twin towers of IMM and common morality.

Although the models cited above do not contain explicit vows to enact as large an aggregate welfare as possible, two clues appear to point in that direction. First, the implication is clear that, if the firm is to practice this "trade," it will require considerable latitude to maneuver in pursuit of its self-interests. Second, the models explicitly prescribe that a choice be made by a firm's strategists, as agents, with regard to economic and noneconomic contributions to the firm's social context.

To claim that corporate strategy rests upon a body of tested principles is to stretch the point, since the field is relatively young. Nevertheless, a survey of its respected literature for a central body of well-advised practices yields at least ten hypothetical imperatives. The implicit morality of corporate strategy can be inferred from these nascent principles, to the effect that: A good corporate strategist follows these practices. How closely these practices adhere to the IMM and common morality can be delineated in terms of their clear or potential violations of each.

1.   Influence what customers will demand through your distinctive competence.

Distinctive competence and the principles of IMM are entirely compatible concepts. Implicit in the theory of perfect competition is the assumption that a firm possesses a distinctive competence to produce efficiently; otherwise, the forces of price competition will drive the firm from the market.

Self-interested pursuit of distinctive competence will clash with the IMM when a firm presumes its competence to include the ability to specify what consumers want and need. One stream of such logic should be familiar: If computer technology can produce it, the consuming public will demand it. In the case of personal computers, this logic appears to be manifest. In the case of the "picture phones" of the 1960's, such competence was missing. In either case, a presumption of what we might call producer sovereignty is evident.

This practice of demand-creating competence clearly violates IMM Commandment 3, the consumer sovereignty requirement; and it implicitly violates Comandments 4, 5, and 6. Creation of consumer demand, in other words, constitutes unfaithfulness to the price system, conscious rent seeking, and mutual concern. What about common morality?

The essence of treating a person as a mere means is to try to influence that person's projects, especially if "influence" involves coercion or any practices other than giving reasons. A reason for people to do X is that doing X helps them to realize their projects. Trying to persuade someone that he or she really wants X, or that X leads to a sexier, happier, more wonderful life, is to treat that person's projects as instrumental. Common morality is violated. To the extent that this implicit commandment of corporate strategy countenances shading the truth, a lack of promise keeping, and the like, it clearly violates common morality.

2.   Use information as a resource.

In the context of free enterprise, market information can be thought of as a social good, whose freely available presence enables market participants to make optimal individual choices. Yet markets are imperfect, because individuals concentrate upon their own projects. The conduct of such projects implies that a given body of information is more valuable to one individual than to another. Self-interest would dictate the advisability of claiming some degree of ownership over this information—in other words, internalizing the benefits—to the exclusion of other potential users.

This clearly violates IMM Commandment 1. Where information is internalized by a firm's management, as owners' agents, regarding an issue of broad moral impact, Commandment 2 can also be violated.

Common morality could be violated here if we interpret it to require giving away information if it involves little cost to us. To the extent to which IMM Commandment 2 is violated, so too, is the requirement of common morality to consult and gain the permission of those whose projects are affected by our actions.

3.   Be alert for, and use, market signals.

The implication that the effective practice of corporate strategy necessitates the internalization of information as a private good is not the only information arena in which corporate strategy and the IMM can part company. Deliberate use of market information channels, through market signaling practices, has been proposed as a method for coping with the uncertainties arising from the interdependence among market participants. A self-interested firm will selectively employ information, choosing from an array of tactics ranging from candid disclosure to bluffing.

These tactics are intended to block information flows, in violation of Commandment 1; imply the need to pay conscious attention to competitors, violating Commandment 6; and need not always contain meaningful information, violating the purposive condition in Commandment 9.

Obviously, to the extent to which market signaling involves misleading others, it violates the ordinary moral requirements to tell the truth and keep promises. Once again, these principles are necessary for the marketplace to work, but not corporate strategy. A firm will be more successful if it systematically misleads its competitors and perhaps its customers.

4. Segment a market and find your niche; use branding to protect your niche.

A logical extension to the purported importance of distinctive competence for the corporate strategist is the imperative that such competence be nurtured and defended. Distinctive competence could be considered an intangible asset for the firm, the key to a corner of the market in which the firm can minimize its environmental uncertainty to some degree. One method for preserving such a niche is to create distinctive product brands.

The practice of niche seeking and niche preservation appears to clash with IMM Commandments 5, 6, and 8, since the underlying intent is not to participate in an open market process. Branding, conceptually, may be a benign manifestation of market segmentation. But when brands become offensive instruments created to attract consumer demand, or to combat the attempted entry of a firm's niche, the IMM principles of consumer sovereignty, mutual unconcern, and free market entry are violated.

The extent to which common morality is violated is precisely the extent to which this commandment inflicts harm on others. The beauty of IMM is that individuals are accorded free entry to the marketplace. This commandment is equivalent to raising the cost of your projects solely for my benefit. One simple and well-placed partial truth such as "Product X helps prevent colds" is permissible under corporate strategy though prevented under both IMM and common morality.

5. Price at a level the "market will bear."

A market niche, by definition, represents a haven for a firm, wherein its distinctive competence is sheltered from broad-based competitive challenge. The strategist's focus becomes the means by which to preserve the niche. Selective use of information and branding represent two barriers to competitive entry. Price can be another. Just as competence can be presumed to include knowing consumer wants and needs, so, too, can competence be logically assumed by strategists to extend to include price specification. "What is the market willing to pay?" replaces price-taking behavior. As price moves from guide and market arbitrator to a strategic tool, IMM Commandments 4 and 5 are clearly abridged. Commandment 6 will likely be violated, as well, to the extent that the firm bases its pricing decisions on the present and expected actions of its competitors.

Curiously enough, as long as customers or suppliers voluntarily agree to pay the price, we can see no violations of common morality. Each market participant values goods and services in terms of how well they fit into particular projects. This should come as no surprise, since it is the price mechanism of IMM which itself violates common morality. We shall return to this point of corporate strategy as voluntary agreements among consenting adults in Chapter 8.

6. Choose your economic and social contribution.

This principle could be restated to say: Choose your external economies. The decisions made by strategists in operationalizing the firm's "social responsibility" essentially involve choices as to what is important to, and valued by, the firm's constituents.

The inconsistency between this approach and IMM should be clear, as it has been the focus of considerable scholarly debate. A firm's conscious selection of social contributions creates market externalities—even if positive effects ensue—which can confound the price mechanism, as discussed previously. Thus, Commandment 7 is violated.

Choice of contribution runs counter to Commandment 6, as well, since explicit concern is being paid to the interests of market participants. This concern becomes more complex when the likely multiplicity of roles assumed by any one actor is recognized. That a consumer can also play the roles of owner, employee (that is, producer of labor services), and regulator simultaneously effectively accentuates this violation. Choice of contribution also potentially violates Commandment 5, if the contribution tactics are linked to a firm's niche-preserving strategies. Finally, Commandment 2 can be violated by this practice, since social contribution choices are value-laden, inherently.

Once again, common morality has little to say here. It would depend on the nature of the particular contribution. Some choices could clearly violate common morality, but we see no reason why they must.

7. Values of top management should be reflected in strategy statements.

A common formulation of this argument runs as follows: The preferences of the Chief Executive Officer should be considered in strategy formulation; after all, he or she must eventually institutionalize these plans. The role of CEO as one of many stakeholders in the strategic process cannot be denied. But, as with broader conceptions of distinctive competence, price setting, market segmentation, and conscious social contribution programs, this corporate strategy imperative reverses the tables on market operation, and suggests that what the firm's managers, as agents, want is what counts. For this approach to even begin to be consistent with IMM Commandment 1, the free flow of information must be assured. But this condition has already been shown to be antithetical to the practice of corporate strategy. In the absence of this condition, Commandments 2, 5, 6, and 8 all stand to be violated.

The extent to which top management values include the denial of the rights of others to pursue their projects will determine whether common morality is violated. The extent to which the moral rules of common morality have become internalized to become moral values of senior management will also determine if there is a problem here.

8. In managing corporate culture, there is opportunity.

Managing corporate culture to create a responsive organizational membership has received considerable recent attention. Aside from the inherent, and often underestimated, difficulties in changing a body of collective beliefs and practices, culture management portends several significant departures from the IMM.

First, implicit in the management of corporate culture is the intent to reinforce the defense of a distinctive competence, through the development of a strongly held collective belief in such a competence. Thus, culture management violates Commandments 4, 5, and 6 by virtue of the company it keeps. Second, the factor markets for labor can become distorted through the practice of culture management. Practitioners of this approach seek to find employees whose values and beliefs match those of the culture of a given firm. In this sense, price as an arbitrator in the labor market is partially replaced by the required congruence of individual and firm beliefs. Commandment 4 is violated in the process.

Third, the selective use of information in devising the instruments of culture management—myths, legends, and so on—and the suggestion in some quarters that culture management is the essence of general management appear to run counter to Commandments 1 and 9.

Common morality gives constraints on what it means to "manage" the corporate culture. Lying and false promises are obviously ruled out. The extent to which the very idea of "corporate culture" is antithetical to treating others as ends, we save until Chapter 8.

9. Use the cost-benefit, time-discounted decision rule.

A considerable body of literature addressing the efficient means of preparing and monitoring corporate strategy plans has paralleled the conceptual development of the field. A common theme in this process is the required quantitative "fit" of each element in a firm's overall strategy. While, in spirit, this attention to accurate information flow is consistent with free enterprise principles, the application of cost-benefit criteria poses two potential IMM violations.

First, undue attention to the quantification of market information can tend to divert attention from the externalities produced by a firm's activities. To the extent that external economies and diseconomies do not readily submit to measurement and quantification, a tendency to lump these phenomena into "qualitative" categories for analytical purposes clashes with Commandment 7. In the same vein, certain decisions of the firm will likely not be quantifiable and will be of such moral import that stockholders must be consulted. Overemphasis on "hard solutions" to strategic problems can, thus, crowd out attention to Commandment 2.

Common morality is quite simple here. As in earlier examples, the degree to which the application of this rule requires us to treat individual persons as interchangeable is the degree to which it violates treating others and their projects as unique.

10. Competitive markets are battlefields.

Free enterprise markets are ruthless in their theoretical prescription. Efficiency conditions must be satisfied by producers if survival as a going concern is to result. Yet this represents a fundamentally different conception of market interaction from that assumed by the corporate strategy model. In the latter view, efficiency shares the beacon role with the drive for market certainty that distinctive competence can purportedly ensure. Since survival is assumed to be a far more likely result in the corporate strategy model, the focus shifts to the nature of that survival. Market share, for example, emerges as a higher-order goal in this context.

The military metaphor is frequently seen across the corporate strategy literature. On the battlefield for scarce and certain market shares, mutual unconcern, freedom of competitive entry, externality avoidance, purposiveness of action, and the prohibition on rent seeking all seem to be out of place. It is in this macroperspective that the divergence between IMM and the imperatives of corporate strategy appears most evident.

The way that we talk makes a difference. Using the military metaphor implies that we see others and their projects as tools to be used, or barriers to be overcome. Killing, maiming, and promoting general harm are forbidden by common morality. Surely the spirit of common morality is that talk of killing, maiming, and promoting general harm should be used carefully.

Without referencing any possibility that misdeeds can be perpetrated in the name of corporate strategy and its link to free enterprise, the gap between corporate strategy's de facto morality and both IMM and common morality appears to be substantial, and it seems to be systematic across all major elements of corporate strategy. What can we conclude?

CONCLUSIONS

We have been sharply critical of current formulations of corporate strategy that are based loosely on economic theory. Given the best possible intentions attendant to, and inherent in, the practice of corporate strategy, no plausible assurance can be given that the dictates of morality will be followed or that social optimality will result. Is this the death knell for corporate strategy? We think not. Rather, the incompleteness of the "theory" of corporate strategy is a good place to start rehabilitating the patient.

One line of response is to argue that even if the outcomes of corporate strategy violate both IMM and common morality, perhaps the *process* of corporate strategy treats others as ends, upholding the integrity of the meaning of a person. Corporate strategy would then be a kind of third-best solution to the marketplace. Perhaps violations of common morality would be only a natural result of human fallibility and the pragmatic fact that some people are evil, routinely violating common morality. In the following chapter we analyze such a "process view" of corporate strategy.

A second response to our criticism of corporate strategy would be to claim that the rules of common morality should be overridden or revised. For example, lying and promise keeping are usually obligations except in certain kinds of business situations. The problem with this argument is IMM. If it could be shown that by following the requirements of corporate strategy, individuals would be better off, in a Pareto sense, then our intuitions about the applicability of common morality could be overridden. But the very nature of corporate strategy also violates the conditions which assure Pareto optimality, namely, IMM.

The only avenue is to seek a new conception of corporate strategy and the corporation which does not violate common morality and to seek a reinterpretation of the virtues of capitalism. We begin this task in Chapter 8.

★ ★ ★ ★ ★ ★ ★ ★ ★ ★ CHAPTER **7**

Ethics and the Strategy Process

INTRODUCTION

In the previous two chapters, we have shown how several popular approaches to corporate strategy fail to help managers deal in a general way with questions of strategy and ethics. We have shown how these shortcomings stem from the general lines of reasoning in these approaches and how they are manifest in both explicit and implicit extensions of such reasoning to questions of strategy and ethics. This chapter presents yet another example of how the current thinking about corporate strategy is not up to the task of linking strategy and ethics: the case of strategic planning and process models (hereafter, "strategic process").[1] But the fact that this analysis comes last in line should not be read as an indication of lesser importance. In fact, we have saved for last the "best" example of how not to reason about strategy if you are interested in ethical issues.

We say that this is the "best" example for two reasons. First, strategic process models abound and have evolved over several decades in many different forms.[2] To many, "strategic management" and "strategic process" (or "planning") are virtually synonymous.[3] In short, a strategic process approach, as we interpret it here, is the most common of the approaches to corporate strategy that we will examine. Every manager in today's world has wrestled with "the planning process." Second, and more important, the strategic process model represents an antithesis to the argument that we will articulate in Chapter 8. This becomes readily apparent when we consider three key assumptions about values—and, hence, the rules derived from those values—that support the strategic process model. These assumptions are: (1) values are general forces that affect strategy and that appear in a finite number of fixed, generic types, such as the organizational goal "maximize shareholder wealth";[4] (2) values are intangible and indistinct creatures, thus not readily amenable to either scientific inquiry or managerial suasion;[5] and accordingly, (3) a person's tendency to reflect upon his or her values and rules poses a threat to the integrity of strategic management processes. Taken together, these assumptions serve to deny the general importance of individuals' reflecting upon the rules regarding how to interact with other individuals doing likewise. Since this posture stands in such marked contrast to the arguments that we have developed here, the case of the strategic process model offers us the "best" opportunity to show how not to link strategy and ethics.

In the section that follows, we take these assumptions and formally interpret them as three basic premises of the strategic process model. On this basis, we then derive three hypotheses of strategic process: the First Hypothesis of Strategic Process, the Second Hypothesis of Strategic Process, and the Value-Free Hypothesis of Strategic Process. We then show, through many contemporary examples, how (1) these hypotheses are in widespread use and (2) the hypotheses support incomplete accounts of the relationship between strategy and ethics.

THE STRATEGIC PROCESS MODEL

Kenneth Andrews, of the Harvard Business School, argues that the whole point of strategic management is for the firm to:

> . . . enter the future on a predetermined course.[6]

In this spirit, he makes clear the central proposition in the strategic process model:

> . . . a business enterprise guided by a clear sense of purpose rationally arrived at and emotionally ratified by commitment is more likely to have a successful outcome, in terms of profit and social good, than a company whose future is left to guesswork and chance.[7]

Andrews draws a telltale distinction between two sets of activities (or processes) that combine to produce a blueprint for successful, overall organizational performance (hence, *strategic* processes):[8]

1. Strategy formulation processes, by which a strategy is "rationally arrived at"
2. Strategy implementation processes, by which a strategy is "emotionally ratified by commitment"

These two processes, although requiring human agents to "rationally arrive at" and "emotionally ratify" a given strategy, are features of the firm, or organization.[9] To the strategic process theorist, the firm is, in fact, a structure of processes derived from the elemental activities of strategy formulation and strategy implementation.[10] The job of maintaining the structure falls on the shoulders of a subset of human agents in the organization, known collectively as "senior management." The leading character in this cast, according to Andrews, is:

> the chief executive officer (who) has as his or her highest function the management of a continuous process of strategic decisions. . . .[11]

This, in a nutshell, is the strategic process model. The question we now want to ask is: What theory of the person is implicit in the model? The answer is powerful and provocative.

THREE HYPOTHESES OF STRATEGIC PROCESS

To understand how the strategic process model accounts for persons, we will pay a visit to the Bison River Company and meet two actors: Jake, the Chief Executive Officer (CEO), and Ben, an ordinary employee.[12] Jake and Ben each possess certain characteristics that have vexed analysts of management and organizations since Day One.[13] We will consider three such characteristics in this section. The strategic process model is designed to overcome the problems created by these characteristics, for the betterment of companies like Bison River. This is accomplished through the creation and maintenance of a structure of processes that guide Jake and Ben through their respective organizational duties. To the extent that Jake and Ben follow these guidelines, the process is deemed appropriate as a necessary condition for Bison River's success.[14] In short, *the central truth of the strategy process model is that people are the problems*. It is not hyperbole to conclude that, as far as the strategic process theorist is concerned, the formulation and implementation of organizational strategy would proceed far more effectively—that is, more easily—if the organization were empty of persons. The saga of Jake and Ben makes this abundantly clear.

Three Human Problems and Three Premisses

First, Jake and Ben both have limited capabilities for receiving, storing, and processing information. The human mind can easily become overloaded.[15] This is a crucial problem for Bison River in Jake's case, because her primary job, as noted above, is to manage the process of charting the company's future course. Jake is a busy executive. She must worry about new competitors, the viability of a key supplier in Honduras, the impending bankruptcy of a major customer, next week's address to the Chamber of Commerce, and telephone messages from the executive producer of *60 Minutes* and someone interested in making a stock tender offer. Jake, like us all, can concentrate on only so many things at once. So, the strategic process theorist draws a conclusion about where to begin with a model that helps Bison River: Jake's activities need to be structured in order to overcome her limitations and lead her to the "right" strategy for Bison River.

Ben likewise presents a problem for Bison River. As an ordinary employee, his role in the company is to faithfully do his part in putting Bison River's strategy into action. But, as an ordinary employee, Ben has neither the familiarity with the company's strategic position, nor the ability to understand it in the technical way that Jake does.[16] This relative ignorance, added to Ben's inherent deficiencies as an information processor, prompts the theorist to draw a conclusion about how to build a model that solves this problem: Structure Ben's activities to overcome his limitations and lead him to act in a manner that "fits" the Bison River strategy.

We can formalize these twin conclusions as a first premise for any model of strategic process:

Structure Premiss

Individual and organizational actions are in part caused by decision-making process structures that accommodate and overcome human psychological limitations.

Causation is partial, because human agents act to varying degrees within the structure. Jake and Ben, in other words, represent the sources of deviation from the proper structure at Bison River.[17] Second, Jake and Ben both tend to make independent judgments about what ends are appropriate for themselves. These value judgments pose a problem for the company, because strategy is an organizational, not an individual, attribute. Suppose that Bison River management, under Jake's direction, has formulated a plan to enter into a joint venture with an Australian firm. At the same time, Bison River management has decided to abandon the company's original and bellwether product by treating it as a "dog" instead of a "cash cow," for resource allocation purposes.

Whenever Jake reflects afterward upon the wisdom of this two-part strategy, she is permitting her own values to intercede, perhaps precariously for Bison River. Ben is likewise prone to reflect upon the implications of the new strategy for his own situation. Suppose that Ben is involved with the implementation of both parts of the strategy. Suppose further that the decision to phase out the original product was accompanied by a new remuneration plan designed to quickly sell off inventories. Ben reasons that he would gain financially by devoting most of his time to the old product. In the process, he could then largely avoid what he considered to be an unchallenging role in the Australian program. Ben, like Jake, is letting his values come between him and his part as a cog in Bison River.

The observant strategic process theorist draws another conclusion from this natural tendency toward self-reflection: Admit that values play a part in determining whether a strategy will work and devise decision-making structures to allow for this proclivity. This conclusion can be formalized as a second premiss guiding the development of any strategic process model:

Constraint Premiss

Individual and organizational values partially constrain the formulation and execution of planned organizational action.

Once again, causation is partial, to allow for varying degrees of self-reflection by the persons involved; and once again, Jake and Ben are the sources of such variability.[18]

Third, both Jake and Ben pursue sets of personal activities that are neither (1) wholly defined by their associations with Bison River nor (2) wholly directed toward what Bison River is trying to accomplish nor (3) directly comparable. Yet, Jake and Ben both believe that they take actions as agents for an entity known as the Bison River Company. Those who monitor their actions, such as the Bison River Board of Directors, build this belief into their monitoring programs. At the same time, suppose that a private citizen named Lynn has called Jake several times to complain about the installation work performed by Ben. Moreover, Lynn has taken her complaint to court and received a substantial damages judgment against Bison River. Jake has authorized Bison River's attorneys to appeal the verdict.

All these circumstances present several problems for the strategic process theorist. It is difficult, first, to determine where "Jake of Bison River" ends and "Jake of Jake's life" begins.[19] She reflects upon the Australian joint venture, for example, not only for "business reasons," but because she will now travel more frequently to look after Bison River's interests. She worries that the travel will impose a considerable cost upon her relationship with her young son, upon her racquetball game, and upon her vegetable gardening.

It is difficult, next, to determine whether the many roles that Ben "fills" are entirely consistent with his employment at Bison River. Ben works at the plant, lives in a neighborhood immediately adjacent to the plant, plays softball in a local league sponsored by a city government that has not always supported Bison River, owns a modest amount of Bison River stock, and is married to the editor of the local newspaper. If an issue arose that activated this nominal split in Ben's loyalties, it is not patently clear how he would decide to act.

It is difficult, third, to determine whether Jake feels more allegiance to the garden or to racquetball, and whether Ben's dinner table discussions with his wife pose any more threat to Bison River than Jake's weekly movie watching with her son. In short, the projects that Jake and Ben pursue are simply not comparable in any meaningful way. Yet, these pursuits could clearly affect how Jake and Ben perform for Bison River.

It is difficult, finally, to determine what to do about Lynn. Lynn has sued Bison River in order to protect her own interests. As the sole proprietor of a law firm, she has no reason to consider herself an agent of Bison River. Yet, her current involvement with the company has a significant effect on the company's ability to carry out the strategy that Jake helped discover.[20]

The strategic process theorist observes these complexities and draws several conclusions. First, although both Jake and Ben play integral parts as the agents for Bison River, neither person's interests can be identified as invariably commensurate with the company's interests. Furthermore, Lynn's interests are antagonistic to Bison River's. So, the theorist concludes, any strategic process model must designate the Bison River organization as the relevant unit for analysis and practice. Second, Lynn is unlike Jake and Ben because she does not participate as an agent in either the derivation, or activation, of Bison River's strategy. That fact, coupled with the fact that Lynn's interests could be satisfied by some third party—such as Bison River's insurance company—leads the theorist to conclude that it is only the interests of Bison River that need to be taken into account.[21] This reasoning can be formalized as a third premiss upon which any strategic process model must be constructed:

Organizational Self-Sufficiency Premiss

Organizational performance is in part caused by the logic of decision-making structures in a single organization directed toward the interests of that organization.

Causation is partial, because the strategic process theorist wants to acknowledge the influence of broad environmental forces, such as shifts in industry structure or political climate, on strategic performance. But causation is not so partial that other identifiable "outside" individuals or organizations directly aid or hinder organizational performance.[22] In the strategic process world, transactions, if they exist at all, are mere data points in a bilateral relationship between an organization and its environment.

An Implicit Theory of the Person

In sum, the strategic process theorist considers how the inherent limitations in the minds of Jake and Ben affect their organizational behavior and then generalizes these effects in terms of three premises, or building blocks, for a model of strategic process. Implicit in these premises is a distinct theory of the person: *Person's are both relatively incompetent and unpredictable when dealing with their world.* They cannot process information with consistent "rationality" (that is, mechanically). They have the annoying tendency to think about themselves. And they will not "stay put" in their activities, but rather, as seen with Jake and Ben, want to move freely between their organization and their life on the outside. An unequivocal statement of this theory of the person comes from no less than Herbert Simon and his Nobel Prize–winning argument:

> The behavior patterns which we call organizations are fundamental, then, to the achievement of human rationality in any broad sense. The rational individual is, and must be, an organized and institutionalized individual. If the severe limits imposed by human psychology . . . are to be relaxed, the individual must, in his decisions, be subject to the influence of the organized group in which he participates. His decisions must not only be the product of his own mental processes, but also reflect the broader considerations to which it is the function of the organized group to give effect.[23]

It should come as no surprise that strategic process theorists pay unabashed homage to Simon.[24]

Finally, we need to reiterate a point attributed to Andrews above. We restate this point as an implication derived from all three premises:

The Expert Corollary

Decision-making process in the organization is the responsibility of senior management.

THREE HYPOTHESES FOR MANAGING STRATEGIC PROCESSES

At this point in our saga, the theorist steps from the shadows and takes his place on center stage. Jake, intent upon being an effective manager, asks for his advice about how to overcome the human-centered problems that plague a company like Bison River. The theorist turns the matter over to his associate, the Corporate Strategy Genie ("Genie," for short), who says, "Jake, I have three hypotheses about how to solve your problems. Think of these as imperatives that any effective strategic manager must adopt." Jake then receives these instructions.

Genie begins, "First, Jake, here is a flow chart that indicates how you should analyze Bison River's opportunities and capabilities. Follow these steps faithfully, and you will formulate the proper strategy for the company. Then, take this other flow chart which shows you how to draw upon Bison River's human resources to put this strategy into practice. Follow these steps faithfully and you will persuade Ben to implement this strategy faithfully."[25]

This advice translates into our first hypothesis:

First Hypothesis of Strategy Process

Corporate strategy must be shaped through faithful adherence to a structure of routinized decision-making processes within an organization.

Genie continues, "Next, Jake, it is entirely proper for you to think about whether you really believe in the strategy that you have just rationally divined for Bison River. After all, a CEO must have her heart in it to do a good job. Others like Ben will look to you for guidance about this strategy. You must make certain that he will not spend a great deal of time rethinking what you and your staff have exhaustively analyzed. So, you must provide credible support for the strategy by taking actions that symbolize your support for it. Think hard on this matter now, and then get on with the execution."[26] This advice translates into the second hypothesis:

Second Hypothesis of Strategic Process

Corporate strategy must be shaped in such a way that constraining values are made to conform to the organization's structurally derived strategy.

Genie moves on to the third imperative: "Finally, Jake, your task is not completed until you have articulated the strategy in terms of how it specifically matches Bison River with its economic environment, how it fits the prevailing and coming political and social trends, and how it affects internal operations at Bison River. The language that you use must be more like the scientist's than the poet's.[27] It must include terms like 'market segment,' 'strategic groups,' 'degree of vertical integration,' 'organizational culture,' 'distribution channels,' 'differentiation,' 'organizational design,' and 'target rate of return on equity.'

"Remember well this dictum. You lead the process designed to rationally discover this strategy. But the strategy is not yours. It belongs to Bison River. The strategy—and the process that you develop to produce and modify it—should be such that if you should leave the company tomorrow, your successor could step in as if nothing had happened. You must accept this for yourself first, and then model this acceptance for Ben."

The third hypothesis can now be stated:[28]

Value-Free Hypothesis of Strategic Process

Corporate strategy must be independent of all intentional actions by individuals and, hence, is independent of anyone's values.

The Strategic Management Genie bows, collects his fee, and disappears.

TELLING A STORY WITH THE STRATEGIC PROCESS MODEL

Jake returns to her desk and finds two notes left by her assistant. One is an urgent telephone call from Lynn. The other is the lead editorial from this morning's local newspaper. The author has delivered a scathing criticism of Bison River for entering the Australian venture allegedly at the expense of the local economy. Jake looks at the notes, ponders what Genie said, and finds her mind filled with a single question: "Is there something missing from this process model?" She decides to conduct a test. She will choose a historical strategic problem and write down two lists. One list contains questions that she wants to ask about the case. The other contains the questions that Genie wants her to ask. Jake has no doubt about which test case fills the bill; she has been studying the AT&T divestiture for a long time.

Breaking Up Ma Bell[29]

On January 8, 1982, officials from the United States Department of Justice and senior managers from American Telephone and Telegraph Company (AT&T) announced an agreement to radically restructure the ways by which telecommunications services would be made available to every telephone user in America. In signing the agreement (formally, the Modified Final Judgment, or MFJ), the parties hoped to end the United States Government's antitrust suit against AT&T, which, although filed in 1974, had only come to trial ten months before January 8, 1982. Although brief—a mere fourteen pages—the divestiture document carried a profound message. The twenty-two Bell System operating companies ("BOCs") were spun off from AT&T and reorganized into seven regional holding companies (RHCs). To the BOCs fell the responsibility for providing basic telephone services in local telephone exchanges, as regulated monopolies. But the BOCs were barred from manufacturing communications equipment and from providing long-distance (that is, interexchange) services. Nonetheless, the BOCs were required to provide "interconnection" facilities for all long-distance carriers, a list which included the BOCs' former parent—AT&T—and such upstarts as MCI and GTE Sprint. Under the terms of the divestiture, Western Electric and Bell Telephone Laboratories would remain as AT&T subsidiaries, and AT&T earnings rates would remain subject to federal regulation. The MFJ also included provisions that permitted AT&T entry into the information processing marketplaces from which it had been formally barred in 1956.

Yet, there was a price to be paid for the brevity of the divestiture agreement. More issues were left unresolved than solved. It was quickly evident to AT&T senior managers that much work remained to be done in order to define what a postdivestiture Bell System would look like. This point became quite clear when, on August 24, 1982, U.S. District Court Judge Harold Greene approved the January 8, 1982, agreement and ordered AT&T senior management to present him with a plan of organization within six months and to activate an approved plan within eighteen months.

1. The first set of questions. Jake took a week to read several published accounts of the AT&T divestiture.[30] She sorted through the questions that those authors had not answered and added her own questions. Soon, her list narrrowed to six issues.

a. *Universal service.* What would be the new "rules of the game" regarding how, and at what prices, local customers should be served, and what types of services should be considered "basic?"

In a postdivestiture America, customers could no longer look to one unified Bell System for universal access to telecommunications services. It would not be unusual for a residential customer to receive local service from a BOC, contract for long-distance services from an AT&T competitor, and buy a telephone in a department store. Thus, it was not patently clear what "universal service" meant after January 8, 1982.[31] In addition, senior managers at the BOCs worried about "bypass," the possibility that business customers could develop their own private telecommunications networks and completely circumvent the local exchanges.

b. *Local interconnection for long-distance services.* What exactly did "equal access" for all long-distance carriers mean?

Access to local exchanges was not a new issue, because MCI and other long-distance carriers had received federal approval to operate networks in competition with AT&T since the late 1960's. But Greene's approval of the MFJ hastened the need for a variety of parties to agree on the terms and conditions regarding pricing and access to the local telephone exchanges, since those exchanges were now operated by independent BOCs.

c. *Divestiture oversight.* Who should monitor telecommunications policy and governance in the United States?

The answer was not patently obvious to Jake, and many others, because legislative, executive, and judicial branches of government at the federal and state levels all had some legal responsibility for telecommunications. The apparently unchallenged role played by Judge Greene in administering the postdivestiture industry heightened debate on the question.[32]

d. *Viability for the BOCs.* What business opportunities should be made available to the local operating companies?
e. *Viability of AT&T.* What business opportunities should be made available to the "new" AT&T?

In many respects, the separation between the BOCs and AT&T was artificial.[33] Both the telephone on Jake's desk and the "local loop" network which enabled Jake to converse with others in the local exchange were also used for carrying long-distance conversations. This, added to a continuing concern among competitors and federal policy makers that a divested AT&T still posed a significant economic threat to competitors, meant that agreements had to be reached about what business opportunities the "new" AT&T and the BOCs could and could not pursue. Since the BOCs were regulated as before by state utility commissions, answers had to be found regarding what constituted a sufficient set of opportunities to ensure that a BOC could be a "going concern." In this way, the issues of BOC viability and universal service were connected.

f. *The "new" Bell System.* What will be the nature of the operating relationship between the "new" AT&T, the RHCs, and the BOCs?

Administrative distinctions aside, the hundreds of thousands of employees working for these entities still coordinated the operation of the nation's primary telecommunications network. But, with the lure of new strategic opportunities for each element of the new Bell System, it was not immediately clear what form that coordination would and should take after January 8, 1982.

2. The second set of questions. Jake put this list aside and, after several days, took out the notes that she had scribbled during Genie's presentation. Drawing upon her knowledge of the AT&T divestiture, she adopted Genie's three imperatives and spelled out a variety of issues.

DECISION-MAKING STRUCTURES

Since Judge Greene had assigned to AT&T senior management the responsibility for delivering a plan of reorganization, Jake reasoned that the following five issues were central in setting up the processes to meet the court-ordered deadlines:

1. How should AT&T senior management organize the schedule for writing a plan of reorganization?[34]
2. How and when should AT&T senior management call upon BOC management to participate in the plan's formulation?[35]
3. How should AT&T senior management keep track of the many events that make up divestiture planning?[36]
4. How should AT&T senior management prioritize and integrate the steps in implementing the plan of reorganization?[37]
5. How and when should AT&T senior management monitor the progress of implementation activities?[38]

Since the loyalty of AT&T employees had attained legendary status in some accounts, Jake reasoned that several issues would pertain to the part that values played in the reorganization process.[39] Thus, she wrote down three more questions:

6. How should AT&T senior management learn about the reactions of AT&T employees to the divestiture?[40]
7. How should AT&T senior management act to symbolize—for AT&T employees—their commitment to reorganizing the company?[41]
8. How should AT&T senior management elicit the cooperation of senior management at the seven newly independent RHCs?[42]

Finally, Jake reasoned that AT&T senior management could not dictate that time stand still while they were involved in meeting Judge Greene's requests. They had important issues to address with regard to how the "new" AT&T would fit its environment. On this count, she listed four more questions:

9. How should AT&T senior management prepare to scan the economic and political environment for opportunities and threats?[43]
10. How should AT&T senior management reorganize the hierarchy at the "new" AT&T in order to fit its environment, with particular attention to the computer business?[44]
11. How should AT&T senior management ensure that attention was given by management at the BOCs and RHCs to the "integrity of the network"?[45]
12. How should AT&T senior management determine the constituent interests to which the "new" AT&T would be responsive?[46]

Jake placed the two lists side by side. She glanced back and forth between them. Slowly, yet surely, a thought dawned on her. *These two lists were completely different and incompatible.* But how did they differ? And was the AT&T divestiture a lone case? She now moved to her desk and retrieved a bulging file of clippings that she regularly collected from the business press.

The Strategic Process Model in Everyday Use

Jake made three piles, to correspond to the three premises of the strategic process model. A number of items caught her attention.

1. *Routinized decision-making processes*

a.   A senior executive at Target Stores defended the elimination of 219 jobs as being necessary to

   . . . streamline our decisionmaking and communications functions, and to reduce expenses. . . . We believe that, as difficult as these decisions were, they are necessary to ensure our success.[47]

b.   The CEO at Owens-Corning Fiberglas Corporation justified an extensive reorganization program:

   The net result will be a company with a more simplified and efficient structure that is sharply focused in its businesses. . . . In our new management structure, activities will be consolidated for greater organizational effectiveness and resources will be focused in support of our new strategic direction.[48]

c.   General Motors Corporation management adopted a restructuring plan in one division because

   . . . we find that the market is increasingly competitive and we have to use the most streamlined approach and the most efficient way to operate in that market.[49]

d.   A reorganization at Lufthansa A. G. reportedly helped improve the German airline's performance:

   The reorganization, among other things permits management to take certain actions without consulting workers for a consensus. "It's rude. It breaks all of the taboos in the company," says one company executive, "but it is necessary."[50]

e.   CBS management eliminated more than thirty positions at its headquarters as a means of

. . . chopping down the fixed costs. . . . There will be a very small central staff. [51]

f. A *Wall Street Journal* article reported how managers at Exxon and Du Pont, among other companies offering early retirement plans, were finding it

. . . hard to construct an offer that exactly the right number of people will accept.[52]

g. The problem of how to merge the work forces following a corporate merger was reportedly solved by managers at Provident Bank and its parent company, PNC Financial Corporation:

The Provident merger became a model used by PNC with its other acquisitions. . . . Meetings were held constantly at all levels to explain changes and assure employees that while some might be assigned to new jobs, few would be let go.[53]

h. Another *Wall Street Journal* article sampled practices regarding

. . . how to cope with or change an employee's frustrating, and often ingrained, behavior.[54]

i. A lawyer advised management at Cenex when it was confronted with a layoff decision,

. . . to conduct layoffs by position, not by personality.[55]

j. The president of Winona Knitting Mills credited a new management process for rescuing the company from the brink of liquidation:

There's no question that that sense of involving people in the operation of the company was one of the things that had to go right for this thing to work.[56]

k. Citing recent trends in crude-oil prices, Exxon Chairman Clifton C. Garvin, Jr., led a reorganization that

. . . will divide its 16 departments into three divisions, two of which will be fully integrated operating businesses or minicompanies. . . . According to . . . the unit's president, Randall Meyer, "Our objective is to combine under one management those activities which are similar in nature. . . . "[57]

l. IBM management announced a headquarters staff reorganization that was

    . . . designed to improve efficiency and internal communications.[58]

2. *Constrain Values to Conform*

a. Amidst a conflict-of-interest controversy, senior managers at the Tennessee Valley Authority proposed a policy that

    . . . would bar loaned managers from positions in which they would supervise employees from their parent companies. . . .[59]

b. A *Wall Street Journal* article attributed this report to a management consulting firm:

    People problems are more important to the long-term success of a merger than financial considerations. . . .[60]

c. A Midwestern advertising agency placed an ad in *The Wall Street Journal* that concluded with these words:

    If you're trying to reach the top, remember this: Your attitude could affect your altitude. [61]

d. An analyst commented on trends in the labor market with this observation:

    Companies now find they cannot afford to own people for a lifetime, particularly in mature and declining industries.[62]

e. General Motors Corporation Chaiman Roger Smith proposed, and won Board approval on, a plan to buy out the shares of dissident Board member H. Ross Perot.[63]

f. A truck driver for a Minnesota firm was fired for refusing to accompany a coworker who smoked. An arbitrator ruled eventually that the worker must be rehired.[64]

g. Howard Fields, an assembly worker at a Ford Motor Company plant in Ohio, was fired for refusing to park his Nissan Maxima car in a parking lot designated for foreign cars.[65]

h. Mark Pavelich, a star player for the New York Rangers professional hockey team, retired because of pressure that his play conform more closely to that ordered by a new coach. According to the team's general manager, a review session with Pavelich immediately prior to his retirement involved

> . . . a lot of one-on-one communication.[66]

i.   A United Parcel Service manager defended the company's close attention to employee productivity this way:

> It's human nature to get away with as much as possible. . . . But we bring workers up to our level of acceptance. We don't go down to their level.[67]

j.   Merrill Lynch and Company management announced a new compensation plan for Merrill Lynch brokers in order to deal

> . . . with a perennial problem: how to make a customer more loyal to the firm than to his broker. By linking the customer more to the firm's services, it also makes its brokers less attractive to raiders from other firms. [68]

k.   A consulting firm executive criticized the use of "contract workers", because

> . . it focuses people's attention on the fluctuation (in the work force) and what it will do to them. . . .[69]

Yet, a Hewlett-Packard manager defends the practice:

> Contractors can be laid off immediately without causing any negative ramifications to morale. . . . (Laying off permanent workers would amount to) changing the corporate culture. . . .[70]

l.   Management at Kimberly-Clark Corporation employ's role-play tests for job applicants on this basis:

> Ten years ago we didn't expect as much from people. Now we have participative organizations that foster a high degree of responsibility, even at the operator level.[71]

m.   Michigan Bell Telephone Company managers reportedly treat an office romance as a "performance issue":

> But as long as a romance doesn't disrupt the workplace, we try not to cross the line and delve into people's inner hearts.[72]

n. A Fujitsu advertisement extolled the purpose of a management training program for a typical new employee:

> Her mind is a Western mind, and she has to get out of it, because if she stays in it she'll never be able to do what she wants to do.[73]

3. *Organizational self-sufficiency*

a. CEO Steven Rothmeier of Northwest Airlines justified the merger with Republic Airlines in this way:

> With this merger, Northwest is better able to compete for both the domestic and international traveler. Why? Because the addition of Republic's fleet of smaller jets complements Northwest's fleet of larger jets. We are now able to match aircraft size with passenger demand, resulting in more efficient service to more cities around the world.[74]

b. The strategy for Cullinet Software, Inc., was recently described as follows:

> The company plans to make its products more compatible with IBM software. And, to lessen the dependence on mainframe software, Cullinet recently bought a mini-computer software company.[75]

Cullinet's CEO remarked that

> . . . the fundamentals are beginning to turn in the right direction.[76]

c. A recent report about Amax Corporation listed CEO Allen Born's accomplishments:

> Since he took over operations nearly a year ago, Mr. Born has turned the ailing concern upside down in a massive restructuring aimed at restoring profit. He already has either sold or is pulling out of almost half of Amax's 16 lines of business. "Shoot the dogs and get rid of the bleeders," he says by way of explanation.[77]

d. After the company's CEO died in a plane accident, this statement was attributed to a company spokesperson:

> The company's management and scientific foundation have been structured to minimize the effect of a tragedy such as this.[78]

e. A general manager at Snyder General commented:

> Our purpose in life is not to eliminate or bust unions. Our purpose is to make quality products and ship it out on time.[79]

f. A Hubinger Company executive defended a lockout of employees at a Keokuk, Iowa, plant:

> We're in an industry that has excess capacity. Without the assurance of continued operations, we think our competitors would take over our customers and we would have difficulty getting back in the marketplace once production resumed.[80]

g. A revised strategy at Union Pacific Corporation was reported in these terms:

> The restructuring plan involves disposal of unproductive oil and gas properties, a write-down on an oil refinery in Corpus Christi, Texas, and proposed incentives to reduce the company's work force, particularly in its rail unit.[81]

h. Burroughs Corporation Chairman W. Michael Blumenthal gave the following reason for a reduction of 9,600 jobs after the merger of Burroughs and Sperry Corporation into Unisys Corporation:

> As a result of the merger, we are able to reduce redundant and duplicative functions and further streamline operations—a process undertaken by both organizations two years ago. In implementing these reductions, steps will be taken to maintain internal efficiency and customer service, as well as minimizing the disruptive impact on employees.[82]

Seque

Jake spends several hours sorting her clippings and, now well into the evening, turns to leave for home. She remembers Ben's wife and Lynn. As she locks the door, one question burns in her mind: "Is there something missing from the strategic process model?"

PROCESS, PROCESS EVERYWHERE . . . BUT NO LINK TO ETHICS

The strategic process model is incomplete on four significant counts, if you are interested in how strategy and ethics are linked. It is incomplete in terms of how certain concepts are defined, and it is incomplete in its internal logic. In this section, we offer a comprehensive critique that clarifies what appears to bother Jake, and perhaps many other "managers" and "nonmanagers" as well. The critique is developed as a comparison between the principles and axioms articulated in Chapter 1 and the premises and hypotheses interpreted above in this chapter. The two lines of argument are placed side-by-side in Table 1.

TABLE 1   A Comparison of Premisses and Conclusions

Values Principle	*Structure Premiss*
Individual and organizational actions are caused in part by the values that the individual and the organization have.	Individual and organizational actions are in part caused by decision-making process structures that accommodate and overcome human psychological limitations.
Interdependence Principle	*Constraint Premiss*
Organizational success is due in part to the choices and actions of those groups that have a stake in the organization.	Individual and organizational values partially constrain the formulation and execution of planned organizational action.
	Organizational Self-Sufficiency Premiss
	Organizational performance is in part caused by the logic of decision-making structures in a single organization directed toward the interests of that organization.
	The Expert Corollary
	Decision-making process in the organization is the responsibility of senior management.
	First Hypothesis of Strategy Process
First Axiom of Corporate Strategy	Corporate strategy must be shaped through faithful adherence to a structure of routinized decision-making processes within an organization.
Corporate strategy must reflect an understanding of the values of organizational members and stakeholders, how those values both coincide and conflict, and how they can be adjudicated.	
	Second Hypothesis of Strategic Process
Second Axiom of Corporate Strategy	Corporate strategy must be shaped in a way that the constraining values are made to conform to the organization's structurally derived strategy.
Corporate strategy must reflect an understanding of the ethical nature of strategic choices.	
	Value-Free Hypothesis of Strategic Process
	Corporate strategy must be independent of all intentional actions by individuals and, hence, is independent of anyone's values.

Strategic Process Model Misses the Specific Part That Values Play in a Person's Life

Values provide the reasons for a person's actions. Genie wants Jake to deny this, which is to say that he wants her to ignore the Values Principle. To Genie, values are indistinct, intangible, and unknowable to anyone but their holders. Does Jake, for example, spend long hours at

Bison River because she savors the salary and perks befitting a CEO, because she enjoys tackling tough problems, or because she likes the view from her penthouse office? Does Ben arise on a summer morning thinking most about a softball game, a major report that he is writing, or the weekend plans that he and his wife have made? Why did Howard Fields buy a foreign-made car? Did he do it because he is a cost-conscious buyer? Or was he trying to vex his Ford supervisors? And why do two coworkers develop an office romance? Do they delight in fueling their eager office gossips? Or do they love each other?

These questions trouble Genie, because he cannot see the answers to them. So, he denies the Values Principle and, in its place, adopts the Structure Premise. In other words, he is content with separating mysterious values from more observable behaviors.[83] But, he pays a price in detaching persons from their values. That price is measured in terms of his forfeiture of the grounds for asking, and understanding the answer to, this question: "Jake, why did *you* do that?"

The Strategic Process Model Misses the Generality of Persons and Their Values

Because Genie denies the Values Principle, he also wants Jake to deny the Interdependence Principle. He reasons that it is difficult enough to determine what values give cause for any one person's actions, let alone for the multitude of agents who comprise an organization. Above all, Genie values simplicity.[84] Interaction and interdependence among persons is too complex for him. Thus, he proposes that Jake adopt the Organizational Self-Sufficiency Premiss instead of the Interdependence Principle. With this second substitution, Genie has deduced the First Hypothesis of Strategic Process, a common phenomenon among Jake's clippings:

1. Lufthansa management attributed part of the company's success to bypassing others affected by the new strategy. No mention was made about what happened to those left out of the decision processes.
2. The streamlined decision-making structures about which Target Stores, Owens-Corning, and Exxon managers speak are features of the company. No mention is made of specific relationships among persons.
3. Senior managers at Provident National, Du Pont, and Exxon reportedly solved their respective companies "social" problems by following specific procedures. No mention was made, however, about whether others' needs were actually satisfied.

None of these accounts, nor any of the ones cited in the previous section, make any provision for interdependencies among persons. Moreover, the Organizational Self-Sufficiency Premise blocks any recognition of interdependence among multiple actors. To Genie, the organization is an actor separate from the persons who act as agents. Many strategic process models contain references to organizations as "organisms" or "living systems."[85] By ascribing action to the organization, Genie leaves no room for either the person or his interaction with others.

Genie completes the argument for the First Hypothesis of Strategic Process by defining values as broad social forces that impinge upon strategy. To Genie, there exists a "true" strategy—a veritable match made in heaven—that awaits the CEO who is sufficiently diligent to discover it. Thus, for Jake to be true to the model, she needs to scan values as broad indicators, lest she overlook any clues for the proper Bison River strategy.[86]

Thus, for reasons of simplification, the strategic process model depicts an organization fitting, more or less aptly, its environment through the instrumental efforts of a CEO who seeks a fitting strategy. There is no room in the model for either values as reasons for persons' actions or for many such persons. Thus, the strategic process model is incomplete twice over, if we are interested in linking strategy and ethics.

The Strategic Process Model Misses the Possibility That Reflection upon Values Strengthens, Not Confuses, Persons

Because Genie rejects the Values and Interdependence Principles, he rejects the First Axiom of Corporate Strategy as well. Understanding values is difficult enough. Adjudication is out of the question. Yet, he is uneasy about this position. He knows that Jake is a person, and surmises that Ben has his own interests as well. Furthermore, he believes that he and the theorist work so well together because they each reflect upon the relationship. In other words, each is in a stronger position—not a more confused position—to advance his own ends because he finds a workable bargain with the other, for mutual gain.[87]

So, reluctantly, Genie substitutes the Second Hypothesis of Strategic Process for the First Axiom. He reasons that values will not go away, as much as he would prefer that outcome. The next-best position, then, is to admit that values have an influence, but to stress that the effective strategic manager has to severely and swiftly curtail those effects. The test that Genie has in mind is this: Values held by organizational members must fit the organization's "values."[88] Once again, Jake's clippings tell many stories about reasoning of this kind:

1. Pavelich, Fields, and Perot, through various processes, were given chances to conform their values to the organization's.
2. Michigan Bell Telephone management made their continued tolerance of office romances contingent upon the fit between the affairs and the organization's values about employee performance.

3. Kimberly-Clark management conducted role-plays in order to test the compatibility of employees with the company's values.
4. Hewlett-Packard managers found that hiring contract employees helped them avoid having to disturb the company's values.
5. The revised Merrill Lynch compensation plan was designed so that brokers would give greater priority to Merrill Lynch values than their own values, including financial goals.

Central to each of these "solutions" is the avoidance of conflict through a management-led attempt to realign employees with company values. Furthermore, the programs seemed designed to discourage employees' own reflection on the matters at hand. There is no suggestion in any of these accounts that better outcomes may have been found through bargaining and reflection by all parties concerned. Genie would applaud these programs because thinking about conflict—the crux of ethical reasoning—diverts attention from the organization's structure.

But the idiosyncracies of the strategic process model go deeper still. To Genie, the actions that count belong to the CEO and the CEO alone. This is plainly evident in Jake's two lists of questions about the AT&T divestiture. Each issue on her first list pointed to (1) a conflict among persons and their interests (2) requiring adjudication (3) without any obvious and simple solution. Each question on her second list, the Genie list, began with "How should AT&T senior management . . . ?"[89] The difference in focus is not accidental. In the strategic process model, we need look no further than to the CEO for guidance about whether a particular action is correct for the company. That dictum applies to aesthetic matters (such as the color of the corporate jet) and to ethical matters (such as whose interests take precedence in a given strategy).[90] Genie wants us to believe that the CEO alone is capable of resolving all such questions, either directly or through the maintenance of an efficient process. Moreover, he wants us to free all others, such as Ben, from responsibility for their actions as corporate agents. Once again, we want to suggest that this is not a very useful way to think about strategy and ethics.

The Strategic Process Model Does Not Take Persons Seriously[91]

Because he denies the First Axiom of Corporate Strategy, Genie also denies the Second Axiom. Managers of strategic process, they argue, should not give questions of ethics a central place in strategic decision processes.[92] To underscore this imperative, Genie asks Jake to substitute the Value-Free Hypothesis of Strategic Process for our Second Axiom. A telltale sign of the Value-Free Hypothesis—the complete absence of actors with intentions of their own—shows up more than a few times in Jake's pile of clippings:

1. The successors to the dead CEO expressed their concerns for the continued viability of the company, referring to "a tragedy such as this . . ." as if this were an everyday event.
2. Northwest's Rothmeier talks about matching demand with capacity, not persons (customers) with other persons (agents of Northwest).
3. Amax's Born is talking about business units, not persons, when he mentions "dogs" and "bleeders."
4. Hubinger's manager defended the lockout on the grounds that the company might be harmed if that action were not taken.
5. The Snyder General executive explained the company's purpose in terms of an inanimate product.
6. The "fundamentals" underlying Cullinet's strategy contained nary a reference to human beings.[93]

At this juncture, two gaps in the strategic process model logic come plainly into view. First, there is an uneasy alliance—if not an internal contradiction—between the Value-Free Hypothesis and the Expert Corollary. Genie wants Jake to put her heart into the strategic process. But she is warned to never lose sight of the priority that Bison River's interests have over her own. He wants her to build a process that (1) results in a strategy statement that excludes any reference to her or any other person and (2) will "outlive" her. In short, Genie asks the CEO to accept a dual standard: exist as an independent person, but don't do it too overtly.[94] Of course, Genie has no such qualms about Ben.

Second, Genie wants Jake to make a trusting leap in logic. He asks her to believe that, if she follows certain steps, she will produce a proper decision for all concerned. While there might be several reasons to doubt this,[95] consider this one example. Suppose that two CEOs follow Genie's instructions to the letter and both discover profitable strategies for their companies. But suppose that one CEO does so by means of the verbal and physical abuse of his staff, which results in several resignations. Is this process justified? The strategic process theorist apparently would say yes. Once again, a general way to link strategy and ethics seems unavailable in Genie's arguments.

Epilogue: The Case of Enlightened Self-Interest

Early the next morning, Jake is poring over her mail, when she hears a knock at the door. It is Genie. Before she can say a word, Jake hears yet one more set of instructions:

"Jake, I read about the Lynn issue. It seems to me that what IBM just did in Greencastle, Indiana, might be a model.[96] They decided to close a distribution center, but then turned around and gave a million dollars or so, and some other services, to the city. So, I have a solution for you. Since Lynn is a lawyer and since Bison River has a capability in communications systems, you should donate a system to the state bar association for a year. It will help them and will improve Bison River's image with them, since Lynn's case has received some high-level attention there. To detemine what kind of system to provide, go through the same steps that I commanded earlier."

Jake says nothing and closes the door. She returns to her desk and finds that an argument is flowing rapidly from her mind to her tablet.

1. Because the strategic process model denies values as reasons for action and the generality of human action, it asks me to forget about Lynn as Lynn. It asks me to act, but only so far as my desires and beliefs parallel those of Bison River.

2. Because the model asks me to deny Lynn's problem, as well as the transaction between us, it asks me to accept that Lynn's interests are interchangeable with those of others and that one transaction is as good as any other.

3. Because someone else's interests could be advanced by such an "enlightened" contribution, and because Bison River's "self-interest" could also gain, Genie asks me to make the donation in lieu of resolving the issue with Lynn to our mutual satisfaction.[97]

Jake pauses and then simply writes "No." She picks up the phone to call Lynn and makes a note to visit the newspaper offices at noontime.

CONCLUSION

We have shown how the strategic process model has been developed and defended and how the logical extensions of this model would deal with strategy and ethics. In the final example, we have also shown how strategic process theorists have attempted to directly apply the model to questions of ethics. In sum, we have shown that the model is broadly incomplete, if you are interested in applying it to questions of strategy and ethics.

By denying the relevance of individual human actors, the values that cause their actions, and the inevitable conflicts among those actions, the strategic process model lacks the rigor to support a general connection between strategy and ethics. And by asking us to believe that faithful adherence to a structure of processes at the organizational level is sufficient for strategic success, strategic process theorists provide us with a model that lacks general relevance for individual persons interested in questions of strategy and ethics. In short, the strategic process model does not give us a very useful way of talking about our lives.

Furthermore, there is little reason to believe that the model can be readily rehabilitated to account generally for strategy and ethics. The premises will not permit theorists to arrive at such a destination. Certainly, some have tried to do so.[98] But, the futility of the effort is manifest in the question typically asked: "How can organizations be made more moral for people?" As we have argued throughout, there is no justifiable reason to distinguish between "organization" and "people." Thus, the rehabilitation effort is predicated upon the wrong question. Jake and many managers already see this when they share the concerns expressed by Firestone Tire and Rubber CEO John J. Nevin:

> You can't close a plant without an awareness that it is having a god-awful effect on a lot of people who aren't responsible for it.[99]

The strategic process model obscures any meaningful way of understanding what that responsibility might be. We now turn to a better way to address the question of strategy and ethics.

★ ★ ★ ★ ★ ★ ★ ★ ★ ★   CHAPTER **8**

The Personal Projects
Enterprise Strategy

INTRODUCTION

For the last seven chapters we have shown how reasoning about ethics and reasoning about strategy go hand in hand. We have articulated at least seven ways of connecting ethics and strategy via the concept of Enterprise Strategy. Along the way we have argued that the temptation to relativism must be avoided, and that we must apply the concept of harms and benefits and the concept of rights wherever possible. We have articulated a way to think about ethics and morality as a set of rules or moral values which needs to be in "reflective equilibrium." And we have analyzed the ethical assumptions behind most current ways of reasoning about strategy.

Implicit in our approach has been a commitment to the concepts of individual rights and the autonomy of the person, concepts which often conflict with the current way of thinking about corporations. In this chapter we want to (finally) defend our position that we need to think of corporations as means to individual ends, as places where individuals with their own personal projects can cooperate in order to accomplish those projects.

First, we set forth our view of persons. Second, we show how corporations can be considered human institutions that enable persons to pursue their projects. We examine several principles which will serve to link the concepts of "corporation" and "person." Finally, we articulate a sketch of what a corporation would look like if it were managed along the lines we envision. We also give some examples of companies that are partially sensitive to our view. Along the way we are going to reinterpret some fundamental ideas like "power" and "authority" and even "participation." And as you may have guessed by now, we also recommend jettisoning some, indeed most, of the current language of corporate strategy.

PERSONS

"What is a person?" Such an innocent and seemingly simple question has a myriad of answers. Before answering the question it is important to notice that there are many kinds of answers. It could be answered in purely biological terms, so that persons are members of the species *Homo sapiens*. It could be answered in anthropological terms; that is, persons are those creatures who live together in communities, use language, build cities, domesticate animals, and kill each other for reasons other than food. The question could be answered in religious terms, so that persons are special creatures of God, or organisms with the potential to be such creatures.

None of these definitions is right or wrong.[1] Each has a different purpose, because the theories and related concepts which go with each give different explanations of persons and their activities. Each explanation enables us to cope with the world in a certain way. Each explanation allows us to do different things. The biological definition allows us to see how persons are like the rest of the plant and animal life on earth. The anthropological definition allows us to see how persons are different from plants and animals, and to discover relevant differences among persons. The religious definition allows us to compare persons with our conception of the gods. So, before we can answer the question "What is a person?" it is important to understand what our purpose is, or what we want to be able to do.

Our purpose in giving an answer to "What is a person?" is to connect some thinking in ethics with the reality of the modern corporation. Our purpose is a normative one, a function of our values and projects: we want to show how an application of an individualistic notion of the person would serve to transform and revitalize our corporations with a sense of purpose and ethics. Ethics is fundamental, and while there are many problems with our view and much work needs to be done to make it more exact and detailed, we believe that it is the minimally defensible view, if you take ethics seriously. There are many other answers to the question from the standpoint of ethics, but ours focuses on the traditions of individualism, and the fundamental autonomy of persons. We believe that the creation of the individual person is the hallmark of Western civilization, and it is one that is worthy of celebration. Rather than extol

Japanese management techniques and the ethics of collaboration, and rather than look to state intervention to solve our problems, we believe that the best hope for persons is to draw on their own creativity and resolve. Such a view requires an explicit theory of the person. We want our answer to "What is a person?" to allow for the maximum amount of liberty so that persons can pursue their own projects in a civilized manner. Corporations, organizations, and other institutions are mere means toward these ends. Thus, our "theory" or "model," or, better yet, our "story" or "narrative," will allow us to see persons and their organizations in a consistent, liberty-enhancing way. We seek a concept of the corporation that is empowering for individuals, not for collectives or states, and that is liberating rather than oppressive and coercive. Hence, our concept of the person is based on the notion of rights.

A person is a being with the ability to formulate and articulate, in some fashion, a set of values or purposes. From these values persons come to want to accomplish certain things, realize certain events, and enter into relationships with others. In short, persons come to have projects.

Persons exist in communities. Except for certain desert-island cases, mostly imaginary, there never has been and there never will be an "individual" who exists outside the context of a community. To say this is not to say much. It is simply true that if persons formulate and articulate values they do so within the context of others. Language guarantees this fact. To speak the same language as another person is to share at least partially in the forms of life of that person. Without shared experiences, communication is not only impossible but irrelevant.[2]

Hence, our claim that persons exist in communities does not commit us to the view that the only projects an individual has are defined by a community, or to the view that the only values a person has are shared ones. Language is not so static. We constantly adopt new ways of talking, because we want to do new things and often the old ways of talking are not adequate.

Some believe that because persons exist in the context of communities, the communities themselves have projects that often take precedence over the projects of individual persons. Nothing could be farther from our minds. Occasionally members of a community may each have the same project or want the same thing, such as freedom from aggression. Such common or joint projects give rise to governance mechanisms. But more times than not, these governance mechanisms become governments or the state, and the common projects of a community are easily perverted. You may believe that government or the state is justified and still believe our view of persons and the Personal Projects Enterprise Strategy, but neither is logically connected to the other.

A consequence of our view that persons pursue projects in the context of a community is the necessity for understanding the historical context of a community and the individuals within it. What projects particular individuals or groups have will be in part a function of how they see their relationship to the community. Within any thriving community there are a large number of persons actively seeking similar things, and there are a smaller number who marginalize themselves in relation to the others because they seek radically different projects. The existence of such an avant-garde poses no problem for us, since we believe that within certain boundaries, persons are free to choose the communities in which they live.[3]

One way of understanding how different persons with different projects coexist is through the concept of "rights." As we explained earlier, Chapter 3, rights are necessary if persons are to be free to pursue their own good. Without some guarantees of noninterference from others, we could accomplish little. We would spend most of our time simply protecting ourselves from physical harm.

In order to be able to pursue their own projects, persons accord certain rights to each other. The exact nature of these rights is debatable, and various conventions will actually arise in different communities. Roughly, these rights must include the right to some level of personal autonomy. By this we mean at least that a person should be free from physical coercion and force in a variety of circumstances, especially where his or her actions do not affect the projects of others, or where freely given consent is obtained when they do affect others. Rights serve as working rules by which we are able to physically carry through on our intentions in a civilized manner, by which we mean the avoidance of physical violence. Rights determine the context of agreements among persons.

But this is a tricky business. If Dawn's project is to physically force her students to study, then realizing that project violates the rights of her students to be free from physical force. Hence, some projects by their very nature will be unrealizable without violating the rights of others. To the extent that persons internalize the rights of community members to personal autonomy, as a moral value, then they will have few unrealizable projects. However, there is an important issue here.

Our concept of a person as having projects is logically connected to a concept of right to autonomy in certain spheres, else persons could have projects without the right to realize any of them, making the concept a useless one. If the right to autonomy is to be a functioning rule, then persons must believe that they have a duty to refrain from interfering with others who are exercising their right to autonomy. Communities which adopt this rule, as a matter of moral development, will be populated by individuals who have what James Buchanan calls an attitude of liberty.[4] They will come to prize liberty, not for its own sake, but for what it allows them to accomplish: their projects. Liberty will become a virtue in these communities.[5] With liberty as a virtue, persons will be hesitant to formulate projects whose realization requires a reduction in the autonomy of others.

Under a system of rights and in a society where liberty is a virtue, persons will be responsible for their actions, in the sense that they will not seek to internalize the benefits of their actions and externalize the costs. The logic is simple. If I know that you are trying to take advantage of me, by misrepresenting your projects, I will not agree to help you more than once, for I will have no assurance that my projects will truly be satisfied. If rights are understood as conventional, rather than natural, it is easy to see that they are self-enforcing. Societies will evolve various ways of dealing with those who routinely and as a matter of course violate the conventions, and these individuals will always exist and will serve a useful role in questioning the conventions themselves. But, for the most part, if persons take their projects seriously, and if they take the right to autonomy seriously, they will seek to take responsibility for their actions, in order to avoid violence and coercion, which they will abhor.

Under our conception, then, persons will be free to make agreements. Since most of our individual projects require the cooperation or acquiescence of others, being able to come to mutually satisfactory arrangements is a key element of the answer to "What is a person?" There are some hidden traps here, for our notion of the person requires that the arrangements be voluntary ones in which each party freely gives consent. And "consent" is a difficult notion. Suffice it to say that there are at least some clear cases of gaining informed consent.

Recall our explanation of the AT&T divestiture. There is little if any evidence that AT&T senior management even attempted to gain the consent of employees, large customers, suppliers, or even subsidiary presidents before agreeing to a covenant which radically changed the rules of the game. Regardless of the final outcome of such a decision, if the reported process was close to the actual facts, it counted as treating others as mere means. Others' projects were not seen as worthy in and of themselves. Others' rights were not seen as necessary to maintaining a system of respect for individual autonomy.

Persons in communities with rights and liberties come to treat each other as ends, rather than as mere means.[6] What it means to treat a person as an end is complex. However, there are several ideas that are relevant. The first is that there is a personal touch to transactions among persons. In choosing to come to some agreement with you, I accept the fact that your projects are important to you, and that while I see your fulfilling your projects as a necessary condition to my fulfilling my projects, you will view me in a similar fashion. Empathy is less a function of the categorical imperative, or the Golden Rule, than a matter of good common sense. Of course, I can always mislead you, but I run the risk of being found out. If we assume with Hobbes that most persons are equal most of the time, and with Lincoln that you can't fool all of the people all of the time, such a strategy of deception will not be a dominant one.

The second fact about treating others as ends is that it does not permit their being used to merely facilitate my own projects, or being used as tools to the accomplishment of ends other than my own. Once you have done your bit to further my project, I still have an obligation, namely, to fulfill my part of the agreement, regardless of the current cost to me.

Suppose that company PQR agreed that it owed an obligation to keep all of its 10,000 workers employed. Suppose that the main project of the management of the company was to be profitable. And suppose that conditions changed so that it could no longer be profitable unless 5,000 of those employees were fired. Absent some condition in the original agreement regarding the contingency of employment, to now fire 5,000 workers amounts to using them as mere means or as tools. Of course, the workers may have freely consented to such a contract, and that brings us to the third point about treating people as ends.

We know that the problem of when a person freely gives his or her consent is difficult.[7] In medical ethics it is so complicated and yet so important that hospitals hire ethicists as well as medical experts to sort out the issue. If a person is unconscious, it is difficult to freely consent to a life-threatening operation. If a person has a longstanding fear of being unconscious, it is equally difficult to consent to necessary surgery. The mere fact of consent to *certain forms* of treatment may well be the best evidence that we could possibly have that a person has lost his or her rational faculties. Yet we also know that there are clear cases of free consent.

In company MNO, employees and customers are routinely consulted and asked for input before radical reorganizations are undertaken. If enough employees or customers object to the proposed change it is postponed or abandoned. In company XYZ, stockholders are carefully consulted before investment decisions in South Africa are made. Additionally, customers and employees are asked for their input. There need not be voting or a veto rule, or even merely a consultation rule, for us to be able to pick out cases where it looks as if persons have given their consent.

None of these conditions are sufficient for treating persons as ends. One additional requirement is that we attempt to convince others by the use of reason rather than coercion.[8] Given our view of persons as project pursuers, this involves giving them reasons and justifying to them and to ourselves how undertaking a certain action is in accordance with their projects, all things considered. The important bottom line to this approach is that we do our best to give reasons and persuade, but that we respect the final decision as one in which the person is merely exercising the rights that we accord him or her. We must accord these rights if we are to live in a community and pursue our own projects and if our own attitude toward liberty requires that we treat others as ends rather than means.

In summary we see persons as essentially beings with values, purposes, and projects. They seek to live together in a way that allows each to realize his or her projects. Hence, they accord fundamental rights to autonomy in some spheres of action, and they come to love liberty and treat each other as ends.

CORPORATIONS

"Corporations are human institutions." Many managers and management thinkers believe this proposition. It is virtually a truism. However, the meaning is dependent on what your view of persons happens to be. If you believe that persons are like herds of sheep, incapable of using reason, or at least severely limited in doing so, then your view of the corporation as a human institution will be different from ours. If you think that persons randomly move from one thing to the next, paying attention only to what commands their attention at the moment, then our view will be foreign to you.

We believe that persons have projects which they want to realize, and that these projects usually represent their attempts to live by the values and purposes which they have. Our view of the corporation is fairly simple. It is a means to facilitate the realization of the projects of certain persons called "corporate members." A corporation is simply one way that we achieve our projects. Stated somewhat differently, persons are only passing through corporations on the way to their respective ends.

What does it mean to "facilitate the achievement of projects?" By serving as *focal points* for the intersection of certain interests, corporations can serve as a place where customers, owners, employees, managers, suppliers, and communities can realize the joint gains of cooperation.[9]

Corporations are fundamentally cooperative institutions, not competitive ones. In our view, if a corporation fails to help person X with project P, then X will search for an alternative and withdraw support from the corporation. Other corporate members do not try to coerce X into staying, nor do they try to prevent other corporations from satisfying X's projects. Such actions can only violate rights. Of course, we are assuming that in a world where persons pursue projects under a system of rights, there is choice. Many times this assumption is false, because some people fail in their duty to accord rights to others. The end result of such cases is always coercion, violence, and a lack of human flourishing.

Corporations are mere means. They are never ends in themselves.

No action is ever taken "for the sake of the corporation." Corporations are fictions, mere placeholders, that stand for *the interests of the members.* When a corporation ceases to serve the interests of its members, it is simply abandoned. In our view, members do not expect the corporation to be immortal, nor do they expect it to expropriate rents from them to ensure its immortality.

Corporations can be thought of as sets of agreements among the members to achieve their projects. Given a notion of a community of persons who pursue their projects with rights to autonomy, these agreements will afford the basic rights in society to all members. If the rights of a particular member are to be violated, that member will have to freely give consent. And because rights violations are serious, the violator must take special care that consent is actually freely given. Recall that persons are responsible for their actions, and due care in judgment must be constantly exercised.

A corporation is governed by its members. Each has the alternative of withdrawing support, and so each is ensured a right to participate in determining the scope of the affairs of the corporation and the entry of new members. Assets which are bought by the collective of corporate members are owned by them, and the sense of "ownership" is that the collective is responsible for the use of these assets and their effects on others.

Because corporate members know that their actions are bound together by their agreements with others, they freely take on the responsibility for the governance of the organization. "Governance" just means what rules and regulations will be used to further projects, and how the inevitable disputes that arise will be solved. There will be many varieties, possibly including the current system of managerialism.

Who are corporate members? There is no definite answer to this question which applies to all corporations at all times. There are many alternatives and corporate forms. Corporations have to start somewhere, and that is with an initial set of projects. It is easy to imagine growth in the list of projects and the list of those affected. Once it has its set of projects, however, the purpose of the corporation is the realization of those projects. Let's see how this works, and in so doing further develop the notion of a Personal Projects Enterprise Strategy.

THE PERSONAL PROJECTS ENTERPRISE STRATEGY

Mr. Meadows has an idea for a baseball bat made out of a new material with which he has some experience in working. As a baseball fan almost from birth, Meadows has had a lifelong project of becoming involved in the game at the national level. Meadows also has a family for which he is partially responsible, and though he loves baseball, he has sadly discovered that it is not edible. So, Meadows needs to make some money to subsist. After working in his basement to make a prototype baseball bat, and after hours of testing it with his daughters, Meadows decides that his project needs the cooperation of others. He contacts a supplier of the material, and he contacts a local minor-league team. They agree that the bats have potential, and that the projects of each will be advanced by cooperating. They draw up some initial terms to which all agree. These terms specify a length of time until they must renegotiate, specific exit conditions for each party, the responsibilities of each including the resources to be contributed, a way to adjudicate any disputes that may arise, and who gets what resources in case of dissolution of the contract. In this case they agree that since Meadows is the expert, he should make all of the decisions regarding the product. They negotiate how the "funds flow" should work, and naturally take into account the available alternatives and the prices of those alternatives.

It is not hard to imagine the joint venture growing, and there are various forms that could emerge. Perhaps Meadows will be left to make decisions about new individuals to involve, but once those individuals are a part of the "corporation," Meadows and others must treat them as ends with projects of their own. Of course, there may be some who will give their permission to be treated as mere means. Imagine Steve, whose project is to spend as much time as possible in singles bars, enjoying his view of the good life for a few years. He wants to minimize his responsibilities to others, for whatever reason. He agrees to work for Meadows Bat Company on the condition that he be paid at some rate and not be involved in decisions that could affect him, except, of course, if he is about to be physically harmed. He views work as a mere means which will allow him to pursue other, more important projects. We see no reason for Meadows not to hire Steve. If the agreement is explicit, and if there are clear exit conditions, and if Meadows can be reasonably sure that Steve is freely consenting, there are no problems.

Suppose, however, that Steve is really down on his luck, that the skills that he has are not in great demand, and that he will agree to almost anything. Meadows is not warranted in treating him as a mere means and must take some care to ensure that Steve's consent is freely given. One way to do this is to build in specific times for contract renegotiation, so that after things get better for Steve, he has a chance to reconsider the terms of the bargain. Remember, Meadows comes from a society which lives together via a system of rights, and most in the society love liberty. Taking advantage of Steve, even if he could get away with it, strikes a most unresponsive chord in Meadows. And, on such an account, "taking advantage" can even include such benevolent actions as drug testing for Steve and his fellow employees, contributing to Steve's favorite charity, and building handball courts for Steve's athletic pleasure, all done in the name of Steve's own good. The point is that doing good for others without their freely given consent can still be treating them as mere means.

We can easily imagine some possible ways that Meadows Bat Company could develop. For instance, suppose that the bats are an outrageous success. At some point Mr. Meadows will hire professional managers, will bring others into the contract to help finance the expansion, and the like. There is a difference between Meadows Bat Company and some other companies we have described. At Meadows Bat Company the parties to the contract remain responsible for the effects of their action. If it is later discovered that Meadows' bats have problems when used normally, resulting in injuries and poor performance, the participants negotiate a settlement of claims and damages. Even if Meadows decides to "sell out," he does so by coming to an agreement with his "partners" as to how the expectations he has created can continue to be met.

Alternatively, it is all too easy to see how Meadows Bat Company can become perverted and stray from the path of the Personal Projects Enterprise Strategy. In return for more money, Meadows might agree to become the agent of the stockholders and agree to subvert the interests of the other groups to those of stockholders. Of course, there is nothing magical about selling out to stockholders. Meadows could strike a deal with any group to try to extract rents from the others. But notice that each attempt to do so involves treating others as mere means. It involves violating the basic compact that is the essence of Meadows Bat Company. And if that compact contains conditions for exit and an agreement to divide the common assets, each attempt to take advantage of others triggers the dissolution of the agreement. Such "self-enforcing agreements" are characteristic of the Personal Projects E-Strategy.

Meadows Bat could become perverted in a more subtle way. A number of "members" could become dependent on Meadows Bat for the accomplishment of all of their projects. And Meadows, having read the latest management treatises on managing the corporate culture, suddenly realizes that indeed there is a corporate culture at Meadows Bat. He begins to reinforce the fact of dependence. Meadows Bat takes on a life of its own and becomes an end in itself. Mission statements are published, company logos are designed, songs are written, and corporate planners are hired. The road to exploitation and coercion is a surprisingly short one, especially if Meadows assures the others that *he* will take the responsibility for how things turn out.

For Meadows Bat to become perverted in this way, not only must Meadows cease to love liberty, but his cohorts must also fail to act on their duty to Meadows and each other to uphold the terms of the original compact. They must come to view each other as vessels, mere means, which are to be filled and emptied at one's leisure, and not a community whose members are free individuals who cherish liberty.

Meadows Bat Company is an example of the Personal Projects E-Strategy. The answer to "What do we stand for?" is alarmingly simple: helping members realize their personal projects. Given our definitions of "persons" and "corporations," the Personal Projects E-Strategy is the only one that is compatible with them. We can reformulate our view as a set of principles which we hope will serve as a focal point of discussion. We believe that some version of these principles must be accepted if a Personal Projects E-Strategy is to be realized and if we are to connect our political and social ideals of autonomous individuals who have inalienable rights with our economic ideals of capitalism as a set of voluntary agreements among consenting adults.

The Principle of Personal Autonomy

Persons have the right to formulate, articulate and pursue projects, unless in doing so they violate the rights of others.

This principle simply formalizes our notion of the person as a being capable of making sustained commitments in the form of projects. It expresses our idea that the right to autonomy is the most basic of human rights. Without such a right, persons are not guaranteed the control of their own bodies. This principle also recognizes that if we are to avoid violence and deceit, we must recognize the similar rights of others. In doing so, it shows how the notion of rights is bound to the idea of persons existing in a community. The next principle is more explicit.

The Principle of Conventional Rights

Persons' rights are a matter of general agreement among members of the community.

This principle represents the explicit denial of any "natural" rights or any single standard of value from which rights can be derived and ordered.[10] Persons and their communities are masters of their own fate. Rights are just the best way we have of living together, flourishing, and avoiding violence and coercion. The philosophical search for the Rosetta Stone of rights is pointless, and should come to an end. This principle does not explain precisely which community is relevant, nor does it specify what counts as general agreement. These matters will be a function of history and culture, rather than logic. To say this is not to embrace relativism, but it is to embrace pluralism, and a view of humans as fallible rather than perfectible.

If rights are a matter of convention and if persons are to be free to pursue their projects, then the projects of others will acquire an importance all their own. This idea is expressed in the following principle:

The Principle of Respect for Persons

Persons have a duty to treat others as ends in themselves, rather than as mere means.

As we discussed earlier, treating others as ends is far from trivial. It means a constant vigilance against the temptation to manipulate and coerce, and it is rooted in a hatred of violence. Free and open discourse, where criticism of ideas is the norm, is the only possible atmosphere. Psychoanalysis as a therapy will be irrelevant in such a society, though not as a discipline. To treat others as ends implies that we must strive to understand ourselves, and this is far from an easy matter. We define ourselves in terms of our history, our culture, and our relationshps with others, so we cannot easily separate the study of self from the study of "the other." Moreover, if we are to accomplish our projects we require the cooperation of the "autonomous other" as expressed in the next principle.

The Principle of Voluntary Agreements

Persons have the right to enter into voluntary agreements with others in order to accomplish their projects.

Intercourse is the basis for civilization. The right to autonomy is uninteresting in isolation, and without the right and ability to cooperate our lives would truly be poor, nasty, brutish, and short. Meadows Bat Company can never be conceived without this principle. Indeed, we believe that it forms the basis for any realistic understanding of capitalism. The usual focus on capitalism as a system of competition through which the strongest survive is a radical perversion of what actually happens in the marketplace.[11] Competition is a second-order property of capitalism. It is a mere placeholder for particular sets of cooperative arrangements, each of which may enable the accomplishment of joint projects. Capitalism is fundamentally concerned with the conditions of cooperation, and only the Personal Projects E-Strategy captures this concern. Without the basic cooperative agreement among factors, there will be no competition. Now it is true that if Meadows Bat is successful, some may be harmed. In particular, the Minneapolis Slugger Company, makers of wooden bats for years, may dissolve. But notice the reason. The customers of Minneapolis Slugger will no longer be able to accomplish their projects, or accomplish them as well. So, they will trigger the exit conditions, dividing the assets, and so forth. What this means is that it is incumbent on each member of the compact that is the corporation to constantly pay attention to the needs of others insofar as they are relevant to the maintenance of the enterprise. "Close to the customer" is to be replaced with "close to the stakeholder." We can formalize this insight with the next principle.

The Principle of Human Institutions

Institutions, for example, corporations, exist as a mere means for the accomplishment of the projects of institutional members.

This principle is logically necessary to our view because when the institution becomes irrelevant to the accomplishment of a member's project, that person simply triggers the exit condition. Either the member is replaced, or the assets are divided, or the contract changes. Meadows Bat is just the intersection of the interests of the members. Any other way of describing the company does violence to the projects of some members. The relevant issue is: Who is a member of Meadows Bat, or any other human institution?

The Principle of Corporate Membership

Corporate members have the right to participate in those decisions which affect the accomplishment of their projects in an important way. Typical corporate members include managers, stockholders, employees, suppliers, customers, and community representatives.

While it is possible to consider a wider notion of membership to include media, government, special interest groups, unions, and the like, we prefer to believe that the very existence of some of these institutions is due to the reliance of managers on enterprise strategies other than the one outlined here. In a community where members see the projects of others as important, they willingly participate in decisions which are important to them. If they are assured that their fellows share the virtue of liberty, they may well delegate a number of decisions, even quite important ones, to them. They are assured of being treated as ends. But they would never agree to give up the right to participate, even if it is not always exercised. Such a move would amount to seeing oneself as a mere means to the accomplishment of others' ends. While such a view may have some descriptive power, it has no place in our view of persons or corporations.

The description of Meadows Bat and the articulation of these principles implies that much of the current thinking about management and corporate strategy can be made optional. It is based on radically different views of the person, and the corporation is too often seen as an end in itself. The Personal Projects E-Strategy is an ideal toward which we strive, if we truly believe that persons ought to be able to pursue their projects in cooperation with others. Some of the greatest barriers to realizing this ideal are simply internal ones, a function of the way we have come to see corporations. In the following section we want to question some of these ideas, so that we can begin the process of setting them aside.

THE IRRELEVANCE OF COMMON NOTIONS OF
MANAGEMENT AND CORPORATE STRATEGY

It should be clear by now that most ways of thinking about corporate strategy depart radically from the Personal Projects E-Strategy.[12] In this section we want to briefly look at why most of these ideas are simply irrelevant to persons following a personal projects approach.

1. Motivation and Leadership

No topic in the history of management thought has had more pages devoted to it than that—or those, depending on how you count it—of motivation and leadership. Motivation and leadership are often lumped together because it is assumed that persons must be motivated and led. Neither is sufficient to spur persons to action. The imagery of motivation and leadership is not pleasant to us. It involves what Harry Levinson called the "Great Jackass Fallacy," that persons are like donkeys who alternatively chase after carrots and receive swift kicks in the rear. William Gomberg used to put the point this way: "The thought of managers motivating each other, is like imagining that they had steering wheels coming out of them, each trying to drive the other around, resulting in madness."[13]

These views portray the concern with motivation and leadership as a lack of concern about persons and their projects, and we agree. If persons are pursuing their own projects, that very fact will motivate them. If you are trying to get persons to do something that is not connected with their own projects, the only possible methods are to coerce them or to make them believe, perhaps falsely, that their projects will in fact be realized. In our view of the person, motivation is either morally wrong or irrelevant. Take your pick.

Leadership isn't irrelevant to our view, but it is different. You might want to say that Meadows is a leader. After all, he marshalls the forces together that become Meadows Bat. But his role is one of coordinator more than leader. The standard idea of leadership involves making things happen that ordinarily wouldn't. Followers invest heavily in their leaders, who often take on godlike qualities. Leaders are heroes, living out a life about which an ordinary follower can only dream. All too often leaders "by coincidence" happen to be those who hold coercive power over others at a particular point in time, such as generals, presidents, and other political figures.

If persons truly are beings who pursue their projects, they are led by themselves. Corporations and communities of such beings are self-governing. At times some individual may become a focal point for others, but others will not transfer their self-esteem to that person. They will be vested in such "leadership" only to the degree that their projects are realized. Infantile fantasies of control will not be replayed through the search for and obedience to charismatic leaders.[14]

Rather than leaders, there will be heroes and heroines, persons whose accomplishments we admire. Stories of such heroic persons will not be full of how they got individuals to sacrifice themselves, but of how they achieved milestones that allowed individual and human flourishing. The focus of such stories will be less on process and more on accomplishment. Those who have the power of coercion or physical force will not be seen as heroic, for accomplishment through the use of force is neither difficult nor good.

2. Power and Authority

Much the same story can be told about power and authority. Power is an interesting concept simply because it signifies that those who have it control those who do not. If we are to understand power in the terms of some social scientists as "influence,"[15] and if we are to understand influence in terms of "giving reasons," then we have no argument with those who promote "power skills" as necessary to effective management. Usually, however, when we say "Mr. Brown really knows how to use power," we do not mean that he is adept at giving others good reasons. Rather, we mean that he is adept at persuading, rewarding, using incentives, "motivating," and "leading."

A more interesting notion of power comes from the analysis of how the projects of Jake (in the example in Chapter 7) are connected with the projects of Ben and Lynn. In this view power is shared interdependence. A person is powerful only in tandem with the other. Absent coercion and violence, this concept is not very helpful. It simply restates the idea that persons may jointly pursue their common aims.

Authority works the same way. In a world in which persons make voluntary agreements, authority is limited to what is specifically agreed upon. In a world where persons come to love liberty in pursuing their projects, they take care that they do not agree to a system of authority whereby the rights of some are systematically denied. To take an extreme case, in such a world, even if Ben were willing to contract with Jake to be her slave, Jake would never agree, since slaveholding involves treating others as mere means. (In fact, "treating others as mere means" is a good definition of slavery for most cases.)

In the Meadows Bat Company example, clearly Meadows has authority. But he has it simply because the others have granted it to him. Barnard's notion of legitimate authority[16] as that which falls into another's "zone of acceptance" is almost correct, but is fatally mistaken. What makes authority legitimate is not the fact that an employee accepts it, but that he or she has agreed to it. We prefer to think about the "zone

"zone of agreement" and to reinterpret authority in these terms. Unfortunately, we can then do without the concept. The language of agreement works all too well. To say that Jake has authority is just to say that the others have agreed to let Jake act in a particular way on this issue or that set of issues. Such authority is not given all at once and forever. Rather, it is always negotiable, and this idea does violence to the ordinary meaning of the term. Authority, like power, motivation, and leadership, is a concept that we can set aside. It is irrelevant to a Personal Projects E-Strategy.

3. Strategy Formulation and Strategy Implementation

Our critique in the previous chapter should have shown you why the terms "strategy formulation" and "strategy implementation" should be banned forever. Briefly, if you think that persons have to be motivated and led, and that power and authority have to be exercised to achieve organizational goals, because these goals differ from the goals of individuals, then it will be useful to divide "corporate strategy" into a cognitive task to be done by senior management (or any other group in power, whose projects are the most important) and a persuasive task, to be done to everyone else. If you think that persons and their projects are interchangeable parts of an organization, then once strategy is formulated, you will see the need to get them to implement it.

Thinking about strategy in this way does not arise in our view of the person and the corporation. Agreements or contracts are negotiated and then executed, but since there is no logical gap between the projects agreed upon and the projects which "motivate" persons, and because parties to the negotiation just are the parties to the execution of the agreement, the so-called implementation gap is nonexistent.

Similar arguments can be made for the concepts of structure following or leading strategy, generic strategies, human resource strategy, and the like. They just won't get us very far if we are interested in persons.

By coming to see persons as capable of pursuing projects, and corporations as vehicles for project realization, we dissolve many of the current puzzles in the strategy literature. They are just irrelevant, and the language that goes along with them is not very useful.

SOME DIFFICULTIES WITH THE PERSONAL PROJECTS E-STRATEGY

We are sure that you have already thought of countless objections to our way of thinking about corporations. At the top of your list is the idea that it just isn't very practical. Our response is that the personal projects view is a description of the way that many small ventures get established. We believe that by formalizing it, as we have here, we can see whether the commitment to the underlying ideas can be sustained. Perhaps they really won't work in practice, and perhaps corporations just cannot be run along the lines we propose here. The price of such an analysis would be severe. The very notion of the autonomous individual in a self-governing community is at stake. We would rather give up the idea of the corporation, and we prefer to be optimists. The principles articulated here are just those embodied in the basic documents of many societies that treasure individual liberty and distrust state authority. They are revolutionary, but in a constitutional sense. We believe that the fruits of such a revolution would lead to human flourishing rather than suffering.

There are some very real problems with our view. The first is that they represent a change in the basic ground rules for the corporation. Transition problems could be massive, as we have seen in a number of political cases. We have no solution for this problem. Our only response is that we find our view of the person to be one that is not optional. Coercion is unacceptable in any form.

Executives sometimes tell us that they would like to treat others as ends, but they would be at a competitive disadvantage. After all, they compete with Third World sweatshops, and others who have lower moral standards. Our response to this objection is to accept the fact that a company that is oriented toward personal projects may not be able to compete with others that are not. But it will be irrelevant. Cooperation, not competition is the basis for capitalism.[17] Perhaps corporations will not have their current size or structure, or have the same perks for some members. But we doubt even this objection. We are convinced by the stories of Tom Peters and others that unleashing the enormous creative potential of persons to pursue their dreams is all there is to the story of human progress.

We are certain that there are other objections, and we want to be certain you understand our response. We have no magic. We simply want to frame the problems of corporate strategy in what we see as fundamentally human terms. Such a reframing of the language of corporate strategy will ensure that ethics enters the picture at the beginning rather than as an afterthought.

A BRIEF SUMMARY AND PROSPECTUS

We have argued that strategy and ethics go hand in hand. Strategy is concerned with purposes and values, and so is ethics. Concepts and models of strategy are necessarily built on some view of ethics, and we will do better to be explicit about the flavor of ethics we want to defend. We have cautioned you against jumping to the conclusions of relativism. Moral reasoning is possible, even necessary, if our civilized society is to continue to solve its conflicts. We have introduced the language of ethics, such as harms and benefits, rights and rules, common morality, and the implicit morality of institutions. We have articulated a concept, Enterprise Strategy, that should be a precursor to corporate strategy, and perhaps even replace it. In Chapters 5, 6, and 7 we tried to show how most of the current thinking about ethics and strategy, or just strategy, is highly suspect. In this chapter we have tried to defend one view of the connection between ethics and strategy, the Personal Projects Enterprise Strategy, by being explicit about our concept of the person and the corporation.

Along the way we have articulated a variety of principles. We have used this rhetorical device to focus attention and debate. Regardless of the final verdict on the personal projects view, we hope that you will use the Values Principle, the Interdependence Principle, the First and Second and Third Axioms of Corporate Strategy, the Principles of Legal and Moral Relativism, the Principles of Promise Keeping, Conventional Rights, Respect for Persons, and the others as a way to continue the debate on the connection of ethics and strategy.

Finally, this book has been a sketch rather than a finished drawing. We hope that there will be others that do a more thorough job of storytelling. In particular the Personal Projects story is a rich and multifaceted one, since it is about our individual search for excellence. We believe that such a search is also a search for ethics, and without ethics, corporate strategy will become another tool of coercion. The search for ethics in corporate strategy is far from over. It is a task in which every executive and business thinker must engage. Only by addressing important business issues in moral terms can we escape the moral low ground on which business resides. The search for ethics is also an individual task of the highest importance. We need to see how our lives hang together in coherent patterns, and we need to justify ourselves to each other. Most important, we need to understand how to treat ourselves and others as persons, as individuals, and as community members, not engaged in some grand common task for the good of humanity, but rather struggling, biting, and kicking against the dark.

★ ★ ★ ★ ★ ★ ★ ★ ★ ★ Endnotes

CHAPTER 1

1. We adopt the following convention in these endnotes. The first time a reference is used, we give the complete citation. On subsequent uses we refer the reader to the bibliography. For example, E. Freeman (1984), *Strategic Management: A Stakeholder Approach*, Boston: Pitman Publishing Inc., is henceforth cited as Freeman (1984).

Business ethics is equally hot in the academic world. The past several years have seen a spate of books, journals, and research centers devoted to a variety of topics. The strangest phenomenon has been the arrival of philosophers in business schools. Even though Alfred North Whitehead was influential in the early days of the Harvard Business School, philosophy has enjoyed little popularity among business students. For a sampling of philosophers' writings on business ethics, see current issues of *Business and Professional Ethics* or *Journal of Business Ethics*.

2. For an account of the Levine situation, see M. Stevens (1987), *The Insiders: The Truth Behind the Scandal Rocking Wall Street*, New York: Putnam's.

3. The Boesky saga goes on and on, affecting much of the current news. For an account, see Stevens (1987).

4. We have analyzed some of the issues in corporate governance, especially hostile takeovers and greenmail, in E. Freeman, D. Gilbert, and C. Jacobson (1987), "The Ethics of Greenmail," *Journal of Business Ethics*, Vol. 6, No. 3, 165–178.

5. South Africa poses a complex issue as we are now seeing. For an account of some recent thinking by a diverse group of commentators, see the spring 1986 issue of *Business and Society Review*, No. 57, edited by S. Prakash Sethi. For a general account of the response of business, see D. Kneale (1986a), "Firms with Ties to South Africa Strike Back at Colleges That Divest," *The Wall Street Journal*, 20 November.

6. Both of these cases are the subject of a great deal of current scholarship. For a summary of the Johns Manville asbestos controversy, see P. Brodern (1985), *Outrageous Misconduct: The Asbestos Industry on Trial*, New York: Pantheon Books. For an account of A.

H. Robins constructed from published materials, see "A. H. Robins Co. and the Dalkon Shield," Charlottesville, Va.: The Darden School Case Studies, UVA E-49.

7. Sexual harassment has been addressed in a number of places. For a sample of the literature see R. Quinn and P. Lees (1984), "Attraction and Harassment: Dynamics of Sexual Politics in the Workplace," *Organizational Dynamics*, Vol. 13, No. 3, 13–46; and G. Sullivan and W. Nowlin (1986), "Critical New Aspects of Sex Harassment Law," *Labor Law Journal*, Vol. 37, spring, 617–624.

8. The classic statement is R. Hayes and W. Abernathy (1980), "Managing Our Way to Economic Decline," *Harvard Business Review*, Vol. 58, No. 4, 67–77. Much literature has followed since that article. For a similar position, see R. Charan and E. Freeman (1980). "Planning for the Business Environment of the 1980s," *Journal of Business Strategy*, Vol. 1, No. 2, 9–19.

9. A recent issue of *Fortune* contains good anecdotal material on the effects of restructuring on management. See M. Magnet (1987), "Restructuring Really Works," *Fortune*, March 2, 1987 and P. Nulty (1987b), "Pushed out at 45 — Now What," *Fortune*, March 2, 1987. Nulty quotes a Bureau of Labor Statistics study that "between 1981 and 1986 almost 500,000 executive, administrative, and management workers lost jobs that they had held for at least 3 years." As one friend of ours in a restructured company puts it, "Restructuring will continue until morale improves!"

10. The literature on the AT&T divestiture is burgeoning. For a sampling of views, see S. Coll (1986), *The Deal of the Century: The Breakup of AT&T*, New York: Atheneum; M. Derthick and P. Quick (1985), *The Politics of Deregulation*, Washington, D.C.: The Brookings Institution; D. Evans (ed.) (1983), *Breaking Up Bell: Essays on Industrial Organization and Regulation*, New York: North-Holland Publishing Company; E. Freeman (1983), "Managing the Strategic Challenge in Telecommunications," *Columbia Journal of World Business*, Vol. 18, No. 1, 8–18; L. Kahaner (1986), *On the Line: The Men of MCI — Who Took on AT&T, Risked Everything and Won!*, New York: Warner; S. Kleinfield (1981), *The Biggest Company on Earth: A Profile of AT&T*, New York: Holt, Rinehart and Winston; A. Phillips (1983), "Regulatory and Interfirm Organizational Burdens in the U.S. Telecommunications Structure," *Columbia Journal of World Business*, Vol. 18, No. 1, 46–52; H. Shooshan (1984), "The Bell Breakup: Putting it in Perspective," in H. Shooshan (ed.) *Disconnecting Bell: The Impact of the AT&T Divestiture*, New York: Pergamon, 8–22; J. Tunstall (1986), *Communications Deregulation: The Unleashing of America's Communications Industry*, Oxford: Basil Blackwell; W. Tunstall (1983) "Cultural Transition at AT&T," *Sloan Management Review*, Vol. 25, No. 1, 15–26; W. Tunstall (1985), *Disconnecting Parties: Managing the Bell System Break-up: An Inside View*, New York: McGraw-Hill; A. von Auw (1983), *Heritage and Destiny: Reflections on the Bell System in Transition*, New York: Praeger; and R. Wiley (1984), "The End of Monopoly: Regulatory Change and the Promotion of Competition," in H. Shooshan (ed.) (1984), *Disconnecting Bell: The Impact of the AT&T Divestiture*, New York: Pergamon, 23–46. Throughout this book our discussion of AT&T is based on these and other public sources, as well as a number of interviews with industry insiders and experts. We alone are responsible for the conclusions that we draw from this host of data.

11. For an account of the scope of the undivested Bell System see Kleinfield, (1981).

12. We believe that the notion of "psychological contract" is a powerful one that has been underutilized in moral theory. Since it relies on a symmetry of expectations, it comes strikingly close to some contract theorists' attempts to find sets of stable expectations which meet certain conditions of fairness. In Nozick's terms, boundary crossings occur when the psychological contract is violated. See H. Levinson (1976), *Psychological Man*, Cambridge: The Levinson Institute; and compare R. Nozick (1975), *Anarchy, State and Utopia*, New York: Basic Books, at 57–59, for an analysis of the concept of "boundary crossings."

13. Our account of the Martin Marietta–Bendix–Allied–United Technologies situation is based strictly on published sources. We have no insider insight into what actually transpired. There is a rather large body of literature on the case. See G. Anders (1982), "First Boston Enjoys Surge as Speculators Expect Big Earnings Gain From Fee as Bendix Advisors," *Wall Street Journal*, 24 September; "The 4 Horsemen: Did Main Characters in Big Takeover Saga Let Egos Sway Them?", *The Wall Street Journal*, 24 September 1982; P. Hartz (1985), *Merger*, New York: William Morrow; A. Hughey (1982), "Allied Corp. Plans Major Debt Reduction, Possible Sale of Bendix's Holdings in RCA," *The Wall Street Journal*, 16

December; P. Ingrassia (1982), "Forget Football. We Have Bendix and U. Tech," *The Wall Street Journal*, 24 September; J. Koten (1982), "Bill Agee of Bendix Corp: Why I Did It," *The Wall Street Journal*, October 2, 1982; M. Krebs (1985), "Allied Reviews Takeover of Bendix," *Automotive News*, 27 May; T. Metz (1982), "The Pacificist," *The Wall Street Journal*, 3 December; "Pac Man Economics," unsigned review and outlook, *The Wall Street Journal*, 27 September 1982; "Our Dream is to Work Together," unsigned Interview with W. Agee and M. Cunningham, *Fortune*, 18 October 1982; and, B. Sloan (1983), *Three Plus One Equals Billions*, New York: Arbor House. We are grateful to Ms. Twyla Greenheck for an admirable job of synthesizing this literature for us.

14. For an account of the decision making process during the episode see Hartz (1985).

15. See T. Peters and R. Waterman (1982), *In Search of Excellence*, New York: Harper and Row, and T. Peters and N. Austin (1985), *A Passion for Excellence*, New York: Random House. In addition, Peters has published numerous columns and pamphlets such as T. Peters (1986), *The Promises*, Palo Alto, CA.: The Tom Peters Companies, which detail the revolution. We have had the opportunity to see Peters talk about the excellent companies many times, and the writing simply cannot give the full effect of the revolution that is taking place in management. Curiously enough there is little excitement about these ideas in large companies, as Peters' most recent examples are from small and medium sized companies.

16. We take as evidence of the revolution those stories so vividly told by Peters and others.

17. The literature on "values" is quite recent. See T. Deal and A. Kennedy (1982), *Corporate Culture*, Reading, MA.: Addison Wesley; G. Cavanaugh (1982), *American Business Values*, Englewood Cliffs, N. J.: Prentice Hall; F. Sturdivant and J. Ginter (1977), "Corporate Social Responsiveness: Management Attitudes and Economic Performance," *California Management Review*, Vol. 19, No. 2, 30–39; and F. Sturdivant (1979), "Executives and Activists: A Test of Stakeholder Management," *California Management Review* Vol. 22, No. 1, 53–59. There is an older tradition in management that is relevant, especially some of the classics such as K. Andrews (1980), *The Concept of Corporate Strategy*, 2nd ed., Homewood, Il.: R.D. Irwin; C. Barnard (1938), *The Function of the Executive*, Cambridge, MA.: Harvard University Press; and P. Selznick (1957), *Leadership in Administration*, New York: Harper and Row.

18. There is a vast literature on organizational environments. Freeman (1984), offers one interpretation of this literature. There seems to be an important distinction in this area. There are those who believe that "environment" does the explaining of organizational action, thereby belittling the importance of strategic choice or simply treating choice on a par with random variations. This group fails to realize that the organization's environment consists of the strategic choices of other organizations. There is a separate group that thinks, as we do, that "environment" is a generic term and must be broken down into names and faces. While managers talk of "the business environment" and often blame it for various infelicities, there is little of substance to this notion. The causal net is not the environment, but specific actions, just as notions of "the economy" are ultimately reducible to microbehavior. Relevant but non trivial arguments to this effect can be found in K. Arrow and F. Hahn (1971), *General Equilibrium Analysis*, San Francisco: Holden-Day; and T. Schelling (1978), *Micromotives and Macrobehavior*, New York: W.W. Norton.

19. Don't think of our principles as "first principles," or anything with "godlike" authority. They are pragmatic rules of thumb, open to revision. In the course of this book, primarily here in the notes, we will end up sketching a pragmatic account of what look, in the main text, to be absolute statements. Principles, like other general statements, even those of physics, are intelligible only in some particular context. And "context" stands for "the practices of an interpretive community." Language, in this sense, is always up for grabs. We follow the accounts of Richard Rorty in Rorty (1979), *Philosophy and the Mirror of Nature*, Princeton: Princeton University Press; Rorty (1982), *Consequences of Pragmatism*, Minneapolis: University of Minnesota Press; Rorty (1983), "Postmodern Bourgeois Liberalism," *Journal of Philosophy*, Vol. 80, No. 10, 583–589; Rorty (1984), "The Historiography of Philosophy," in R. Rorty, J. Schneewind, and Q. Skinner (eds.) (1984), *Philosophy in History*, Cambridge: Cambridge University Press, 49–75; Rorty (1984a), "Texts and Lumps," *New Literary History* Vol. 16, No. 1, 1–16; and, Donald Davidson in Davidson (1984), "On the Very Idea of a Conceptual Scheme," *Inquiries into Truth and Interpretation*, New York: Oxford University

Press, 183–198; and, Stanley Fish in Fish (1980), *Is There a Text in This Class?*, Cambridge: Harvard University Press; Fish (1984), "AntiProfessionalism," *New Literary History*, Vol. 16, No. 1, 89–108; and S. Knapp and W. Michaels (l982), "Against Theory," *Critical Inquiry*, Vol. 8, No. 4 732–742.

20. We follow the argument of Donald Davidson in Davidson (1980a) "Actions, Reasons and Causes," in *Essays in Action and Events*, New York: Oxford University Press, 3–19, that values can be both reasons and cause. We are grateful to Edwin Hartman for making this point to us. For an application to the Harvard way of doing strategy see E. Freeman, D. Gilbert, and E. Hartman (1988, in press) "Values and the Foundations of Strategic Management," *Journal of Business Ethics*.

21. Of course, in one sense this principle is trivial, since without stakeholders there is no organization. "Organization" cannot be defined without a membership and exclusion rule. See W. Evan (1966), "An Organization Set Model of Interorganizational Relations," in M. Tuite, M. Radnor, and R. Chisholm (eds.) (1966), *Interorganizational Decision Making*, Chicago: Aldine, 181-200. For an attempt to do without "organization" as a predicate, see the fascinating work of Steven Cheung in Cheung (1983), "The Contractual Nature of the Firm," *Journal of Law and Economics*, Vol. 26, No. 1, 1–21. For an attempt to apply the insights of Cheung's contract theory to the problem of corporate legitimacy see E. Freeman and W. Evan (1987 in press) "Stakeholder Management and the Modern Corporation: Kantian Capitalism," in T. Beauchamp and N. Bowie (eds.) (1987, in press) *Ethical Theory and Business*, 3rd edition, Englewood Cliffs: Prentice Hall.

22. There is no difference on our view between axioms and principles. Fix some axioms and see what follows, see note 19, *supra*.

23. Ethics also has a personal side which involves trying to see one's life as a coherent whole. See H. Barnes (1967), *An Existentialist Ethics*, Chicago: University of Chicago Press. We return to this idea in Chapter 2.

24. To see how this follows, note that we assume that strategy results in some action which affects the ability of persons to carry out their project. To deny this also denies the Interdependence Principle. However, to say that most questions of corporate strategy are ethical is not to say very much. Most interesting questions of human interaction are questions of ethics. We don't always have to "do ethics"; rather, we can hold some principles as fixed points, so long as we are aware of the need to justify these principles as being ethical in nature. This is even true in that most hallowed area of academic discourse: science. For an analysis of the value judgments in science, see R. Rudner (1953), "The Scientist Qua Scientist Makes Value Judgments", *Philosophy of Science*, Vol. 20, No. 1, 1–6. The amazing point is that stating that corporate strategy and ethics are logically related comes as news to both researchers and managers.

25. Another way to put this point is that individual goals are the primary units of analysis. It is not that corporate goals and projects do not exist, nor that they are decomposable into individual goals, but that they are explainable in terms of individual goals. Such an explanation can be accomplished without a radical form of reductionism. See D. Davidson (1980d) "Mental Events," in *Essays on Actions and Events*, New York: Oxford University Press, 207–227, and Rorty (1979). We are grateful to Edwin Hartman for clarifying this point.

26. For a comprehensive account of the critique of the modern corporation, see E. Herman (1981), *Corporate Control, Corporate Power*, Cambridge: Cambridge University Press; and R. Nader and W. Taylor (1986), *The Big Boys: Power and Position in American Business*, New York: Pantheon Books.

27. The attack on corporate strategy is led by Hayes and Abernathy (1980), R. Pascale and A. Athos (1981), *The Art of Japanese Management*, New York: Simon and Schuster. Wickham Skinner has been a voice in the wilderness for a number of years about the disregard for manufacturing as a key variable in strategy. For an early and prescient attempt to rectify the concept of corporate strategy, see the articles which led to his recent brilliant book, W. Skinner (1985), *Manufacturing: The Formidable Competitive Weapon*, New York: Wiley.

28. Ironically enough, the academics in strategy are experiencing booming times. Strategic Human Resources Management, Strategic Information, and International Competitive Strategy are the latest genres of strategy. The job market in these specialties is up. Strategy professors have taken refuge in becoming "more empirical and scientific," and that attitude is a best seller in business schools. But the real point of the critique is that the

current language of strategy is optional. We can simply set it aside and not lose much if we focus on people and their relationships to each other and the organizational systems in place.

29. Another way to put this point is that the formulation-implementation distinction is not useful. It leads managers to thinking about strategy as a cognitive task followed by a persuasive task. D. Gilbert (1987a), *Strategy and Justice*, Minneapolis: Ph.D. Dissertation, Department of Strategic Management and Organization, Carlson School of Management, University of Minnesota, explores these issues in greater detail.

30. Strategy academics trace the evolution of the field as quite recent. See I. Ansoff (1977), "The State of Practice in Planning Systems," *Sloan Management Review*, Vol. 18, No. 2, 1–28; D. Schendel and C. Hofer (1979) "Introduction" in D. Schendel and C. Hofer (eds.) (1979), *Strategic Management: A New View of Business Policy and Planning*, Boston: Little Brown, 1–12. D. Gilbert, E. Hartman, J. Mauriel, and E. Freeman (1988, in press), *The Logic of Strategy*, Boston: Ballinger, gives a slightly more historical account. See also M. Horwitch (1988, in press), *Postmodern Management*, New York: Basic Books, for a more accurate and convincing view.

31. We insist on thinking of corporate strategy as metaphor rather than an indentifiable and discrete set of sentences that describes all actions of a particular organization in a certain arena and only those actions. If you begin to think of corporate strategy as a metaphor, it will become easier to connect to areas of the humanities such as ethics, literature, art and the like. If you insist on thinking of corporate strategy as a concept capable of the same kind of precision as "heat" and "pressure," you will waste a lot of time searching for the equivalent of Boyle's law.

32. These questions are adapted from P. Lorange (1980), *Corporate Planning: An Executive Viewpoint*, Englewood Cliffs: Prentice Hall Inc. We are grateful for many conversations with Lorange in which he convinced us of the power of these simple questions.

33. It is crucial to connect the actual budgets, blueprints, and concrete actions of specific individuals to the broader questions of direction. Usual models of strategy disconnect these questions, or see the third one as a question of "implementation" or "persuasion." Freeman (1984), and E. Freeman and D. Gilbert (1987) "Managing Stakeholder Relationships," in P. Sethi and C. Falbe (eds.) (1987), *Business and Public Policy: Dimensions of Conflict and Cooperation*, Lexington: D. C. Heath, try to show how a close reading of Graham Allison (1970) *Essence of Decision*, Boston: Little Brown, implies that the transactional level must be logically connected to the rational level of decision making.

34. For a summary of recent work on strategic control, see P. Lorange and M. Scott-Morton (1986), *Strategic Control*, St. Paul: West Publishing.

35. Thus, strategy is essentially game-theoretic. Events are functions of my expectations of your behavior, and your behavior is a function of your expectations of my behavior, and so on. T. Schelling (1960), *The Strategy of Conflict*, Cambridge: Harvard University Press, is still the best book available on business strategy, even though it is about the arms race. We develop this theme below in Chapter 5.

36. We talk about "strategy as purpose," and later, in Chapter 3 we will talk about "ethics and values" and "moral values." Distinguishing between "purpose" and "value" is arbitrary, though some might say that values are more basic than purpose. If you think of purposes as resulting in certain "projects" to be accomplished, perhaps we agree. The point is that they are all the same kind of intentional concept. "Purpose" seems more in line with the jargon in strategy, and "value" seems more in line with the jargon in ethics.

37. Once again, purpose functions as a theoretical term in explanations. You simply can't give a proper account of human action without it. For a clear and concise view of explanation, see J. Elster (1983), *Explaining Technical Change*, New York: Cambridge University Press. *Pace* J. Pfeffer (1982), *Organization*, Boston: Pitman Publishing.

38. What we have said here, and will say later in this section, is fairly standard in accounts of intentionality in the philosophical literature. See J. Searle (1984), *Minds, Brains, and Science*, Cambridge: Harvard University Press, for a readable introduction. However, we caution that the issue is bitterly contested once one leaves the surface. See Rorty (1979) for a historical treatment.

39. There are no better examples of this point than in the classics such as A.

Chandler (1962), *Strategy and Structure*, Boston: MIT Press; A. Chandler (1977), *The Visible Hand*, Cambridge: Harvard University Press; A. Sloan (1969), *My Years with General Motors*, New York: Doubleday; and, Barnard (1938).

40. For a theoretical view that much of business success and failure can be explained by attention to demographic variables, see J. Pfeffer (1983), "Organizational Demography," in L. Cummings and B. Staw (eds.) (1983), *Research in Organization Behavior*, Greenwich Conn.: JAI Press, 5, 299–357.

41. Purpose or values make it possible for us to come to terms with life, to justify our lives, to see life as a coherent whole. Imagine giving a justification of your life and your projects without reference to a purpose or to a value. You would not have an answer when faced with the question "Why did you do that?" For an account of values as answers to "why" questions, see chapter 3, *infra*.

42. Andrews (1980) is the exemplar of this view, though he has recently changed his mind.

43. For an account of the Britt–People Express–Frontier saga, see W. Carley and T. Agins (1985), "People Express Merger Might Cause Problems," *The Wall Street Journal*, 14 October; W. Carley (1986), "People Express is a Victim of its Fast Growth," *The Wall Street Journal*, 25 June; W. Carley (1986b), "Struggling to Survive, People Express Alters Operations and Image," *The Wall Street Journal*, 31 July; A. Salpukas (1986), "People Express Beaten at its Own Game," *Minneapolis Star and Tribune*, 29 June; A. Salpukas (1985), "People Express to get Britt," *New York Times*, 28 December.

44. Else you cannot ever tell if a purpose has been realized. We believe that such a view is the essence of rationality.

45. For an account of the TWA story see C. Loomis (1986), "The Comeuppance of Carl Icahn," *Fortune*, 17 February, 19–25; and, D. Hertzberg (1986), "TWA Names Carl Icahn as Chairman, but His Victory is Seen as Bittersweet," *The Wall Street Journal*, 6 January.

46. For an account of the Apple Computer story, see P. Gray (1986), "Apple Computer and Jobs Reach Pact Barring Sale of New Machine Until 1987," *The Wall Street Journal*, 20 January.

47. Hormel and Company's dispute with the union is chronicled in M. Charlier (1986), "Hormel and Union Are Locked in Battle that Carries High Stakes for Both Sides," *The Wall Street Journal*, 23 January; N. St. Anthony (1986), "P-9 Trusteeship gets Judge's Approval; Local Leadership Out," *Minneapolis Star and Tribune*, 3 June; and, D. Hage (1986b), "On Anniversary, P-9 Militants Haven't Given Up, But Rest of Austin Looks Ahead," *Minneapolis Star and Tribune*, 17 August.

48. For a related concept, the value chain, see M. Porter (1985), *Competitive Advantage*, New York: The Free Press. See Chapter 5, *infra*, for a critique of this view.

49. Gilbert (1987a) explores the concept of "web of bargains" in much more detail, and connects it to the strategy literature.

50. O. Williamson (1985), *The Economic Institutions of Capitalism*, New York: The Free Press, gives a simple account of safeguards. E. Freeman and W. Evan (1987), "Corporate Governance: A Stakeholder View," unpublished manuscript, extend the notion to include an analysis of who pays for the safeguards. Also see E. Freeman (1987), "Review of Williamson's *The Economic Institutions of Capitalism*," *Academy of Management Review*, Vol. 12, No. 2, 385–387.

51. This section is based on our fanatical following of several major league baseball teams, through direct research and through such publications as *Baseball America* and *The Sporting News*.

CHAPTER 2

1. There are many excellent discussions of relativism. This chapter adds little new to the philosophical literature. It is heavily indebted to Nancy Gifford's excellent book, *When*

In Rome, see N. Gifford (1983), *When In Rome: An Introduction to Relativism and Knowledge*, Albany, N.Y.: SUNY Albany Press. For the classic statement see R. Brandt (1959), *Ethical Theory*, Englewood Cliffs, N.J.: Prentice Hall. For more recent and much more in-depth discussions, see P. Foot (1982), "Moral Relativism," in J. Mieland and M. Kraus (eds.) (1982), *Relativism: Cognitive and Moral*, Notre Dame, IND.: University of Notre Dame Press, 152–166, and G. Harman's "Moral Relativism Defended" in the same volume at 189–204. Also, see A. Goldman (1977), *The Moral Foundations of Professional Ethics*, Totowa, N.J.: Rowman and Littlefield, at 8–20.

2. These conversations are based on real cases which are disguised. They represent four types of problems we have seen in our years of talking with managers in business.

3. For a more comprehensive account see Gifford (1983).

4. On the notion of "right for X" and "true for X" see Brandt (1959).

5. To make this claim is not to claim that "absolutism" is the alternative. See Chapter 3 for our view on how moral theory works.

6. We do not claim that there are four logically distinct versions of relativism again, ours are taken from Gifford (1983). Rather, we have drawn a pragmatic distinction among the types of conversations which seem to prevail in the business world.

7. See Gifford (1983), at 18.

8. This section is based on our interpretation of Gifford (1983), at 32–38; Also see C. Harris (1986), *Applying Moral Theory*, Belmont, Mass.: Wadsworth; and, Brandt (1959).

9. Harris (1986), at 19.

10. For a penetrating discussion of the philosophical issues associated with the concept of "tolerance," see J. Wisdom (1970) "Tolerance" in *Paradox and Discovery*, Berkeley: University of California Press, 139–147.

11. We are indebted to Edwin Hartman for making this point emphatically to us.

12. There is a connection between the process of coming to have a belief, and its association with relativism, and the whole process approach to strategy which is largely responsible for the disconnection between ethics and strategy. See Chapter 7.

13. A more precise way of putting this point is that naive relativism rests on a mistaken concept of truth and reasoning. As Rorty would put it, all we have are our descriptions or beliefs, but the very purpose of intellectual discourse is to find sets of beliefs that help us to better cope with the world.

14. For a credible statement of role relativism, see N. Bowie (1982), *Business Ethics*, Englewood Cliffs: Prentice Hall Inc., at 3–16. Also see K. Baier (1984), "Duties to One's Employer," in T. Regan (ed.) (1984), *Just Business*, New York: Random House, 60–99. The problem is that this whole approach makes business ethics issues depend in a crucial way on a larger moral theory, rather than serve as data points for considered judgments in reflective equilibrium in the theory. Baier has argued that obligations are presumptive, but the problem is that managers want to know what to do. They cannot wait until we have a broader theory. They cannot take every situation as a call for a full-scale "Are you a utilitarian or a Rawlsian?" type of analysis.

15. Erving Goffman has given a powerful statement of this view. See E. Goffman (1981), *Forms of Talk*, Philadelphia: University of Pennsylvania Press; Goffman (1971), *Relations in Public*, New York: Basic Books; Goffman (1969), *Strategic Interaction*, Philadelphia: University of Pennsylvania Press; and Goffman (1959), *The Presentation of Self in Everyday Life*, Garden City: Doubleday. For our response see E. Freeman and D. Gilbert (1986) "Orwell and Organizations," Charlottesville, unpublished manuscript.

16. Alan Goldman has put the point this way. When a particular profession is so important to the smooth functioning of society then particular rights claims can be overridden. Goldman believes that the notion of "public morality" is more appropriate for business and medicine than the professional model. He argues that only judges and teachers fulfill the criteria for professional morality. See Goldman (1977).

17. For one answer, see Bowie (1982). But there is a problem here: How does one evaluate the role itself? If it is to be evaluated from the standpoint of moral theory, then what is the point of roles? If not, then the status quo interpretation of roles and their place in society always wins the day.

18. The history of this concept goes back a long way, to W. D. Ross (1930), *The Right and the Good*, Oxford: Clarendon Press. For a critique, see Brandt (1959).

19. Once again, Edwin Hartman is responsible for the clarity of our understanding here.

20. The classic pieces are Stanley Milgram (1975), *Obedience to Authority*, New York: Harper and Row; and P. Zimbardo (1969), *The Cognitive Control of Motivation*, Glenview, Ill.: Scott, Foresman.

21. There are no better statements of this view than Aldous Huxley (1932), *Brave New World*, New York: Harper and Row; and George Orwell (1948), *1984*, 1961 edition, New York: Harcourt Brace Jovanovich. See also Orwell's brilliant essay, G. Orwell (1968), "Inside the Whale," in *The Collected Essays, Journalism and Letters of George Orwell*, Volume 1, edited by Sonia Orwell and Ian Angres, New York: Harcourt Brace Jovanovich.

22. It would be difficult to defend this version of relativism as an autonomous position distinct from naive and cultural relativism. Norms of practice are clearly related to social roles and underlying cultures. Again, our task is to create heuristics, not truths of logic.

23. For an account of Union Carbide's problems in Bhopal see B. Meier and J. Stewart (1985), "A Year After Bhopal, Union Carbide Faces A Slew of Problems," *The Wall Street Journal*, November 26; M. Miller and B. Meier (1986), "India Files Suit Against Carbide in Bhopal Court," *The Wall Street Journal*, September 8; and M. Miller (1986), "Two Years After Bhopal's Gas Disaster, Lingering Effects Still Plague Its People," *The Wall Street Journal*, December 5.

24. For an account of the Texaco–Pennzoil–Getty situation, see C. Reich (1986), "The Litigator: David Boies, The Wall Street Lawyer Everyone Wants," *New York Times Magazine*, June 1; A. Sullivan (1987), "Texaco Banks on Kinnean to Steer Firm Out of Financial Legal Crises," *The Wall Street Journal*, February 3; R. Bennett (1987), "Winning Friends for Texaco When It Needs Them Most," *New York Times*, February 22.

25. The best example is a set of cases known as Sedek Industries (A)–(H), Cambridge, Mass.: Harvard Business School Case Studies, 9-584-132 to 9-584-140.

26. For a deep discussion of pluralism, see the essays in *Critical Inquiry*, Vol. 12, No. 3, spring 1986.

27. See the stories in Peters and Austin (1985).

28. For a substantive discussion of this issue, see the Winter 1986 issue of *Business and Society*, edited by Prakash Sethi. Also see the stories and novels of Nadine Gordimer and J. M. Coetzee, such as N. Gordimer (1980), *A Soldier's Embrace*, London: Jonathan Cape; and Gordimer (1984), *Something Out There*, London: Jonathan Cape; and J. Coetzee (1977), *In the Heart of the Country*, London Secker and Warburg; and Coetzee (1982), *Waiting for the Barbarians*, New York: Penguin Books. Analytical discussions cannot depict the *Geist* of the times, and thus are of marginal help in actually coping with the situation.

29. It is sometimes thought that CR is not a moral view at all. Rather, CR simply points out the fact that what appears in one set of circumstances to be the morally correct decision is not the morally correct decision in another set of circumstances. Once again, our reply is that managers certainly believe that it is a separate moral theory, and while this belief may be false, it must be met on its own ground.

30. Yet there is little or no discussion on these matters in books about international business.

31. See J. Rawls (1971), *A Theory of Justice*, Cambridge, Mass.: Harvard University Press, at 363, for an analysis of civil disobedience.

32. For an interesting view of the Dresser case see B. Crawford and S. Lenway (1985), "Decision Modes and International Regime Changes: Western Collaboration on East-West Trade," *World Politics*, Vol. 37, No. 3, 375–402.

33. Rorty is clear on the distinction between postmodernism, or pragmatism, with which we are in substantial agreement, and relativism in "Postmodern Bourgeois Liberalism" (1983), at 589:

> The second objection is that what I have been calling "postmodernism" is better named "relativism," and that relativism is self-refuting. Relativism certainly is self-

refuting, but there is a difference between saying that every community is as good as every other and saying that we have to work out from the networks we are, from the communities with which we presently identify.

CHAPTER 3

1. While we will sometimes put our argument in terms of language—that we need to use the language of ethics in reasoning about business decisions—the same point can be made nonlinguistically in terms of action. We believe, however, that it is important to understand that the very words that we use determine how we see the world. If we persist in not using moral language to describe the business world, it follows that we see that world through amoral lenses. So, it is not enough to act in a way that is consistent with some moral theory or other. We have to articulate and defend such a theory, and show how this or that case follows or does not follow from adherence to it. This account of language as a tool which helps us to cope with the world follows L. Wittgenstein (1953), *Philosophical Investigations*, E. Anscombe (trans.), Oxford: Basil Blackwell. For a postmodern rendition of Wittgenstein, see the references to Richard Rorty, Chapter 1, note 19, *supra*.

2. For a powerful statement of this view, see Mark Pastin (1986), *The Hard Problems of Management*, San Francisco: Jossey Bass.

3. See Chapter 1, note 10.

4. All of this plainly follows from our discussion of "strategy as purpose" in Chapter 1.

5. Of course, rules would still emerge in a society where violence is an accepted way of solving disputes. Only in cases where there are literally no common understandings would there be no rules.

6. The failure to describe essentially moral phenomena in moral terms is itself a moral issue. Scholars and researchers in management should be held accountable for their amoral description of moral phenomena, if our argument is correct.

7. The focus in this chapter is on using the language of ethics to make decisions. In Chapter 4, below, we will address the problem of justification. Of course, there is no difference between these issues. For pedagogical purposes we prefer to put the same point, about the connection between ethics and strategy, in several different ways.

8. For the very best philosophical thinking on the issue of whether corporations can be moral agents see Peter French (1984), *Collective and Corporate Responsibility*, New York: Columbia University Press; and K. Goodpaster and J. Mathews (1982), "Can A Corporation Have A Conscience", *Harvard Business Review*, Vol. 60, No. 1, 132–141. We hold this issue in abeyance for the time being.

9. We follow Robert Nozick (1975), *Anarchy, State and Utopia*, New York: Basic Books, on the issue of entitlements, though the issue is complicated.

10. See Gilbert (1987a) for a more complete discussion of these issues.

11. Not all stable expectations create rights, especially if the behavior harms others in an important way or coerces them. The issues are complex here. Nozick (1975), sorts through them one way, and Rawls (1971) another. The definitive statement on rights is Ronald Dworkin (1980), *Taking Rights Seriously*, Cambridge, Mass.: Harvard University Press. There is naturally a large literature here.

12. See Rawls (1971) for a spate of arguments against such views. It is worth noting that John Stuart Mill would be appalled at the suggestion that utilitarianism could ever justify slavery. See Mill (1949 ed.), *Utilitarianism*, Oxford: Basil Blackwell, at Chapter 4.

13. For the notion of "rights as trumps" as applied to business see Alan Goldman (1977), at 24–33.

14. A rule respects my rights if and only if I am a guaranteed winner (or nonloser) when the rule is followed. Simple rules such as "always do what is in Jones's interest" clearly respect Jones's rights given standard assumptions about "interests," "rights," "knowledge of Jones's interests and rights," and "Jones's right to decide about Jones." Ethics is the search

for rights-respecting rules which are more complex in the sense that more than one person's interests are covered by the rule.

15. Some believe that we can define "The Good" (capitals intended) as some absolute concept to which all humans should aspire, the *summum bonum* of life. This excess Platonic baggage, often institutionalized by religions, represents a way of philosophizing which should be set aside for all the reasons given by Rorty and others.

16. Note that we are complete and total relativists about "the good." Each person is entitled to his or her own conception of the good. But it does not follow that each person is entitled to realize that conception. Another way to put this point, epigramatically, is "relativists about the good, and absolutists about rights."

17. Here is the reason that we find so much current thinking in organization studies unconvincing. Power is a means. Naturally it may get corrupted, through self-deception and bad faith, to become an end in itself. We find too little discussion of ends in this literature.

18. We follow Davidson here. See Davidson (1980a), at 13.

19. There is a large literature on "intrinsic value" and the logic of this concept which is at the foundation of so much of social science. For a sample of the philosophical literature, see B. Hansson (1968), "Fundamental Axioms for Preference Relations," *Synthese*, Vol. 18, No. 4, 423–442; and G. von Wright (1963), *The Logic of Preference*, Edinburgh: Edinburgh University Press.

20. See D. Davidson (1980b), "How Is Weakness of the Will Possible," in *Essays on Actions and Events*, New York: Oxford University Press, 21–42; and D. Davidson (1980c), "Intending," in *Essays on Actions and Events*, New York: Oxford University Press, 83–102.

21. Compare what we have said about values with Deal and Kennedy (1982), Chapter 1 note 17 *supra*, and D. Siebert (1984), *The Ethical Executive*, New York: Simon and Schuster.

22. Andrews and the original framers of the Harvard Policy Model realized this fact. See Freeman, Gilbert, and Hartman (1988, in press), "Values and the Foundations of Strategic Management," *Journal of Business Ethics*, for an account of the role of values in the Harvard Policy Model. Also see Chapter 7.

23. For a survey, see R. Martin and J. Nickel (1983), "Recent Work on the Concept of Rights," in K. Lucey and T. Machan (eds.) (1983), *Recent Work in Philosophy*, Totowa, N.J.: Rowman and Allanheld.

24. This definition rules out animals and others who do not speak a language. Whether a collective can be an agent is more complex.

25. For an account of the Apple story, see A. Pollack (1985a), "Jobs Resigns as Apple's Chairman," *New York Times*, September 18, A. Pollack (1985b), "Now Sculley Goes It Alone At Apple," *New York Times*, September 22; and B. Uttal (1985), "The Adventures of Steve Jobs (cont'd)," *Fortune*, 14 October.

26. For a fascinating and often overlooked way to take the concept of moral rules to its logical conclusion see Bernard Gert (1970), *The Moral Rules: A New Rational Foundation for Morality*, New York: Harper and Row. Because Gert dared to give some answers, some moral philosophers did not take this book seriously.

27. For the concept of common morality see A. Donagan (1977), *The Theory of Morality*, Chicago: University of Chicago Press. Our use which can substitute "conventional" for "common" follows C. McMahon (1981), "Morality and the Invisible Hand," *Philosophy and Public Affairs*, Vol. 10, No. 3, 247–277.

28. The classic piece in moral philosophy is J. Searle (1964), "How to Derive 'Ought' From 'Is'," *Philosophical Review*, Vol. 73, No. 1, 43–58.

29. This section follows Rawls (1971).

CHAPTER 4

1. See Chapter 1, note 10, *supra*.

2. There is no mention of ethics in the volume of *The Columbia Journal of World*

Business devoted to the industry, and little in the literature referred to in note 1 *supra*. Gilbert (1987a) is the first full-blown analysis of the ethical issues in such a monumental decision that affected millions of people.

3. See C. Brown (1953), "Recasting the Bell System," *Columbia Journal of World Business*, Vol. 18, No. 1, 5–7.

4. Another way to put this point is to distinguish between "stated" reasons and "reasons in force," or between the press release and the reality.

5. Davidson (1980b and 1980c) argues that any explanation of human behavior that is intentional, or purposeful, will appeal to such values or purposes. Compare J. Pfeffer (1982), *Organizations*, Boston: Pitman Publishing, at Chapter 2. For a brilliant Davidsonian critique see E. Hartman (1988, in press), *Foundations of Organization Theory*, Boston: Ballinger Publishing.

6. It is not clear from Brown's remarks that he actually believes this claim. There is a note of remorse, and he sometimes writes as if he and AT&T were victims of forces beyond their control. The jury is still out, but it looks as if the Bell Operating Companies are substantially better off than AT&T.

7. The business press of the time abounds with speculation. For a sample, see the references in Chapter 1, note 10 *supra*.

8. Many who fervently defend the stockholder theory do not do so on moral grounds. There is a whole genre of literature on "agency theory" which is written as if the whole problem is a technical one, amoral in nature. Nevertheless, the stories in this genre are peppered with language such as "shirking," "control," and "monitoring costs." For an introduction to this literature see J. Pratt and R. Zeckhauser (eds.) (1985), *Principals and Agents: The Structure of Business*, Cambridge: Harvard Business School Press. For a recent critical analysis see J. Horrigan (1987), "The Ethics of the New Finance," *Journal of Business Ethics*, Vol. 6, No. 3, 97–110. There is growing evidence that agency theory will at last come under moral scrutiny. Recently a group of agency theorists and moral philosophers met under the sponsorship of Professor Norman Bowie's Center for the Study of Values, at the University of Delaware, for a two-day conference to explore the ethical implications of agency theory. A book is planned from the conference, to be edited by N. Bowie and E. Freeman, which will be the first major ethical assessment of agency theory.

9. Things are slightly more complex. There is a whole literature on the question "Why be moral?" Our view is that if the critic admits that "morality" and "moral reasons" have some meaning, in a nonrelativistic manner, then the critic is committed to the proposition that morality gives the best possible reasons for acting. We can claim this without making a specific claim about whose interests ultimately win the day. For a sample of this debate, see K. Baier (1958), *The Moral Point of View*, Ithaca: Cornell University Press. For a different view, from the existentialist perspective, see Barnes (1967).

10. See Chapter 3, note 12, *supra* on utilitarianism. There are many different forms of the disease.

11. In fact there were some pretty clear winners and losers in the case. Bendix stockholders did fairly well. Martin Marietta was saddled with a great deal of debt, and the jury is still out on Allied.

12. For the classic analysis of ethical egoism see J. Kalin (1968), "In Defense of Egoism," in D. Gauthier (ed.) (1968), *Morality and Rational Self Interest*, Englewood Cliffs, N.J.: Prentice Hall. For a summary of more recent developments see T. Machan (1985), "Recent Work in Ethical Egoism," in K. Lucey and T. Machan (eds.) (1985).

13. See Chapter 1, note 14 *supra*.

14. Peters openly admits that part of the reason for the emphasis on profits is that it is the only way executives will take his claims about people seriously. (Private communication.)

15. Autonomy is far from a clear-cut concept. See R. Nozick (1969), "Coercion," in S. Morgenbesser et al (eds.) (1969), *Philosophy, Science and Method*, New York: St. Martin's Press, at 440–472; and L. Haworth (1986), *Autonomy: An Essay in Philosophical Psychology and Ethics*, New Haven: Yale University Press.

16. See H. Barnes (1967).

17. For a brief history of the concept of "enterprise strategy" see Freeman (1984), at Chapter 4.

18. Of course, not much else will help either. Ethics starts with authenticity, not with deceit, bad faith, and self-deception. Such a company would have to admit to not adopting an ethical (descriptive) posture toward the world. Note that its actions would still be able to be judged from an ethical point of view. They would have no coherence.

19. These strategies, with the exception of the Personal Projects E-Strategy, were originally framed in Freeman (1984) for a different purpose. The approach there was completely a process approach, vulnerable to the criticisms we level at that genre in Chapter 7.

20. The best statement of this view is M. Friedman (1962), *Capitalism and Freedom*, Chicago: University of Chicago Press. For a critique of the philosophical foundations see E. Freeman and W. Evan (1987, in press).

21. There are two possible kinds of arguments here: property rights, and the utilitarian one. Only the property rights arguments are relevant to this E-strategy.

22. Of course, you can always tell a story like this. "Really the capital markets don't give the true value of long-run thinking. Some die-hard shareholders do see the value, and they will be rewarded in the end." Such stories approach the level of gospel and their believers have the same apostolic fervor. At some point *simplicity* rears its ugly head. Pragmatists, like us, know that we can believe literally any proposition to be true, but the question is which ones are useful. Simply put, if we convolute the story enough, we will be better off with another story. E. Freeman and W. Evan (1987, in press) is an attempt to show that the story of managerial capitalism is so convoluted as to be in dire need of repair.

23. For our view on corporate governance see E. Freeman, D. Gilbert, and C. Jacobson (1987).

24. See A. Berle and G. Means (1932), *The Modern Corporation and Private Property*, New York: Harcourt, Brace, Jovanovich. Also, see the June 1983 volume of *Journal of Law and Economics* for a reassessment of Berle and Means' argument by eminent scholars.

25. Since managers have an obligation to do what is in their own individual self-interest, according to egoism, they have an obligation to maximize their continued existence in the corporation. To force them to do otherwise would go against the truth of psychological egoism, the view that humans can do nothing other than act in their self-interest. For a much more sophisticated defense of egoism which does not depend on psychological egoism, see E. McClennen (1988), *Rationality and Dynamic Choice: Foundational Explorations*, St. Louis: Washington University, unpublished manuscript.

26. See note 8 *supra*.

27. O. Williamson (1964), *The Economics of Discretionary Behavior*, Englewood Cliffs, N.J.: Prentice Hall, is a brilliant example.

28. But why focus on these groups and not others? The answer is probably due to our beliefs about the importance of these groups. If corporations were more a part of communities and if we came to see relationships with suppliers as cooperative rather than competitive, then we would have a full-blown stakeholder theory.

29. Ask a group of managers, off the record, or a group of MBA students on the record, how many are motivated by making money for stockholders. The answer is always laughter. Add customers and employees and making money for stockholders, and the laughter is not so loud. This phenomenon is probably a function of Rawls' Aristotelian Principle: that all things being equal, human beings prefer complex tasks to simple ones. See Rawls (1971), at 426, for an analysis of the Aristotelian Principle, the view that "other things equal, human beings enjoy the exercise of their realized capacities (their innate or trained abilities) and this enjoyment increases the more the capacity is realized, or the greater the complexity."

30. It was an appalling revelation to discover that by using "stakeholder" as the unit of analysis, we could be more careful utilitarians. Indeed, it was the motivating force behind the joint effort in this book. See D. Gilbert (1987b) "Three Genres of Stakeholder Research," Lewisburg: Bucknell University, unpublished manuscript, and E. Freeman and D. Gilbert (1987), "Managing Stakeholder Relationships," in P. Sethi and C. Falbe (eds.) (1987),

Business and Public Policy: Dimensions of Conflict and Cooperation, Lexington: D. C. Heath.

31. It is often thought, especially by executives, that serving society is the essence of ethics, even at sacrifice to self. We desperately need a historical and cultural explosion of this myth.

32. In the management literature there has always been an emphasis on "public service." See, for example, C. Barnard (1938), where he argues that executives must set their private values aside and cultivate morality in other managers.

33. See the references in Chapter 1, note 10, *supra*.

34. For an account of the service crisis, see Kleinfeld (1982).

35. For a discussion of the difference of the wide and narrow definition of 'stakeholder' see Freeman (1984), at 54–56.

36. See R. Pascale and A. Athos (1981).

37. See Rawls (1971).

38. For accounts of Control Data under Norris see J. O'Toole (1985), *Vanguard Management: Redesigning the Corporate Future*, Garden City: Doubleday; B. von Sternberg (1986), "A Job At Control Data Has Lost Its Luster," *Minneapolis Star and Tribune*, March 24; R. Broderick (1985), "The Dream Turns Sour," *Corporate Report Minnesota*, Vol. 16, No. 9, 45–52, 56–59, 142–146; and "Bill Norris: The View From the 14th Floor," *Corporate Report*, Vol. 9, No. 1 (January 1978), 28–34.

39. For an account of the IBM story, see D. Kneale (1986b), "IBM Will Close Distribution Site To Trim Costs," *Wall Street Journal*, November 12.

40. We think that the paradigm of this strategy is in partnerships and small entrepreneurial firms. We explore this idea in more detail in Chapter 8.

41. The relevant question for researchers is how to describe the corporate behavior that they observe. Unfortunately there are many alternatives, making management theory a matter of choosing a narrative, rather than one of finding out the "truth" about organizations.

42. On a scale of advertising jingles to psychoanalysis, E-Strategy is more like psychoanalysis.

43. If Freud taught us anything, he showed us how what may appear to be obvious is rather less than straightforward. Everything that we believe in our hearts may not be the real reason for our behavior.

44. See D. Siebert (1984).

CHAPTER 5

1. See M. Friedman (1962).

2. See E. Freeman (1984) for one account of the history of this concept. We are grateful to Professors Lee Preston, University of Maryland, William Frederick, University of Pittsburgh, and Edwin Epstein, University of California, Berkeley, for many helpful conversations regarding the intellectual history of the corporate responsibility movement. We do not believe that they would agree with the account here, and certainly not the conclusions.

3. It is ironic that the very methods of moral philosophy which we have discussed in Chapter 3 were being highly refined by Harvard philosopher John Rawls during this time. There was evidently an uncrossable bridge in Cambridge.

4. William Frederick has outlined the history of this concept in a nice paper. See W. Frederick (1986), "Toward CSR-3: Why Ethical Analysis is Indispensible and Unavoidable in Corporate Affairs," *California Management Review*, Vol. 28, No. 2, 126–141.

5. The key statement of this view is Robert Ackerman (1975), *The Social Challenge to Business*, Cambridge: Harvard University Press.

6. For a definitive discussion of these issues, see the excellent annual volumes edited

by Lee Preston (ed.) (1979–1987), *Research in Corporate Responsibility and Social Policy*, Greenwich, Conn.: JAI Press, Volumes 1–9.

7. For examples, see the case studies in J. Mathews, K. Goodpaster, and L. Nash (eds.) (1985), *Policies and Persons*, New York: McGraw Hill, especially Part 3, at 169–374.

8. The work of Thomas Schelling is rich with insight here. See Schelling (1960), Schelling (1978), Schelling (1984), *Choice and Consequences*, Cambridge, Mass.: Harvard University Press.

9. Brams argues that biblical stories can be understood in game theoretic terms if one assumes that God, Adam and Eve, and Abraham, for example, acted rationally. Muzzio argues that we can explain Watergate by understanding the alternatives, outcomes, preferences and context of choices available to the "players" in such key situations as "The Saturday Night Massacre Game," "The Tapes Game," and "The Conspiracy Game." Schotter gives a game-theoretic account of the emergence and evolution of social institutions, making precise some of the insights of Hayek. Hardin argues that many generic social situations can be modeled as Prisoner's Dilemma games, and applies this particular approach to political situations such as disarmament. Finally, Axelrod has shown how stable, cooperative institutions can emerge from the narrow self-interests of players in repeated Prisoner's Dilemma games. The relevant references are S. Brams (1980), *Biblical Games*, Cambridge, Mass.: MIT Press; D. Muzzio (1982), *Watergate Games*, New York: New York University Press; A. Schotter (1981), *The Economics of Social Institutions*, New York: Cambridge University Press; R. Hardin (1982), *Collective Action*, Baltimore: Johns Hopkins University Press; R. Axelrod (1984), *The Evolution of Cooperation* New York: Basic Books; and F. Hayek (1948), *Individualism and Economic Order*, Chicago: University of Chicago Press.

10. While strategic analysts using game theory can make no predictive claims for their theories, they are empowered to offer explanatory claims. Schelling (1960) counsels theorists to expect such powerful explanatory utility, tempered by predictive weakness. The good news regarding explanation follows from game theory's conservative assumptions about human behavior. The weakly predictive aspect follows from the problematic game theory assumption that the players have knowledge of the game theory model. Some movement is already evident in the direction of rethinking corporate strategy in game-theoretic terms. J. McDonald (1975), *The Game of Business*, New York: Anchor Press, analyzes several classic business cases according to general game-theoretic principles. Porter's (1980), *Competitive Strategy*, New York: Free Press, analysis of market signaling is essentially game-theoretic, in the case of the long series of moves in the Kodak-Polaroid instant camera game. N. Fraser and K. Hipel (1980), "Metagame Analysis of the Poplar River Conflict," *Journal of Operational Research Society*, Vol. 31, No. 5, 377–385, use meta-game analysis to analyse a particular environmental conflict. Freeman (1984) argues that many interactions with activist stakeholder groups can be seen as a Prisoner's Dilemma game and argues that the current restructuring of the telecommunications industry can be seen as a bargaining game; see Freeman (1983).

11. The limited, perhaps nonexistent, role ascribed to values in strategy models can be traced to a more basic factor, namely, that *identifiable* strategic players have been overlooked as the activators in strategic situations. A brief history of the strategy field reveals the begrudging acceptance of a multiple–strategic-actor perspective. During the early days of the field, planners and researchers were concerned with forecasting the external environment (for three views see I. Ansoff (1977), D. Schendel and C. Hofer (1979), and Freeman (1984)). The early models took the environment as a relatively static entity, something which managers predicted and to which they responded. A firm gained competitive advantage, in this view, through superior predictive skill. During the mid-1960's and 1970's, researchers began to understand the importance of key constituents, or stakeholders, in the firm and developed methods of understanding their behavior in generic terms. The Business Intelligence Program, developed by SRI, International, is a case in point. Here, firms obtained generic information on the changing values of critical stakeholder groups. This information was reformulated and several scenarios were constructed that broadly defined the firm's environment. But in a turbulent and complex external environment, such generic information is still insufficient. To execute strategies under complex environmental conditions, strategic managers need detailed information on specific groups. Fulfillment of this need

dictates a move past identifying stakeholders, toward formulating and implementing key transactions with them. Further, the formalization of such interdependence only makes sense if the process is grounded in the preferences of stakeholders and firms for specific strategic outcomes. Hence, the stakeholder concept, bolstered by a game-theoretic approach, sets the stage for considering the interdependent nature of strategic management.

12. S. Foote (1984), "Corporate Responsibility In A Changing Legal Environment," *California Management Review*, Vol. 26, No. 3, 217–228. We are grateful to Professor Foote for several helpful conversations which have served to clarify a number of points throughout this chapter.

13. Foote (1984) at 222.

14. E. Gatewood and A. Carroll (1981), "The Anatomy of Corporate Social Response: The Rely, Firestone 500 and Pinto Cases," *Business Horizons*, Vol. 24, No. 5, 9–16.

15. R. Ackerman (1975).

16. S. Brams (1980) at 179–180, footnote 4.

17. In fact, it is a theorem of two-person game theory that any two-by-two game where one player has the first move is equivalent to a two-by-four game where the second player has a dominant strategy.

18. This is the Gatewood and Carroll interpretation.

19. Foote (1984).

20. Foote (1984).

CHAPTER 6

1. We borrow this term from C. McMahon (1981).

2. See J. Rawls (1971) at 158, on slavery.

3. C. McMahon (1981), at 260.

4. P. Samuelson (1970), *Economics*, New York: McGraw Hill.

5. C. McMahon (1981), at 255.

6. McMahon (1981), at 257.

7. McMahon (1981), at 259.

8. See J. Hirschliefer (1958), "On the Theory of Optimal Investment Decisions," *Journal of Political Economy*, Vol. 66, No. 4, 329–352.

9. The issue is complicated by arguments such as M. Friedman (1953), *Essays in Positive Economics*, Chicago: University of Chicago Press. He argues that "reality" of assumptions is less important than the "explanatory power" of the assumptions. Things are trickier still when we realize that assuming that economic actors are omniscient and automatically know prices explains perfect markets, yet it is logically impossible for humans to be omniscient. Such is the point of the distinction between humans and gods.

10. We follow L. Lomasky (1984), "Personal Projects as the Foundation for Basic Rights," *Social Philosophy and Policy*, Vol. 1, No. 2, 35–55, and his account of projects and persons. His more recent book, L. Lomasky (1987), *Persons, Rights and the Moral Community*, New York: Oxford University Press, is a more complete statement of his view. Unfortunately, it appeared after this book was already in production.

11. L. Lomasky (1984), at 52.

12. A. Gewirth (1984), "The Epistemology of Human Rights," *Social Philosophy and Policy*, Vol. 1, No. 2, 1–24.

13. L. Lomasky (1984), at 46.

14. F. Scherer (1980), *Industrial Market Structure and Economic Performance*, New York: Houghton Mifflin.

15. See R. Lipsey and K. Lancaster (1956), "The General Theory of the Second Best," *Review of Economic Studies*, Vol. 24, No. 1, 11–32.

16. How to make the best of a less than ideal market economy has been the avowed and elusive aim of American antitrust regulators for nearly a century. Grounded in the language of the law and the legacy of judicial precedent, and empowered with preemptive and *ex post* coercive sanctions, this overt public policy practice is administered in the name of effective, or workable, competition as the desired end.

Summarily, an individual actor's direct attempts to influence the operation of a market are proscribed by law. Monopolistic trade restraints violate Commandments 1, 3, 4, 5, 6, 8, 9, and 10 of the IMM. Unfair trade practices run counter to Commandments 1, 4, 5, 6, 7, 8, 9, and 10. And price discrimination clashes with Commandments 4, 5, 6, 7, 8, 9, and 10. In principle, therefore, federal antitrust policy represents an approach to preserving free enterprise conditions for market participants. In practice, almost from the very outset, the rights-protection implications in the statute have frequently been overridden by direct attempts to fix specific market problems, rather than to fix the market mechanism itself. As a result, the rights of individual actors to expect the protection of certain market characteristics fostering free enterprise have been subordinated to higher, utility concerns. At issue is the doctrine of the so-called Rule of Reason. This tradition in antitrust basically holds that the language of the law is not absolute, but, instead, is subject to reinterpretation on a case-by-case basis. Beginning with the 1911 Standard Oil ruling, the twin tests of intent of the parties and inherent effects have been employed by the Supreme Court to decide whether corrective action is necessary. If the intent or inherent effect is deemed worthy, no violation has occurred, all other things being equal. This amounts to saying that the precepts of the IMM are negotiable—a policy which might not instill much hope that workable competition lies around the corner. Nor is the de facto morality of antitrust policy convincing as a consistent guide for market behavior. Carried to an extreme, the Rule of Reason has enshrined such memorable reasoning as that delivered in the 1933 Appalachian Coal majority opinion (from Breit and Elzinga):

> The mere fact that the parties to an agreement eliminate competition between themselves is not enough to condemn it. . . .

Use of legal channels for attempting second-best solutions is replete with other problems. Among them is the implication that a weakened moral resolve is permissible, given the nominal presence of the law on a particular issue. The inherent lags in, and costs attendant to, an institution such as antitrust complicates matters. In conclusion on this point, the seeming inadequacy of one second-best approach stems from a fundamental aversion on the parts of its practitioners to permitting the market to operate freely. Any result approximating Pareto optimality seems unlikely. If a purported second-best solution administered from outside the marketplace is subject to the dilution that antitrust displays, what can be said for an internally generated solution?

17. For a complete analysis of portfolio models, including their strengths and weaknesses, see D. Gilbert, E. Hartman, J. Mauriel, and E. Freeman (1988, in press). Also see P. Haspelagh (1982), "Portfolio Planning: Uses and Limits," *Harvard Business Review*, Vol. 60, No. 1, 58–73; and Y. Wind and V. Mahajan (1981), "Designing Product and Business Portfolios," *Harvard Business Review*, Vol. 59, No. 1, 155–165. There is much more to be said regarding these models. Our goal is not to tell the whole story here, but rather to sketch the plot so that we can analyze the main characters.

18. Things are slightly more complicated. There are two main kinds of risk, "systematic" and "unsystematic." You can diversify away the systematic risk, by selecting businesses which balance each other in terms of the normal business cycle, in a manner similar to diversifying a stock portfolio by buying securities in various sectors of the economy. Such is the well known theory of "betas" and the like. There is a great deal of debate between finance theorists and strategy scholars about whether unsystematic risk can be managed. See R. Bettis (1983), "Modern Financial Theory, Corporate Strategy and Public Policy: Three Conundrums," *Academy of Management Review*, Vol. 8, No. 3, 406–415; T. Naylor and F. Tapon (1982), "The Capital Asset Pricing Model: An Evaluation of its Potential as a Strategic Planning Tool," *Management Science*, Vol. 28, No. 10, 1166–1173; and C. Woo (1984), "An Empirical Test of Value-Based Planning Models and Implications," *Management Science*, Vol. 30, No. 9, 1031–1050.

19. For an analysis of the usefulness of the concept of Strategic Business Unit (SBU)

as developed by General Electric and McKinsey see D. Gilbert, E. Hartman, J. Mauriel, and E. Freeman (1988, in press).

20. The real world rarely accommodates a perfect model, so that in reality this is a major problem. Many firms use portfolio theory even though they are organized quite differently. The difficulty is that one cannot tell if the right strategy has been followed or if the wrong allocation is responsible for the results.

21. See M. Porter (1980), and M. Porter (1985), *Competitive Advantage*, New York: Free Press, and the references to more technical literature on which these books are based.

CHAPTER 7

1. For a more comprehensive interpretation and critique of "strategy through process," see D. Gilbert (1987a). This chapter has been developed, in part, around the arguments made in E. Freeman and D. Gilbert (1986) (1985); D. Gilbert and E. Freeman (1985) "Flight from Meaning: A Critical Interpretation of Management Classics," unpublished manuscript; and, E. Freeman, D. Gilbert and E. Hartman (1988, in press). The designation "strategic process" is intended to encompass such common analytical concepts as strategy formulation, strategy implementation, and strategic planning. D. Schendel and C. Hofer (1979), and E. Freeman and P. Lorange (1985), "Theory Building in Strategic Management," in R. Lamb and P. Srivastava (eds.) (1985), *Advances in Strategic Management*, Volume 3, Greenwich, Conn.: JAI Press, 9–38, give accounts of how to sort through these concepts. Also see Andrews (1980), at viii-ix, on this subject. The argument in this chapter is developed around the strategic process models proposed by K. Andrews (1980), P. Lorange (1980), *Corporate Planning: An Executive Viewpoint*, Englewood Cliffs, N.J.: Prentice Hall; P. Lorange and R. Vancil (1976), "How to Design a Strategic Planning System," *Harvard Business Review*, Vol. 54, No. 5, 75–88; R. Vancil and P. Lorange (1975), "Strategic Planning in Diversified Companies," *Harvard Business Review*, Vol. 53, No. 1, 81–93; H. Mintzberg (1973), "Strategy Making in Three Modes," *California Management Review*, Vol. 16, No. 2, 44–53; H. Mintzberg (1979), "Organizational Power and Goals: A Skeletal Theory," in D. Schendel and C. Hofer (eds.) (1979); H. Mintzberg (1980), *The Nature of Managerial Work*, Englewood Cliffs, N.J.: Prentice Hall; H. Mintzberg (1983), *Power In and Around Organizations*, Englewood Cliffs, N.J.: Prentice Hall; B. Quinn (1980), *Strategies for Change: Logical Incrementalism*, Homewood, Ill.: R. D. Irwin; and D. Schendel and C. Hofer (1979).

2. For one brief survey of these models see J. Bryson, E. Freeman and W. Roering (1986), "Strategic Planning in the Public Sector: Approaches and Directions," in B. Checkoway (ed.) (1986), *Strategic Perspectives on Planning Practice*, Lexington: D. C. Heath, 65–85.

3. See L. Fahey and K. Christensen (1986), "Evaluating the Research on Strategy Content," *Journal of Management*, Vol. 12, No. 2, 167–183, for an account that divides "strategic management" into "process" and "content" genres. Our argument covers both genres, since both "process" and "content" are couched in the same view of the firm as a decision-making ("process") structure wherein the matches between the firm and its environment are given certain names ("content"). See Gilbert (1987a) for a fuller articulation of this conception of the firm.

4. We have already addressed, in Chapter 5, a particular manifestation of this assumption: the general rule "practice corporate social responsiveness." The field's contentment with treating values as general forces, but not action-causing features of persons, stems from a long debate about whether or not organizations have goals a priori. Taking the cue from the argument made by R. Cyert and J. March (1963), *A Behavioral Theory of the Firm*, Englewood Cliffs, N.J.: Prentice Hall, that organizational goals are residual byproducts of internal political processes, strategic process theorists have come to eschew a direct focus on goals, or values. Instead, they have argued that power (see Mintzberg (1983)) or rational processes (see Lorange (1980) for a model statement) are more manipulable concepts. Quinn (1980), at 181, provides a vivid statement in this regard:

> Since there is no objectively right answer concerning the proper ultimate ends for an organization, sensible practice dictates giving top priority to the *processes* through which such choices are made.

In short, conventional wisdom in the model proposes that values are "just there." O. Williamson (1975), *Markets and Hierarchies*, New York: Free Press, chooses the apt metaphor of "atmosphere" to make this very point.

5. This reflects the classic positivist justification for social sciences in general and, in particular, the scientific study of management and organization. Strategic process theorists, among others, have long looked to H. Simon (1945), *Administrative Behavior*, New York: Free Press, at 253 for instance for support in this regard:

An administrative science . . . is concerned purely with factual statements. There is no place for ethical assertions in the body of a science.

Moreover, according to Simon (1945), at 49:

Strictly speaking, it is not the decision itself which is evaluated, but the purely factual relationship that is asserted between the decision and its aim.

6. Andrews (1980), at viii.

7. Andrews (1980) at 46. Despite this central reference to "purpose," Andrews honors Simon's assertion (see note 5, *supra*) and never examines the purpose per se, but rather the processes of formulating any purpose.

8. Chandler (1962), at 13, is generally credited with making this distinction, although Barnard (1938), at 215, made much the same case.

9. We will use the terms "firm" and "organization" interchangeably. In fact, we believe that the common practice of treating these as separate entities is one manifestation of a persistent belief that values can only be meaningfully ascribed at a very broad level of discussion. In other words, firms ("in the interests of stockholders") are often distinguished from, for example, government agencies ("in the interests of all interest groups") on such a basis. If we see values as reasons for an individual's actions, the distinction between "firm" and "organization" becomes meaningless.

10. See Gilbert (1987a) for a more comprehensive account.

11. Andrews (1980), at 170.

12. We deliberately specify only two actors to show how the strategic process theorist looks at persons as occupants of two basic kinds of organizational roles: strategic managers and all others. Ben is "ordinary" insofar as his role is expendable, and he is replaceable in his role, in the structure.

13. We introduce this lengthy analysis with a quote from D. Katz and R. Kahn (1966), *The Social Psychology of Organization*, New York: John Wiley, at 34:

Much of the energy of organizations must be fed into devices of control to reduce the variability of human behavior and to produce stable patterns of activity.

14. Lorange (1980), at 281, equivocates about how analysts and managers can ever determine the effectiveness of a process per se. Note that we do not deny process as a necessary condition in a general sense, but rather we take issue with, first, the argument that process is a cause of human action and, second, that it is a sufficient condition for justifying collective effort.

15. For a particularly axiomatic account of the limitations in human action, see A. Van de Ven (1986), "Central Problems in the Management of Innovation," *Management Science*, Vol. 32, No. 5, 590–607.

16. Lorange and Quinn both argue that the strategic decision-making process is something of an inner sanctum for senior management. Lorange expressly doubts the usefulness of including functional managers, and Quinn (1980), at 67–69, counsels CEO's to keep others in the dark about their intentions. For a contrary view, see T. Peters (1985), "'Backroom' folks need infomation," *Minneapolis Star & Tribune*, March 19.

17. Andrews (1980), at 152, is unequivocal about the importance of structuring persons' actions, asserting that:

Put another way, behavior is the outcome of *processes* of measurement, evaluation, motivation, and control.

To this end at 132:

Man-made and natural organizational *systems* and *processes* are available to influence individual development and perfomance.

Quinn (1980), at 68, argues that effective strategic managers incrementally structure their subordinates' behaviors, lest overload of this kind occur:

Oddly enough, when lower levels demand clearer goals, they are often unwittingly working against their own desire for increased freedom and personal growth.

Lorange (1980), at 12, asserts that:

. . . the overriding purpose of corporate planning . . . [is] to assist a company's line management to carry out its strategic decision-making tasks.

If properly done, at 63:

. . . the planning process should . . . facilitate innovative and creative managerial behavior.

Schendel and Hofer (1979), at 53, are explicit about the importance of structuring decision processes:

. . . goals do not just arise out of thin air. They must have some source if they are to motivate the kind of fundamental action associated with strategy. It is, therefore, fair to ask whether there is some organizational process or processes that might be called goal formulation processes. . . .

Mintzberg (1983), at 7, deals with structure in a different way, arguing that power structures are causal forces:

In other words, goals do not have lives of their own, independent of actions. Hence, we are safer talking about power than about goals

. . . we focus on those behaviors that are dictated by roles. (p. 30)

It is only through studying power as manifested in actual decisions and actions that we come to understand goals. (p. 7)

18. To Andrews (1980), at 44, values constrain strategic decision-making processes, because values are distinct from more rational entities:

It is entirely possible that a strategy may reflect in an exaggerated fashion the values rather than the reasoned decisions of responsible managers . . .

Still, he advises us, at 79, to live with this "problem":

We should in all realism admit that the personal desires, aspirations, and needs of the senior managers of a company actually do play an influential role in the determination of strategy.

Quinn (1980), at 17, concurs with the inevitability of this phenomenon:

Ultimately top management—or the "dominant coalition" running the enterprise— also implements in its major decisions a set of goals representing its own personal and interpersonal trade-offs among many competing objectives.

But he urges managers, at 69, to tread with care in revealing their values too soon.

Lorange (1980), at 37, concurs on the general subject of goals:

The objectives-setting stage provides a vehicle for the CEO and the division managers to be explicit about their aspirations for the organization. . . . Undoubtedly, we are dealing here with important constraints in terms of setting realistic aspirations for strategic change.

Schendel and Hofer (1979), at 16, are sufficiently unsettled by the mystery of values that they analytically separate goal formulation processes from strategy formulation processes:

. . . because personal values and social mores are almost always much more influential in goal formulation than in strategy formulation . . .

Mintzberg (1983), at 255, sees "All goals as constraints. . . ."

19. Katz and Kahn (1966), at 57, treat this multiplicity of roles as if it were an unpardonable sin:

Since the individual is involved in a social system with only a part of himself, he might readily behave less as a member of any given organization and more in terms of some compromise. . . . There must be a clarity of demands and constraints imposed upon him so that he will give unto Caesar what is Caesar's.

Barnard (1938), at 88, asserted that this "split personality" problem was unavoidable:

. . . Every participant in an organization may be regarded as having a dual personality—an organizational personality and an individual personality.

20. By the definition in Freeman (1984), Lynn is a "stakeholder" of Bison River, even though she is not an agent for the company. This example shows how the designation "stakeholder" gives a more general account than "organizational member."

21. See Gilbert (1987a) for a definition of "self-sufficient firm" and an analysis of the concept's shortcomings.

With regard to organizational "being," Andrews (1980), at 133, seeks to generate a strategy which can "animate structure":

> . . . [in] a thriving company—itself a living system . . .

that is separate from persons, at 27:

> Most crucially, where corporate [*sic*] capability leads, executives do not always want to go.

but personlike at 63:

> But just as it is essential, though difficult, that a maturing person achieve reasonable self-awareness, so an organization can identify approximately its central strengths and critical vulnerability.

Quinn (1980), at 164, as well, describes the organization as a kind of entity:

> Consequently, the essence of strategy . . . is to *build a posture* that is so strong (and potentially flexible) in selective ways that the organization can achieve its goals despite the unforeseeable ways external forces may actually interact when the time comes.

Lorange (1980), at 54–55, like Andrews and Quinn, seeks to breathe life into an organization:

> The model specifies a logical sequence of steps that should be carried out in order to make the process come alive within a corporation.

Schendel and Hofer (1979), at 17, describe the strategic management problem as a matter of:

> . . . the reconciliation of social/political processes used in implementation with analytical/rational processes used in strategy formulation and evaluation . . .

within a context where, at 63:

> . . . yet, organizations act and indeed form, and with a purpose. Can it not be said then that organizations may not have goals . . .?

Mintzberg (1983), at 22, likewise, sees the organization as the relevant level of analysis for his argument:

> It is built on the premise that organizational behavior is a power game in which various players, called *influencers*, seek to control the organization's decisions and actions. . . . Thus, to understand the behavior of the organization, it is necessary to understand which influencers are present, what needs each seeks to fulfill in the organization, and how each is able to exercise power to fulfill them.

In the midst of this, he asserts that at 29:

> . . . there is an eleventh actor in the organizational power system, one that is technically inanimate but in fact shows every indication of having a life of its own, namely the *ideology* of the organization . . .

22. Porter (1985), for example, is unwilling to make this extension. The buyer situated at the other end of his "value chain" concept is merely an abstraction serving as an indicator for the firm.

23. Simon (1945), at 102.

24. See Lorange (1980), Mintzberg (1983), and Schendel and Hofer (1979) for discussions of "organizational goals."

25. See A. Van de Ven (1980), "Problem Solving, Planning, and Innovation, Part II, Speculations for Theory and Practice," *Human Relations*, Vol. 33, No. 10, 757–779, which argues that when collective problem solving is subject to complex and turbulent conditions, the parties involved should concentrate upon following a specified process.

Andrews (1980), at 109, states the First Hypothesis in this way:

> The successful implementation of strategy requires that executives shape to the peculiar needs of their strategy the formal structure of their organization, its informal relationships, and the processes of motivation and control which provide incentives and measure results.

That strategy formulation is itself a *process of organization*, rather than the masterly conception of a single mind, must finally become clear.

Quinn (1980), at 145, puts the First Hypothesis this way:

> Constantly integrating the simultaneous incremental processes of strategy formulation and implementation is the central art of effective strategic management.

Lorange (1980), at 46, says this:

> Unless there is a clear and logical relationship between objectives setting, strategic

programming, and budgeting, the decision-making purpose which should be the aim of the corporate planning activity will be sacrificed.

Schendel and Hofer (1979), at 17, claim that:

. . . the implementation task is inherently behavioral in nature. . .an administrative task. . . .

Finally, Mintzberg (1980), at 152, approaches the First Hypothesis with this definition of strategy:

. . . the reprogramming of the system by which important organizational decisions are made and interrelated, that is, strategy-making.

26. Both Andrews (1980) and D. Seibert (1984), seem to believe that, when it comes to thinking about one's values, enough is enough. Seibert asserts, at 36, that self-reflection is a sign of weakness in executives.

The imperative of reigning values appears again and again in Andrews' argument. He first establishes the priority of interests, at 17:

The perspective demanded for successful organizational leaders embraces both the *primacy* of organizational goals and the *validity* of individual goals. (emphasis added)

Once a strategy is set, the constraint imperative is set in motion, at 27:

If purpose is detemined, then the resources of a company can be mobilized to accomplish it. . . . The organizational processes of performance measurement, compensation, management development . . . must be directed toward the kind of behavior required by organizational purpose.

toward this end, at 120:

To keep individual purposes and needs as well as departmental substrategies consistent with corporate strategy . . .

lest this occur, at 85:

You should obviously not warp your recommended strategy . . . in order to adjust it to the personal values you hold. . . .

Quinn (1980), at 90, puts the Second Hypothesis this way:

Effective goal processes . . . obtain maximum identity between people's personal goals and their role goals.

Quinn, at 119, urges managers to:

. . . coopt or neutralize serious opposition, if necessary. . . .

Lorange (1980) at 53 asserts that:

. . . our approach is that the incentives that are under the discretion of the company should be administered in such a way that they *ameliorate* some of the [manager's] goal incongruence. . . . (emphasis added)

In this way, at 37:

. . . planning should . . . attempt to improve lackluster aspirations.

Schendel and Hofer (1970), at 54, state the Second Hypothesis in this form:

The essence of the problem that any goal formulation process must solve is making sense out of a collection of individual members' personal goals, as well as those goals of the parties or actors that can influence the organization. Some consistency among these goals is necessary before effective behavior can result.

Mintzberg (1979), at 63, argues that:

. . . social norms impinge on the internal influencers . . .

and in Mintzberg (1983), at 66:

Social norms are vague and unenforceable. . . .

The Second Hypothesis follows in this form in Mintzberg (1980), at 95:

The manager must act as the focus for organizational values. Influencers exert pressures on him to have the organization serve their ends. The manager must interpret the values of each influencer, combine all these to determine the true power system, and then infom his subordinates of this in the form of organizational preferences to guide them in their decision-making.

27. For a discussion of the fallacy in this distinction, see Rorty (1984b).

28. See Freeman, Gilbert, and Hartman (1988, in press) for an analysis of "value free" versions of strategic management models.

Andrews (1980), at 64–65, urges that persons understand their values as transparent:

Essential to *effective membership* in an organization is the capacity as an individual to *see*

78. "Ribi's Chairman Is Killed in a Plane Crash in Idaho," *The Wall Street Journal,* September 3.

79. J. Marcotty (1986), "Fridley Firm Sold; New Owner Fires Workers, Asks Them Back," *Minneapolis Star & Tribune,* September 4.

80. D. Hage (1986a), "Employers' 'Right' to Lock Workers Out Faces Test," *Minneapolis Star & Tribune,* June 1.

81. D. Machalaba (1986a), "Union Pacific to Restructure Certain Assets," *The Wall Street Journal,* June 12.

82. S. Gross (1986), "Sperry's New Owner Plans to Cut 9,600 Jobs," *Minneapolis Star & Tribune,* October 9.

83. Simon (1945), at 45–49.

84. Andrews (1980), at 129, makes a major point of "simplicity": Simplicity is the essence of good art; a conception of strategy brings simplicity to complex organizations.

85. See Andrews (1980), at 54, and Barnard (1938), at 79, for example.

86. Andrews (1980) and Quinn (1980) repeatedly claim that a "true" or "real" strategy exists for a firm, if opportunities are properly scanned and competencies matched to the best product or market decision.

87. See Gilbert (1987a) for an argument that it is advantageous to think about strategy "through the means of convention."

88. We are not sure what it means to say that an organization has values. If it is difficult to know one's own values and more difficult to know another's, as Genie presumes, how is the stipulation that "organizations have values" any more meaningful?

89. We selected the account in Tunstall (1985), at 13, precisely to show this argument in action:

... the largest corporation in the world completed the formidable assignment of managing its own divestiture.

[The process worked] ... by means of the organizational hierarchy. (p. 59)

90. See Freeman, Gilbert, and Hartman (1988, in press) for a critique of this argument.

91. This wording is taken directly from Rawls (1971), at 27, assessment of utilitarianism:

Utilitarianism does not take seriously the distinctions between persons.

The strategic process model bears telltale signs of a classic utilitarian argument: indistinct and interchangeable persons led by some visible hand to produce the greater net good for some institution. In the case of the strategic process model, the visible hand is the process structure and the institution is the organization.

92. As evidence of this, in note Andrews (1980), where matters of ethics come last. Moreover, at 22, he makes reference to "social responsibility *substrategies*" (emphasis added). Lorange (1980) and Quinn (1980) ignore the matter of ethics altogether.

93. Andrews (1980), at 22, provides an example of what a strategy statement should "say." There are, however, no references to any human beings in that statement.

94. Barnard (1938), at 283, accepts the "dual personality" problem as given and then asks executives to make strategic decisions "... derived largely from within themselves." This seems to imply a third personality.

95. For one example, see Gilbert (1987a).

96. D. Kneale (1986b), "IBM Will Close Distribution Site to Trim Costs," *The Wall Street Journal,* November 12.

97. Andrews (1980), at 99–100.

98. See, for example, R. Golembiewski (1965), *Men, Management and Morality: Toward a New Organizational Ethic,* New York: McGraw Hill.

99. R. Winter (1987), "Firestone's Restructuring Bid Works Well—To a Point," *The Wall Street Journal,* January 14.

CHAPTER 8

1. Definitions cannot be right or wrong. They are part of a narrative, and narratives have uses that allow us to cope with the world better or less well. This is true even in science.

2. Indeed communication arises because of shared experiences and the need to coordinate if basic projects are to be realized. For a definitive account of the way that language arises through convention, see D. Lewis (1969), *Convention*, Cambridge: Harvard University Press.

3. See S. Fish (1980), R. Rorty (1983), and the Spring–Summer 1986 issue of *Salmagundi* on the role of intellectual life in society.

4. James Buchanan (1986), "An Attitude of Liberty," address given to the George Mason University Liberty Fund Conference, Fairfax, July. We are grateful to participants at this conference for helping us to clarify some of our ideas on liberty.

5. We have said little about virtue in this book. Much recent work in moral philosophy is aimed at rehabilitating the idea, but at the expense of rights. We believe such a defense rests on a mistake. Rights make civilized society possible. Only within a framework of rights can *individuals* be virtuous.

6. This is a complicated matter that has worried philosophers since Kant. Our account is based on A. McIntyre (1981), *After Virtue*, Notre Dame, Ind.: University of Notre Dame Press, at chapter 1; J. Lomasky (1984); and O. O'Neill (1985), "Between Consenting Adults," *Philosophy and Public Affairs*, Vol. 14, No. 3, 252–277.

7. Of course, this is an understatement. The entire field of medical ethics is preoccupied with this issue.

8. See A. McIntyre (1981). For the best available analysis of coercion see R. Nozick (1969).

9. Thus, we follow Thomas Schelling in adopting a solution to the bargaining problem that is the corporation by focusing on "focal points" rather than optimality conditions. See Schelling (1960).

10. We follow the interpretation in Rorty (1983), and are happy to be admitted to the "postmodern bourgeois liberal" camp. We just think that such a narrative will look a lot like a modern-day Jeffersonian narrative.

11. See E. Freeman and W. Evan (1987, in press).

12. We have saved a careful and scholarly development of a similar concept of corporate strategy for another occasion. For a related statement that goes well beyond the text see Gilbert (1987a).

13. For years until his death in 1986, Gomberg taught a course on "managerial philosophy" at Wharton, influencing, more or less, generations of students. As a former labor union leader, he had an extremely simple and direct view of motivation research with which we are in large agreement.

14. See M. Kets de Vries (1980), *Organizational Paradoxes: Clinical Approaches to Management*, London: Tavistock Publications.

15. See J. Pfeffer (1981), *Power in Organizations*, Boston: Pitman Publishing, and J. Kotter (1979), *Power in Management*, New York: AMACOM.

16. See C. Barnard (1938).

17. See E. Freeman and W. Evan (1987, in press).

Bibliography ★ ★ ★ ★ ★ ★ ★ ★ ★

ACKERMAN, R. (1975), *The Social Challenge to Business*, Cambridge, Mass.: Harvard University Press.

"A. H. Robins Co. and the Dalkon Shield," Charlottesville, Va.: The Darden School Case Studies, UVA E-049.

ALLISON, G. (1970), *The Essence of Decision*, Boston: Little Brown.

ANDERS, G. (1982), "First Boston Enjoys Surge As Speculators Expect Big Earnings Gain from Fee as Bendix Advisor," *The Wall Street Journal*, Sept. 24, 1982.

ANDREWS, K. (1980), *The Concept of Corporate Strategy*, 2nd ed., Homewood, Ill.: R. D. Irwin.

ANSOFF, I. (1977), "The State of Practice in Planning Systems," *Sloan Management Review*, Vol. 18, No. 2, pp. 1–28.

ARROW, K., and F. HAHN (1971), *General Equilibrium Analysis*, San Francisco: Holden-Day.

AXELROD, R. (1984), *The Evolution of Cooperation*, New York: Basic Books.

BAIER, K. (1958), *The Moral Point of View*, Ithaca, N.Y.: Cornell University Press.

BAIER, K. (1984), "Duties to One's Employer," in T. Regan (ed.), *Just Business*, New York: Random House, pp. 60–99.

BERNARD, C. (1938), *The Function of the Executive*, Cambridge, Mass.: Harvard University Press.

BARNES, H. (1967), *An Existentialist Ethics*, Chicago: University of Chicago Press.

BARNES, P. (1986), "CBS is Continuing to Cut Staff, Focus on Core Businesses," *The Wall Street Journal*, Sept. 22, 1986.

BENNETT, A., and D. SEASE (1986), "To Reduce Their Costs, Big Companies Lay Off White-Collar Workers," *The Wall Street Journal*, May 22, 1986.

BENNETT, R. (1987), "Winning Friends for Texaco When It Needs Them Most," *The New York Times*, Feb. 22, 1987, Section 3.

BERLE, A. and G. MEANS (1932), *Modern Corporation and Private Property*, New York: Harcourt Brace Jovanovich.

BETTS, R. (1983), "Modern Financial Theory, Corporate Strategy and Public Policy: Three Conundrums," Academy of Management Review, Vol. 8, No. 3, pp. 406–415.

"Bill Norris: The View from the 14th Floor," Corporate Report, Vol. 9, No. 1 (January 1978), pp. 28–34.

BOWIE, N. (1982), Business Ethics, Englewood Cliffs, N.J., Prentice-Hall.

BRAMS, S. (1980), Biblical Games, Cambridge, Mass.: MIT Press.

BRANDT, R. (1959), Ethical Theory, Englewood Cliffs, N.J., Prentice-Hall.

BREIT, W. and K. ELZINGA (1982), The Anti Trust Casebook, New York: The Dryden Press.

BRODERICK, R. (1985), "The Dream Turns Sour," Corporate Report Minnesota, Vol. 16, No. 9, pp. 45–52, 56–59, and 142–146.

BRODEUR, P. (1985), Outrageous Misconduct: The Asbestos Industry on Trial, New York: Pantheon.

BROWN, C. (1983), "Recasting the Bell System," Columbia Journal of World Business, Vol. 18, No. 1, pp. 5–7.

BRYSON, J., E. FREEMAN, and W. ROERING (1986), "Strategic Planning in the Public Sector: Approaches and Directions," in B. Checkoway (ed.), Strategic Perspectives on Planning Practice, Lexington, Mass.: D.C. Heath, 1986, pp. 65–85.

BUCHANAN, J. (1986), "An Attitude of Liberty," address given to the George Mason University Liberty Fund Conference, Fairfax, Va., July 1986.

CAREY, S. (1986), "Lufthansa Jettisons Bureaucratic Baggage," The Wall Street Journal, Sept. 30, 1986.

CAREY, W. (1986a), "People Express is a Victim of Its Fast Growth," The Wall Street Journal, June 25, 1986.

CAREY, W. (1986b), "Struggling to Survive, People Express Alters Operations and Image," The Wall Street Journal, July 31, 1986.

CAREY, W., and T. AGINS (1985), "People Express Merger Might Cause Problems," The Wall Street Journal, Oct. 14, 1986.

CAVANAUGH, G. (1982), American Business Values, Englewood Cliffs, N.J.: Prentice-Hall.

CHANDLER, A. (1962), Strategy and Structure, Boston: MIT Press.

CHANDLER, A. (1977), The Visible Hand, Cambridge, Mass.: Harvard University Press.

CHAKAN, R., and E. FREEMAN (1980), "Planning for the Business Environment of the 1980s," Journal of Business Strategy, Vol. 1, No. 2, pp. 9–19.

CHARLIER, M. (1986), "Hormel and Union Are Locked in Battle That Carries High Stakes for Both Sides," The Wall Street Journal, Jan. 23, 1986.

CHEUNG, S. (1983), "The Contractual Nature of the Firm," Journal of Law and Economics, Vol. 26, pp. 1–21.

COETZEE, J. (1977), In the Heart of the Country, London: Secker & Warburg.

COETZEE, J. (1982), Waiting for the Barbarians, New York: Penguin.

COLL, S. (1986), The Deal of the Century: The Breakup of AT&T, New York: Atheneum.

CRAWFORD, B., and S. LENWAY (1985), "Decision Modes and International Regime Changes: Western Collaboration on East-West Trade," World Politics, Vol. 37, No. 3, pp. 375–402.

Critical Inquiry, Vol. 12, No. 3, (spring 1986).

CYERT, R., and J. MARCH (1963), A Behavioral Theory of the Firm, Englewood Cliffs, N.J.: Prentice-Hall.

DAVIDSON, D. (1980a), "Actions, Reasons and Causes," in Essays in Action and Events, New York: Oxford University Press, 1980, pp. 3–19.

DAVIDSON, D. (1980b), "How Is Weakness of the Will Possible," in Essays on Actions and Events, New York: Oxford University Press, 1980, pp. 21–42.

DAVIDSON, D. (1980c), "Intending," in Essays on Actions and Events, New York: Oxford University Press, 1980, pp. 83–102.

DAVIDSON, D. (1980d), "Mental Events," in Essays on Action and Events, New York: Oxford University Press, 1980, pp. 207–227

DAVIDSON, D. (1984), "On the Very Idea of a Conceptual Scheme," in Inquiries into

Truth and Interpretation, New York: Oxford University Press, 1984, pp. 183–198.

DAVIS, B. (1986), "FCC Chairman Calls for Deregulating Some Local Phone Firms in 3-Year Test," The Wall Street Journal, Oct. 15, 1986.

DEAL, T., and A. KENNEDY (1982), Corporate Culture, Reading, Mass: Addison-Wesley.

DERTHICK, M., and P. QUICK (1985), The Politics of Deregulation, Washington, D.C.: The Brookings Institution.

DONAGAN, A. (1977), The Theory of Morality, Chicago: University of Chicago Press.

DWORKIN, R. (1980), Taking Rights Seriously, Cambridge, Mass.: Harvard University Press.

ELSTER, J. (1983), Explaining Technical Change, New York: Cambridge University Press.

EVAN, W. (1966), "An Organization Set Model of Interorganizational Relations," in M. Tuite, M. Radnor, and R. Chisholm (eds.), Interorganizational Decision Making, Chicago: Aldine, 1966, pp. 181–200.

EVANS, D. (ed.) (1983), Breaking Up Bell: Essays on Industrial Organization and Regulation, Amsterdam: North-Holland.

FAHEY, L., and K. CHRISTENSEN (1986), "Evaluating the Research on Strategy Content," Journal of Management, Vol. 12, No. 2, pp. 167–183.

FISH, S. (1980), Is There a Text in This Class? Cambridge, Mass.: Harvard University Press.

FISH, S. (1984), "AntiProfessionalism," New Literary History, Vol. 16, No. 1, pp. 89–108.

FOOT, P. (1982), "Moral Relativism," in J. Mieland and M. Kraus (eds.), Relativism: Cognitive and Moral, Notre Dame, Ind.: University of Notre Dame Press, 1982, pp. 152–166.

FOOTE, S. (1984), "Corporate Responsibility in a Changing Legal Environment," California Management Review Vol. 26, No. 3, pp. 217–228.

"Ford Worker Fired over Foreign-Car Parking Dispute," Minneapolis Star & Trib-une, Aug. 1, 1985.

"The 4 Horsemen: Did Main Characters in Big Takeover Saga Let Egos Sway Them?" The Wall Street Journal, Sept. 24, 1982.

FRASER, N., and K. HIPEL (1980), "Metagame Analysis of the Poplar River Conflict," Journal of Operational Research Society, Vol. 31, No. 5, pp. 377–385.

FREDERICK, W. (1986), "Toward CSR-3: Why Ethical Analysis is Indispensible and Unavoidable in Corporate Affairs," California Management Review, Vol. 28, No. 2, pp. 126–141.

FREEMAN, E. (1983), "Managing the Strategic Challenge in Telecommunications," Columbia Journal of World Business, Vol. 18, No. 1, pp. 8–18.

FREEMAN, E. (1984), Strategic Management: A Stakeholder Approach, Boston: Pitman.

FREEMAN, E. (1987), "Review of Williamson's The Economic Institution of Capitalism," Academy of Management Review, Vol 12, No. 2, pp. 385–387.

FREEMAN, E., and D. GILBERT (1986), "Orwell and Organizations," unpublished manuscript.

FREEMAN, E., and D. GILBERT (1987), "Managing Stakeholder Relationships," in P. Sethi and C. Falbe (eds.), Business and Public Policy: Dimensions of Conflict and Cooperation, Lexington, Mass.: D.C. Heath, 1987.

FREEMAN, E., and P. LORANGE (1985), "Theory Building in Strategic Management," in R. Lamb and P. Srivastava (eds.), Advances in Strategic Management, Vol. 3, Greenwich, Conn.: JAI Press, pp. 9–38.

FREEMAN, E., and W. EVAN (1987), "Corporate Governance: A Stakeholder View," unpublished manuscript.

FREEMAN, E., and W. EVAN (1987, in press), "Stakeholder Management and the Modern Corporation: Kantian Capitalism," in T. Beauchamp and N. Bowie (eds.), Ethical Theory and Business, 3rd ed. Englewood Cliffs, N.J.: Prentice-Hall.

FREEMAN, E., D. GILBERT, and E. HARTMAN (1988a, in press), "Values and the Foundations of Strategic Management," Journal of Business Ethics.

FREEMAN, E., D. GILBERT, and C. JACOBSON (1987) "The Ethics of Greenmail," *Journal of Business Ethics* Vol. 6, No. 3, pp. 165–178.

FRENCH, P. (1984), *Collective and Corporate Responsibility*, New York: Columbia University Press.

FRIEDMAN, M. (1953), *Essays in Positive Economics*, Chicago: University of Chicago Press.

FRIEDMAN, M. (1962), *Capitalism and Freedom*, Chicago: University of Chicago Press.

GATEWOOD, E., and A. CARROLL (1981), "The Anatomy of Corporate Social Response: The Rely, Firestone 500 and Pinto Cases," *Business Horizons*, Vol. 24, No. 5, pp. 9–16.

GERT, B. (1970), *The Moral Rules: A New Rational Foundation for Morality*, New York: Harper & Row.

GEWIRTH, A. (1984), "The Epistemology of Human Rights," *Social Philosophy and Policy*, Vol. 1, No. 2, pp. 1–24.

GIFFORD, N. (1983), *When In Rome: An Introduction to Relativism and Knowledge*, Albany, NY: SUNY-Albany Press.

GILBERT, D. (1987a) *Strategy and Justice*, Minneapolis: Ph.D. Dissertation, Department of Strategic Management and Organization, Carlson School of Management, University of Minnesota.

GILBERT, D. (1987b) "Three Genres of Stakeholder Research," unpublished manuscript.

GILBERT, D., and E. FREEMAN (1985), "Flight from Meaning: A Critical Interpretation of Management Classics," unpublished manuscript.

GILBERT, D., E. HARTMAN, J. MAURIEL, and E. FREEMAN (1988, in press), *The Logic of Strategy*, Boston: Ballinger.

"GM Will Restructure Service Parts Units," *Wall Street Journal*, Oct. 29, 1986.

GOFFMAN, E. (1959), *The Presentation of Self in Everyday Life*, Garden City, N.Y.: Doubleday.

GOFFMAN, E. (1969), *Strategic Interaction*, Philadelphia: University of Pennsylvania Press.

GOFFMAN, E. (1971), *Relations in Public*, New York: Basic Books.

GOFFMAN, E. (1981), *Forms of Talk*, Philadelphia: University of Pennsylvania Press.

GOLDMAN, A. (1977), *The Moral Foundation of Professional Ethics*, Totowa, N.J.: Rowman and Littlefield.

GOLEMBIEWSKI, R. (1965), *Men, Management and Morality: Toward a New Organizational Ethic*, New York: McGraw-Hill.

GOODPASTER, K., and J. MATHEWS (1982), "Can a Corporation Have a Conscience," *Harvard Business Review*, Vol. 60, No. 1, pp. 132–141.

GORDIMER, N. (1980), *A Soldier's Embrace*, London: Jonathan Cape.

GORDIMER, N. (1984), *Something Out There*, London: Jonathan Cape.

GRAHAM, E. (1986), "My Lover, My Colleague," *The Wall Street Journal*, March 24, 1986.

GRAY, P. (1986), "Apple Computer and Jobs Reach Pact Barring Sale of New Machine until 1987," *The Wall Street Journal*, Jan. 20, 1986.

GROSS, S. (1986), "Sperry's New Owner Plans to Cut 9,600 Jobs," *Minneapolis Star & Tribune*, Oct. 9, 1986.

HAGE, D. (1985), "Judge Upholds Company's Right to Lay Off Workers," *Minneapolis Star & Tribune*, Dec. 31, 1985.

HAGE, D. (1986a), "Employers' Right to Lock Workers Out Faces Test," *Minneapolis Star & Tribune*, June 1, 1986.

HAGE, D. (1986b), "On Anniversary, P-9 Militants Haven't Given Up, but Rest of Austin Looks Ahead," *Minneapolis Star & Tribune* Aug., 17, 1986.

HANSSON, B. (1968), "Fundamental Axioms for Preference Relations," *Synthese*, Vol. 18, No. 4, pp. 423–442.

HARDIN, R. (1982), "Collective Action," Baltimore: Johns Hopkins University Press.

HARMAN, G. (1982), "Moral Relativism Defended," in J. Mieland and M. Kraus (eds.), *Relativism: Cognitive and Moral*, Notre Dame, Ind.: University of Notre Dame Press, 1982, pp. 189–204.

HARRIS, C. (1986), *Applying Moral Theory*, Belmont, Calif.: Wadsworth.

HARTMAN, E. (1988, in press), *Foundations of Organization Theory*, Boston: Ballinger.

HARTZ, P. (1985), *Merger*, New York: Morrow.

HASPELAGH, P. (1982), "Portfolio Planning: Uses and Limits," *Harvard Business Review*, Vol. 60, No. 1, pp. 58–73.

HAWORTH, L. (1986), *Autonomy: An Essay in Philosophical Psychology and Ethics*, New Haven, Conn.: Yale University Press.

HAYEK, F. (1948), *Individualism and Economic Order*, Chicago: University of Chicago Press.

HAYES, R., and W. ABERNATHY (1980), "Managing Our Way to Economic Decline," *Harvard Business Review*, Vol. 58, No. 4, pp. 67–77.

HERMAN, E. (1981), *Corporate Control, Corporate Power*, Cambridge: Cambridge University Press.

HERTZBERG, D. (1986), "TWA Names Carl Icahn as Chairman, but His Victory Is Seen as Bittersweet," *The Wall Street Journal*, Jan. 6, 1986.

HIRSCHLIEFER, J. (1958), "On the Theory of Optimal Investment Decisions," *Journal of Political Economy*, Vol. 66, No. 4, pp. 329–352.

HORRIGAN, J. (1987), "The Ethics of the New Finance," *Journal of Business Ethics*, Vol. 6, No. 3, pp. 97–110.

HORWITCH, M. (1988, in press), *Postmodern Management*, New York: Basic Books.

HUGHEY, A. (1982), "Allied Corporation Plans Major Debt Reduction, Possible Sale of Bendix's Holdings in RCA," *The Wall Street Journal*, Dec. 16, 1982.

HUXLEY, A. (1932), *Brave New World*, New York: Harper & Row.

HYMOWITZ, C., and T. SCHELLHARDT (1986), "Merged Firms Often Fire Workers the Easy Way—Not the Best Way," *The Wall Street Journal*, Feb. 24, 1986.

"I Am an Employee," *The Wall Street Journal*, Oct. 10, 1986.

"IBM to Cut Many Positions, Move Staffs to Reduce Costs," *The Wall Street Journal*, Oct. 29, 1986.

INCRASSIA, L. (1986), "Cullinet Struggles with Problems Caused by Strategic Miscues and Overconfidence," *The Wall Street Journal*, Aug. 1, 1986.

INCRASSIA, P. (1982), "Forget Football. We Have Bendix and U. Tech," *The Wall Street Journal*, Sept. 24, 1982.

"An Interview with Steven G. Rothmeier, Northwest Chairman and CEO," *Northwest Worldperks Update*, Oct. 1986, p. 2.

"Judge Defends Monitoring of AT&T, Bell Companies," *The Wall Street Journal*, Oct. 24, 1986.

KAHANER, L. (1986), *On the Line: The Men of MCI—Who took on AT&T, Risked Everything and Won!* New York: Warner.

KALIN, J. (1968), "In Defense of Egoism," in D. Gauthier (ed.), *Morality and Rational Self Interest*, Englewood Cliffs, N.J.: Prentice-Hall.

KATZ, D., and R. KAHN (1966) *The Social Psychology of Organization*, New York: John Wiley.

KETZ DE VRIES, M. (1980), *Organizational Paradoxes: Clinical Approaches to Management*, London: Tavistock Publications.

KLEINFIELD, S. (1981), *The Biggest Company on Earth: A Profile of AT&T*, New York: Holt, Rinehart & Winston.

KNAPP S., and W. MICHAELS (1982), "Against Theory," *Critical Inquiry*, Vol. 8, No. 4, pp. 732–742.

KNEALE, D. (1986a), "Firms with Ties to South Africa Strike Back at Colleges That Divest," *The Wall Street Journal*, Nov. 20, 1986.

KNEALE, D. (1986b), "IBM Will Close Distribution Site to Trim Costs," *The Wall Street Journal*, Nov. 12, 1986.

KOTEN, J. (1982), "Bill Agee of Bendix Corp: Why I Did It," *The Wall Street Journal*, Oct. 4, 1982.

KOTTER, J. (1979), *Power in Management*, New York: AMACOM.

KREBS, M. (1985), "Allied Reviews Takeover of Bendix," *Automotive News*, May 27, 1985.

"Labor Letter," *The Wall Street Journal*, Aug. 26, 1986.

LEVIN, D., and D. BUSS (1986), "GM Plans Offer to Pay $700 Million to Buy Out Its Critic H. Ross Perot," *The Wall Street Journal*, Dec. 1, 1986.

LEVINSON, H. (1976), *Psychological Man*, Cambridge, Mass.: The Levinson Institute.

LEWIS, D. (1969), *Convention*, Cambridge, Mass.: Harvard University Press.

LIPSEY, R., and K. LANCASTER (1956), "The General Theory of the Second Best," *Review of Economic Studies*, Vol. 24, No. 1, pp. 11 and 32.

LOMASKY, L. (1984), "Personal Projects as the Foundation for Basic Rights," *Social Philosophy and Policy*, Vol. 1, No. 2, pp. 35–55.

LOMASKY, L. (1987), *Persons, Rights and the Moral Community*, New York: Oxford University Press.

LOOMIS, C. (1986), "The Comeuppance of Carl Icahn," *Fortune*, Feb. 17, 1986.

LORANGE, P. (1980), *Corporate Planning: An Executive Viewpoint*, Englewood Cliffs, N.J.: Prentice-Hall.

LORANGE, P., and M. SCOTT-MORTON (1986), *Strategic Control*, St. Paul: West Publishing.

LORANGE, P., and R. VANCIL (1976), "How to Design a Strategic Planning System," *Harvard Business Review*, Vol. 54, No. 5, pp. 75–88.

MACHALABA, D. (1984a), "Union Pacific to Restructure Certain Assets," *The Wall Street Journal*, June 12, 1982.

MACHALABA, D. (1986b), "United Parcel Service Gets Deliveries Done by Driving Its Workers," *The Wall Street Journal*, April 22, 1986.

MACHAN, T. (1983), "Recent Work in Ethical Egoism," in K. Lucey and T. Machan (eds.), *Recent Work in Philosophy*, Totowa, N.J.: Rowman & Allanheld.

MAGNET, M. (1987), "Restructuring Really Works," *Fortune*, March 2, 1987.

MARCOTTY, J. (1986), "Fridley Firm Sold; New Owner Fires Workers, Asks Them Back," *Minneapolis Star & Tribune*, Sept. 4, 1986.

MARTIN, R., and J. NICKEL (1983), "Recent Work on the Concept of Rights," in K. Lucey and T. Machan (eds.), *Recent Work in Philosophy*, Totowa, N.J.: Rowman & Allanheld.

MATHEWS, J., K. GOODPASTER, and L. NASH (eds.), (1985), *Policies and Persons*, New York: McGraw-Hill.

MCLENNEN, E. (1988), *Rationality and Dynamic Choice: Foundational Explorations*, unpublished manuscript.

MCDONALD, J. (1975), *The Game of Business*, New York: Doubleday Anchor.

MCINTYRE, A. (1981), *After Virtue*, Notre Dame, Ind.: University of Notre Dame Press.

MCMAHON, C. (1981), "Morality and the Invisible Hand," *Philosophy and Public Affairs*, Vol. 10, No. 3, pp. 247–277.

MEIER, B., and J. STEWART (1985), "A Year after Bhopal, Union Carbide Faces a Slew of Problems," *The Wall Street Journal*, Nov. 26, 1985.

METZ, T. (1982), "The Pacificist," *The Wall Street Journal*, Dec. 3, 1982.

MILGRAM, S. (1975), *Obedience to Authority*, New York: Harper & Row.

MILL, J. (1949 ed.), *Utilitarianism*, Oxford: Blackwell.

MILLER, M. (1986), "Two Years after Bhopal's Gas Disaster, Lingering Effects Still Plague Its People," *The Wall Street Journal*, Dec. 5, 1986.

MILLER, M., and B. MEIER (1986), "India Files Suit against Carbide in Bhopal Court," *The Wall Street Journal*, Sept. 8, 1986.

MINTZBERG, H. (1973), "Strategy Making in Three Modes," *California Management Review*, Vol. 16, No. 2, pp. 44–53.

MINTZBERG, H. (1979), "Organizational Power and Goals: A Skeletal Theory," in D. Schendel and C. Hofer (eds.), (1979), *Strategic Management: A New View of Business Policy and Planning*, Boston: Little, Brown.

MINTZBERG, H. (1980), *The Nature of Managerial Work*, Englewood Cliffs, N.J.: Prentice-Hall.

MINTZBERG, H. (1983), *Power in and around Organizations*, Englewood Cliffs, N.J.: Prentice-Hall.

MUNDT, D. (1985), "Truck Driver Who Refused to Ride with Smoker Must Be Rehired, Ruling Says," *Minneapolis Star & Tribune*, Oct. 15, 1985.

MUZZIO, D. (1982), Watergate Games, New York: New York University Press.

NADER, R., and W. TAYLOR (1986), The Big Boys: Power and Position in American Business, New York: Pantheon.

NAYLOR, T., and F. TAPON (1982), "The Capital Asset Pricing Model: An Evaluation of Its Potential as a Strategic Planning Tool," Management Science, Vol. 28, No. 10, pp. 1166-1173.

NOZICK, R. (1969), "Coercion," in S. Morgenbesser et al. (eds.), Philosophy, Science and Method, New York: St. Martin's, pp. 440-472.

NOZICK, R. (1975), Anarchy, State and Utopia, New York: Basic Books.

NULTY, P. (1987a), "Now Managers Will Manage," Fortune, Feb. 2, 1987.

NULTY, P. (1987b), "Pushed Out at 45—Now What?" Fortune, March 2, 1987.

O'NEILL, O. (1985), "Between Consenting Adults," Philosophy and Public Affairs, Vol. 14, No. 3, pp. 252-277.

ORWELL, G. (1948), 1984, New York: Harcourt Brace Jovanovich, 1961.

ORWELL, G. (1968), "Inside the Whale," in S. Orwell and I. Angres (eds.), The Collected Essays, Journalism and Letters of George Orwell, Vol. 1, New York: Harcourt Brace Jovanovich.

O'TOOLE, J. (1985), Vanguard Management: Redesigning the Corporate Future, Garden City, N.Y.: Doubleday.

"Our Dream Is to Work Together," unsigned interview with W. Agee and M. Cunningham, Fortune, Oct. 18, 1982.

"Pac Man Economics," unsigned review and outlook, The Wall Street Journal, Sept. 27, 1982.

PASCALE, R., and A. ATHOS (1981), The Art of Japanese Management, New York: Simon & Schuster.

PASTIN, M. (1986), The Hard Problems of Management, San Francisco: Jossey-Bass.

PETERS, T. (1985), "Backroom' Folks Need Information," Minneapolis Star & Tribune, March 19, 1985.

PETERS, T. (1986), The Promises, Palo Alto, Calif.: The Tom Peters Companies.

PETERS, T., and N. AUSTIN (1985), A Passion for Excellence, New York: Random House.

PETERS, T., and R. WATERMAN (1982), In Search of Excellence, New York: Harper & Row.

PFEFFER, J. (1981), Power in Organization, Boston: Pitman.

PFEFFER, J. (1982), Organizations, Boston: Pitman.

PFEFFER, J. (1983), "Organizational Demography," in L. Cummings and B. Staw (eds.), Research in Organization Behavior, Greenwich, Conn.: JAI Press, Vol. 5, pp. 299-357.

PHILLIPS, A. (1983), "Regulatory and Interfirm Organizational Burdens in the U.S. Telecommunications Structure," Columbia Journal of World Business, Vol. 18, No. 1, pp. 46-52.

POLLACK, A. (1985a), "Jobs Resigns as Apple's Chairman," The New York Times, Sept. 18, 1985.

POLLACK, A. (1985b), "Now Sculley Goes It Alone at Apple," The New York Times, Sept. 22, 1985.

PORTER, M. (1980), Competitive Strategy, New York: Free Press.

PORTER, M. (1985), Competitive Advantages, New York: Free Press.

PRATT, J., and R. ZECKHAUSER (eds.) (1985), Principals and Agents: The Structure of Business, Cambridge, Mass.: Harvard Business School Press.

PRESTON, L. (ed.) (1979-1987), Research in Corporate Responsibility and Social Policy, Greenwich, Conn.: JAI Press, Vol. 1-9.

QUINN, B. (1980), Strategies for Change: Logical Incrementalism, Homewood, Ill.: R.D. Irwin.

QUINN, R., and P. LEES (1984), "Attraction and Harassment: Dynamics of Sexual Politics in the Workplace," Organizational Dynamics, Vol. 13, No. 3, pp. 13-46.

RAWLS, J. (1971), A Theory of Justice, Cambridge, Mass.: Harvard University Press.

REIBSTEIN, L. (1986a), "More Companies Use Free-Lancers to Avoid Cost, Trauma of Layoffs," The Wall Street Journal, April 18, 1986.

REIBSTEIN, I. (1986b), "More Firms Use Personality Tests for Entry-level, Blue-Collar Jobs," *The Wall Street Journal*, Jan. 16, 1986.

REIBSTEIN, I. (1986c), "What to Do When an Employee Is Talented—and a Pain in the Neck," *The Wall Street Journal*, Aug. 8, 1986.

REICH, C. (1986), "The Litigator: David Boies, The Wall Street Lawyer Everyone Wants," *The New York Times Magazine*, June 1, 1986.

"Ribb's Chairman Is Killed in a Plane Crash in Idaho," *The Wall Street Journal*, Sept. 3, 1986.

RORTY, R. (1979), *Philosophy and the Mirror of Nature*, Princeton, N.J.: Princeton University Press.

RORTY, R. (1982), *Consequences of Pragmatism*, Minneapolis: University of Minnesota Press.

RORTY, R. (1983), "Postmodern Bourgeois Liberalism," *Journal of Philosophy*, Vol. 80, No. 10, pp. 583–589.

RORTY, R. (1984a), "The Historiography of Philosophy," in R. Rorty, J. Schnee-wind, and W. Skinner (eds.), *Philosophy in History*, Cambridge: Cambridge University Press, 1984, pp. 49–75.

RORTY, R. (1984b), "Texts and Lumps," *New Literary History*, Vol. 16, No. 1, pp. 1–16.

ROSS, W. (1930), *The Right and the Good*, Oxford: Clarendon Press.

RUDNER, R. (1953), "The Scientist qua Scientist Makes Value Judgments," *Philosophy of Science*, Vol. 20, No. 1, pp. 1–6.

ST. ANTHONY, N. (1986), "P-6 Trusteeship Gets Judge's Approval; Local Leadership Out," *Minneapolis Star & Tribune*, June 3, 1986.

ST. ANTHONY, N. (1987a), "Target Cutting 219 Jobs by Friday," *Minneapolis Star & Tribune*, Jan. 8, 1987.

ST. ANTHONY, N. (1987b), "Winona Knitting Workers Turned Firm Around from the Bottom Up," *Minneapolis Star & Tribune*, Jan. 4, 1987.

Salmagundi, spring–summer 1986 issue.

SALPUKAS, A. (1985), "People Express to Get Britt," *The New York Times*, Dec. 28, 1985.

SALPUKAS, A. (1986), "People Express Beaten at Its Own Game," *Minneapolis Star & Tribune*, June 29, 1986.

SAMUELSON, P (1970), *Economics*, New York: McGraw-Hill.

SCARDINO, A. (1986), "Merrill Lynch Changes Compensation Plan," *Minneapolis Star & Tribune*, Feb. 26, 1986.

SCHELLING, T. (1960), *The Strategy of Conflict*, Cambridge, Mass.: Harvard University Press.

SCHELLING, T. (1978), *Micromotives and Macrobehavior*, New York: W. W. Norton, & Co. Inc.

SCHELLING, T. (1984), *Choice and Consequences*, Cambridge: Harvard University Press.

SCHELSINGER, J. (1986), "Owens-Corning Fiberglas Consolidates Divisions as Part of Restructuring Plan," *The Wall Street Journal*, Sept. 23, 1986.

SCHENDEL, D., and C. HOFER (1979), "Introduction," in D. Schendel and C. Hofer (eds.), *Strategic Management: A New View of Business Policy and Planning*, Boston: Little-Brown, pp. 1–12.

SCHERER, F. (1980), *Industrial Market Structure and Economic Performance*, New York: Houghton Mifflin.

SCHOTTER, A. (1981), *The Economics of Social Institutions*, Cambridge: Cambridge University Press.

SEARLE, J. (1964), "How to Derive 'Ought' From 'Is'," *Philosophical Review*, Vol. 73, No. 1, pp. 43–58.

SEARLE, J. (1984), *Minds, Brains, and Science*, Cambridge, Mass.: Harvard University Press.

Sedek Industries (A)–(H), Cambridge, Mass.: Harvard Business School Case Studies, 9-584-132 to 9-584-140.

SELZNICK, P (1957), *Leadership in Administration*, New York: Harper & Row.

SHOOSHAN, H. (1984), "The Bell Breakup: Putting it in Perspective," in H.

Shooshan (ed.), *Disconnecting Bell: The Impact of the AT&T Divestiture*, New York: Pergamon, 1984, pp. 8–22.

SIEBERT, D. (1984), *The Ethical Executive*, New York: Simon & Schuster.

SIMON, H. (1945), *Administrative Behavior*, New York: Free Press.

SKINNER, W. (1985), *Manufacturing: The Formidable Competitive Weapon*, New York: John Wiley.

SLOAN, A. (1969), *My Years with General Motors*, New York: Doubleday.

SLOAN, B. (1983), *Three plus One Equals Billions*, New York: Arbor House.

STEVENS, M. (1987), *The Insiders: The Truth Behind the Scandal Rocking Wall Street*, New York: Putnam's.

STURDIVANT, F. (1979), "Executives and Activists: A Test of Stakeholder Management," *California Management Review*, Vol. 22, No. 1, pp. 53–59.

STURDIVANT, F., and J. GINTER (1977), "Corporate Social Responsiveness: Management Attitudes and Economic Performance," *California Management Review*, Vol. 19, No. 2, pp. 30–39.

SULLIVAN, A. (1986a), "Amax Chief's Revamping Approaches Payoff," *The Wall Street Journal*, May 27, 1986.

SULLIVAN, A. (1986b), "Exxon's Sleeker Look Starting to Emerge," *The Wall Street Journal*, June 2, 1986.

SULLIVAN, A. (1986c), "Exxon to Cut Some Operations in U.S., Overseas because of Falling Oil Prices," *The Wall Street Journal*, March 19, 1986.

SULLIVAN, A. (1987), "Texaco Banks on Kinnear to Steer Firm Out of Financial Legal Crises," *The Wall Street Journal*, Feb. 3, 1987.

SULLIVAN, G., and W. NOWLIN (1986), "Critical New Aspects of Sex Harassment Law," *Labor Law Journal*, Vol. 37, Spring 1986, pp. 617–624.

TUNSTALL, J. (1986), *Communications Deregulation: The Unleashing of America's Communications Industry*, Oxford: Blackwell.

TUNSTALL, W. (1983), "Cultural Transition at AT&T," *Sloan Management Review*, Vol. 25, No. 1, pp. 15–26.

TUNSTALL, W. (1985), *Disconnecting Parties: Managing the Bell System Break-Up: An Inside View*, New York: McGraw-Hill.

"TVA Proposes Ethics Plan on Contracted Employees," *The Wall Street Journal*, Oct. 27, 1986.

UTTAL, B. (1985), "The Adventures of Steve Jobs (Cont'd)," *Fortune*, Oct. 14, 1985.

VANCIL, R., and P. LORANGE (1975), "Strategic Planning in Diversified Companies," *Harvard Business Review*, Vol. 53, No. 1, pp. 81–93.

VAN DE VEN, A. (1980), "Problem Solving, Planning, and Innovation, Part II: Speculations for Theory and Practice," *Human Relations*, Vol. 33, No. 10, pp. 757–779.

VAN DE VEN, A. (1986), "Central Problems in the Management of Innovation," *Management Science*, Vol. 32, No. 5, pp. 590–607.

VECSEY, G. (1986), "Pavelich and 'The System,'" *The New York Times*, March 14, 1986.

VON AUW, A. (1983), *Heritage and Destiny: Reflections on the Bell System in Transition*, New York: Praeger.

VON STERNBERG, B. (1986), "A Job at Control Data Has Lost Its Luster," *Minneapolis Star & Tribune*, March 24, 1986.

VON WRIGHT, G. (1963), *The Logic of Preference*, Edinburgh: Edinburgh University Press.

WILEY, R. (1984), "The End of Monopoly: Regulatory Change and the Promotion of Competition," in H. Shooshan (ed.), *Disconnecting Bell: The Impact of the AT&T Divestiture*, New York: Pergamon, 1984, pp. 23–46.

WILLIAMSON, O. (1964), *The Economics of Discretionary Behavior*, Englewood Cliffs, N.J.: Prentice-Hall.

WILLIAMSON, O. (1975), *Markets and Hierarchies*, New York: Free Press.

WILLIAMSON, O. (1985), *The Economic Institutions of Capitalism*, New York: Free Press.

WIND, Y., and V. MAHAJAN (1981), "Designing Product and Business Portfolios," *Harvard Business Review*, Vol. 59, No. 1, pp. 155–165.

WINTER, R. (1987), "Firestone's Restructuring Bid Works Well—to a Point," *The Wall Street Journal*, Jan. 14, 1987.

WISDOM, J. (1970), "Tolerance," in *Paradox and Discovery*, Berkeley: University of California Press, pp. 139–147.

WITTGENSTEIN, L. (1953 ed.), *Philosophical Investigations*, E. Anscombe (trans.), Oxford: Blackwell.

WOO, C. (1984), "An Empirical Test of Value-Based Planning Models and Implications," *Management Science*, Vol. 30, No. 9, pp. 1031–1050.

ZIMBARDO, P. (1969), *The Cognitive Control of Motivation*, Glenview, Ill.: Scott, Foresman.

INDEX